Italian Icon

The history of Alitalia
and antecedents

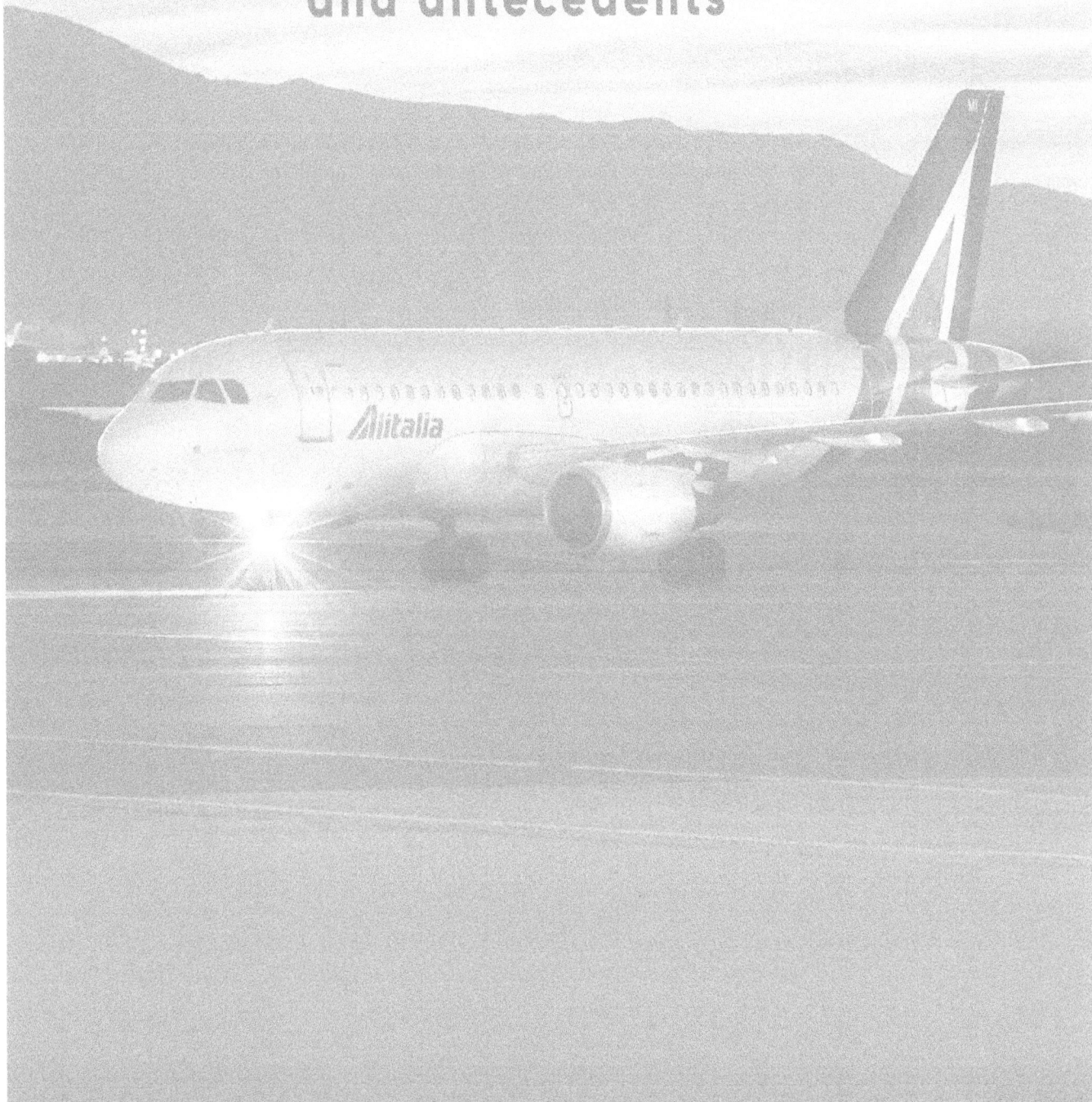

Cover photo of Alitalia Airbus A319 taken at Cagliari/Elmas by Stefano Garau

ISBN 978-0-9573744-5-4

Design and layout by Graham Hobster, Moncton, Canada

Introduction

Alitalia, an icon of Italy's aviation scene, is no more, having succumbed after 75 years carrying the Italian flag across the world. After a relatively measured start in 1946 and the 'golden age' of the 1950s and 1960s, the state-owned airline became stuck on a roller coaster ride that offered no smooth landing.

The airline staggered from crisis to crisis and its eventual demise in 2021 became inevitable. The reasons are not difficult establish. State interference and mismanagement, a bloated workforce, powerful unions and failed partnerships led to heavy losses, massive debts, and several bankruptcies and bailouts. The Covid-19 pandemic also hastened the end. The last flight on 14 October was viewed as a sad day by many, with others experiencing relief that the bottomless pit that had swallowed nearly EUR 13 billion of government money, had now been filled in. Yet, the endless problems should not overshadow Alitalia's contribution to Italy's visual presence in many parts of the world.

Politics had also shaped Italy's air transport development in the inter-war years with the rise of Benito Mussolini's *Partido Nazionale Fascista* (National Fascist Party) essentially controlling development. Although several airlines began operations in 1926, these were soon amalgamated into a single government airline, Ala Littoria, in 1934, conceived as Mussolini's showcase of the new Italy and to serve his short-lived colonial expansion around the Mediterranean and the Red Sea. Only Avio Linee Italiane (ALI), controlled by the powerful Fiat empire, refused to be swallowed up and retained its independence, although it also became impressed in the military in World War Two after Italy joined the conflict on the side of Germany. After 1945, Alitalia and Linee Aeree Italiane (LAI) became the two main airlines until a forced merger in 1957 left Alitalia the sole flag-carrier.

A day after Alitalia's last flight, a new airline, ITA Airways, entered the fray with a first flight from Milan/Linate to Bari. Also government-owned but intended to be privatised, at least partially, nothing has changed other than it is a much slimmed down operation but only time will tell if it can achieve the success that had eluded Alitalia. It is interesting to note that ITA Airways has bought the Alitalia name for a large sum to prevent it being used by another carrier. Maybe a resurrection cannot be ruled out. At least for now it is a new dawn for Italy's air transport sector.

Günter Endres

Acknowledgements

I am greatly indebted to Maurice Wickstead for his invaluable help with historic records and photographs made freely available. To Luigino Caliari who generously provided information and the majority of pre-war and wartime photos from his vast collection, and to Leonardo Pinzauti who filled many gaps in photographic coverage of the immediate post-war years. Without their important contributions, it would have been impossible to complete this work. Alitalia too has been helpful with more recent photographs. A special thank you also to Diego Meozzi for his excellent work on the Alitalia fleet on his website azfleet.info.

Of course, the task of sourcing sufficient photographs to adequately illustrate such a book is always onerous and much credit must go to the many photographers and organisations across the world who kindly and unselfishly permitted their use, many by liberal licensing through Wikimedia Commons. To ensure the completeness of the coverage, I have included rare and difficult to obtain photographs where the photographer was either unknown, or has not responded to a request for permission to publish, and I am hoping for their understanding.

All are listed below, but please accept my sincere apologies for any inadvertent omissions.

Guido Allieri, Peter Bakema, Aldo Bidini, David Carter, Marco Dotti, Alain Durand, Roberto Falciola, Ken Fielding, Angelo Gialarella/Archive Ottogalli), Michel Gilliand, Geoffrey Goodall, Clinton Groves, Perry Hoppe, Darren Koch, JetPix, Alan Lebeda, Paul J Morton, David Parker Brown, Enrico Pierobon, Adrian Pingstone, Bob Proctor, Jon Proctor, Robbie Shaw, Sean D Silva, Tom Singfield, Paul Spijkers, Peter Tonna, John Visanich, Konstantin von Wedelstaedt, Anna Zvereva

There is, of course, one other person who deserves my heartfelt gratitude, and that is my best friend and collaborator Graham Hobster in Canada, whose skilful and visually pleasing layouts are designed to inform and enhance the enjoyment of the reader.

Sources

Castellani Antonio: *Il Gabbiano in Camicia Nera – storia della LATI*; LoGisma, 2015
Civoli Massimo: *S.A.S. I Servizi Aerei Speciali della Regia Aeronautica 1940-1943*; IBN Istituto Bibliografico Napoleone, 2014
Gianvanni Paolo: *Itrasporti Aerei in Italia dalla Guerra All'era del Getto 1945-1960*; Edizioni Aeronautiche Italiane Srl, Florence
Caprotti, Federico: *Profitability, Practicality and Ideology: Fascist Civil Aviation and the Short Life of Ala Littoria, 1934–1943*; The Journal of Transport History 32.1 (2011): 17–38
D'Agostino, Carlo and Tomarchio Mario; *La prima compagnia aerea commerciale italiana*; Aviani and Aviani Edition
Roselli Alberto: *The air links between Italy and Eastern Africa, June-November 1941*; Storiaverita.org

First experimental postal service flown by Lieutenant Mario de Bernardi between Turin and Rome

Alitalia's Origins

Italy was a latecomer to the field of Europe's commercial aviation and the reason for this tardiness is not hard to find and dates back to the First World War. Having first sided with Germany and Austro-Hungary in the Triple Alliance and was expected to join when war broke out on 28 July 1914, it instead adopted a wait-and-see attitude, before entering the conflict on 26 August 1915, much to the dismay of the Socialist Party, but on the side of the Triple Entente – Britain, France and Russia - which had promised large sections of territory on the Adriatic Sea region, including Tyrol, Dalmatia and Istria, as well as subsidies and loans, signed in the secret Treaty of London. It was too tempting an offer from Britain to refuse, but Italy's war experience proved disastrous, ending with shame and heavy loss of life. The high cost had also plunged the country into a recession, unemployment soared, and to add humiliation to its woes, Italy never received all the promised rewards of territory in the Treaty of Versailles. Its failure to stand up to the 'big three' at Versailles was exploited by the Fasci Italiani di Combattimento, which was founded by Benito Mussolini, the self-styled Il Duce, in Milan in March 1919, and resulted in much civil unrest. Mussolini then created his Partido Nazionale Fascista (National Fascist Party) and seized power from a weakened Government on 31 October 1922. He went on to transform the nation into a one-party dictatorship and oversaw a period of intervention in the economy through large-scale nationalisation

In spite of Wilbur Wright's visit to Rome on 1 April 1909, which had generated great excitement, shared by King Victor Emmanuel III, flying activities were limited to the army and navy. It was not until 22 May 1917 that the first experimental mail flight was undertaken, when Lt. Mario de Bernardi, employing a Pomilio PC-1 reconnaissance biplane of the *Corpo Aeronautico Militare* (Military Aviation Corps), left Turin for Rome with 218 kg (480 lb) of mail and La Stampa newspapers, completing the 523-km (325-mile) straight line distance in four hours and three minutes. Driving rain, which had delayed the scheduled first service date of 20 May, also pushed the

return flight to 27 May, but this did not go to plan, as a gale forced the aircraft to land on the beach at Lavagna, some 150 km short of Turin, and the mail had to delivered to its destination by surface transport. This was followed on 5 June by a regular service between Brindisi and Valona (now Vlorë in Albania), operated by the *Regia Marina* with FBA Type H floatplanes. On 27 June 1917, a service between Naples and Palermo was added, principally because the presence of Austrian submarines in the area prevented safe passage between the two cities by boat. The aircraft, possibly an FBA floatplane, was piloted by Ruggero Franzoni, the Italian aeronautical pioneer.

FBA Type H seaplane operated the first postal service between Naples and Palermo

Pomilio PC-1 reconnaissance biplane of the Corpo Aeronautico Militare

Other military airmail flights were operated between 27 June and 31 September 1917 between Civitabecchia and Terranova Pausania on the island of Sardinia, between 25 November 1918 and November 1919 by the Trans Adriatic Naval Airport Service over the Venice-Trieste-Pula-Fiume route, a Padua-Vienna service inaugurated on 2 March 1919 with Caproni aircraft and flown three times a week, and a Turin-Milan-Venice line was active during 1920. Another mail flight was undertaken in June 1925 between Livorno and Rome, flown with a SIAI S.16 from the No.144 Hydroplane Squadron of the *Regia Aeronautica Italiana* (Italian Royal Air Force), to coincide with the 12th Philatelic Congress in Livorno. Limited passenger and mail service had started in May 1919, when two SCA (Stabilimento Costruzioni Aeronautiche) M-class semi-rigid airships were used between Rome and Naples, but disaster struck on 2 August that same year, when a large Caproni Ca.48 triplane, flown by two military pilots on a Milan/Taliedo-Venice/St Nicola service, crashed on the return flight at Verona, causing the death of all 15 people on board. Structural failure of the wings in mid-flight at an altitude of 915 m was the most likely cause.

With the economy improving and funds more readily available, and Mussolini's intent to showcase his new Italy, emphasis was directed towards modernisation of its aviation assets, both civil and military. A priority was the development of its seaplane construction capability, which it had developed during the war. Claude Dornier had demonstrated his new flying-boats but was forbidden by the Treaty of Versailles to build these in Germany. As a result, Claude Dornier had to leave Germany and find suitable working conditions elsewhere. An Italian officer of the *Inter-Allied Aeronautical Commission of Control* (IAACC) had drawn Dornier's attention to Italy, where a suitable site was at hand near Pisa in the small village of Marina di Pisa at the mouth of the River Arno, which was occupied by

Postage stamps overprinted to commemorate the Rome-Turin and Naples-Palermo services in May and June 1917

Società Anonima Industrie Meccaniche Gallinari, a builder of FBA (Franco-British Aviation) seaplanes under licence during the war. On 17 December 1921, the Italian Banca Commerciale Italiana formed a new company: the Società Anonima Italiana Costruzioni Meccaniche (SAICM), which acquired the licence to build the Dornier Wal, known in Italy as the Wal Cabina, which went on to form some of the fleets of the fledgling airlines yet to be established. The first Italian-built Wal made its maiden flight on 6 November

SVA.9 two-seat unarmed reconnaissance biplane of 107 Squadriglia at Pisa engaged on a Pisa-Piacenza-Milan-Turin mail service

1922, having received a blessing from the Bishop of Pisa. On 5 November, 1925, SAICM changed its name to Costruzioni Meccaniche Aeronautiche Società Anonima (CMASA), led by Engineer Guido Guidi.

Belated start

Under the auspices of the *Direzione Generale dell' Aeronautica Civile*, which had already been established in 1919, plans were finally being made for the opening of civil air services in Italy, backed up by a number of innovative aircraft and engine manufacturers, particularly in the area of seaplane designs, which would provide the emerging airlines with state-of-the-art equipment with which to get started. In August 1925, the government issued authorisation for five routes, all with generous subsidies. These were:

- Line No.1: Trieste-Venice-Milan-Turin
- Line No.2: Trieste-Zara (now Zadar, Croatia)
- Line No.3: Naples-Palermo
- Line No.4: Brindisi-Athens-Istanbul
- Line No.5: Venice-Klagenfurt-Graz-Vienna

On 31 January 1926, the Royal Decree of 18 October 1923 was finally converted into law, enabling the start of regular air services, with considerable financial contribution from the State. Line No.1 was awarded to Società Italiana Servizi

Aerei (SISA), with a 50 per cent subsidy up to a maximum of 38,000 km. In exchange, the company committed itself to uplifting some 50 kg of mail along the line for the *Regie Poste* (Post Office).

To SISA goes the credit of having been the first airline to have been founded in Italy, and also the first to start scheduled services, although this was not until several years later. The airline was established in 1921 at Lussinpiccolo (now Mali Lošinj on the island of Lošinj, Croatia), by brothers Alberto and Oscar Cosulich, third-generation scions of a dynastic family maritime business, originally

SISA FBA floatplane on the River Po by the Umberto I Bridge at Turin

founded in 1857 and based at Trieste. Among the interests of the entrepreneurial Cosulich siblings was a hotel complex in the coastal spa town of Portorose (now Portorož in Slovenia), which was to become part of the operation. The brothers' increasing curiosity about aviation led to the purchase of an FBA Type H floatplane decommissioned by the *Regia Marina* (Royal Navy), with the aim of conducting local pleasure flights for hotel guests and transporting them to nearby Trieste, or even as far as Venice. The venture, begun in 1922, proved moderately successful and, with the addition of two more FBA floatplanes, some 1,200 flying hours were accrued in the first year. The FBA Type H was a single engine biplane, with the 127 kW (170 hp) Hispano-Suiza 8A water-cooled engine mounted between the wings with a pusher propeller. It provided accommodation for the pilot and two passengers.

Looking to expand the venture, a flight school was opened at Portorose in 1924, and a contract was obtained from Italy's *Ministero dell'Aeronautica* (Ministry of Aviation) to train military pilots. A number of successful students would go on to become crew members on General Italo Balbo's long-distance aerial cruises of the early 1930s. This increased activity saw the SISA fleet enlarged to 25 FBA Type H floatplanes, and the construction of hangars, a slipway and other necessary facilities. Aeronautical workshops were also constructed at Monfalcone on the Gulf of Trieste, taking their name from the shipyard complex, Cantieri Navali Triestini, which would be responsible for a large number of innovative seaplane designs, initially by Engineer Raffaele Conflenti (formerly with SIAI, and CAMS of France) The

second of these was the four-passenger Cant 10ter flying-boat, designed specifically for SISA, which acquired most of the 16 examples built. The Cant 10ter was a conventional biplane design with unstaggered wings of equal span, with the 300 kW (400 hp) Lorraine-Dietrich engine mounted in pusher configuration, replacing the 186 kW (250 hp) Fiat A.12 engine fitted to the first three aircraft. The open single-seat cockpit was on the port side immediately forward of the wing, and the cabin for four passengers was in the bows, with five rectangular windows in each side. It had a cruising speed of 150 km/h.

Having been awarded Route No.1 Trieste-Turin, months of intense activity followed, including the establishment of marine bases and passenger facilities, including on the River Po in one of the more picturesque parts of Turin, on the River Ticino at Pavia, and, at first, utilising using the transalpine railway station in Trieste from which passengers were transported to the aircraft by boat. Emergency stopovers were also identified along the route at Adria, Ostiglia, Casalmaggiore, Piacenza and Casale Monferrato. Altogether 27 test flights were conducted over the route, with the first on 15 May 1924 in an FBA piloted by Count Luigi Maria Ragazzi, general manager of SISA. The two years after the first test flight were used to install meteorological and radio-telephony stations on the waterways of Venice, Pavia and Turin, and training of pilots and engineers. Along the proposed route, suitable locations were identified and prepared, where the seaplanes could land in case of technical problems or poor weather conditions. These were at Adria, Ostiglia,

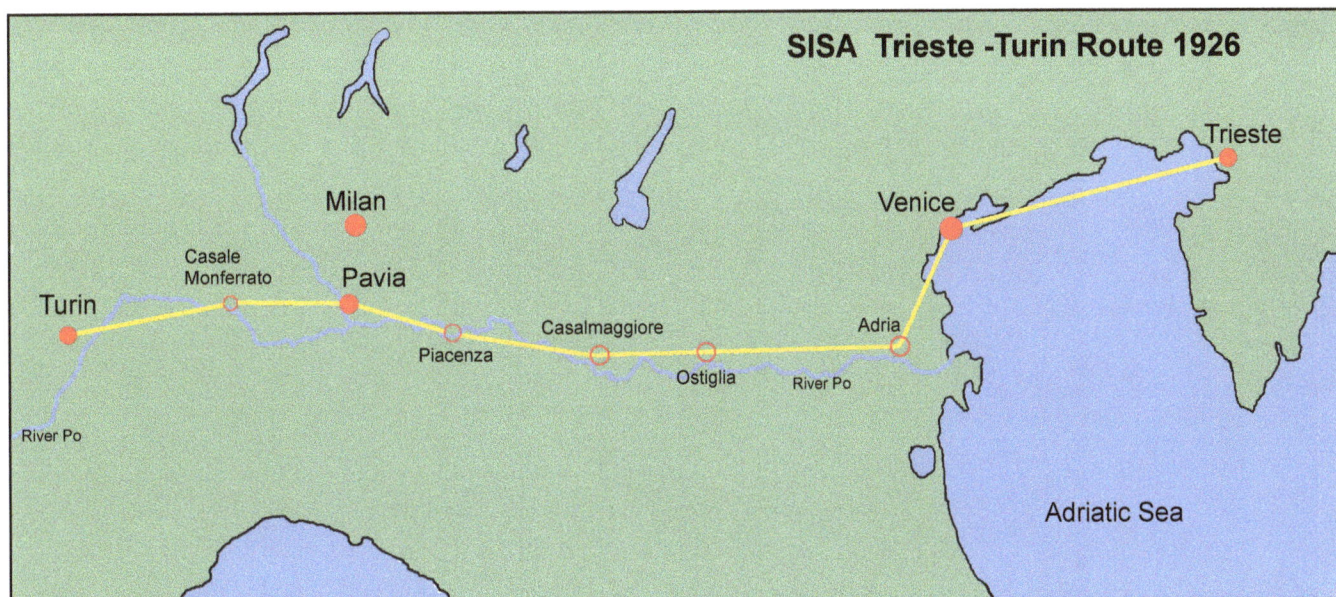

SISA Trieste -Turin Route 1926

Grand inaugural

Casalmaggiore, Piacenza and Casale Monferrato. All was in place by March 1926. On the 28th of the month, two Cant 10ter – I-OLTD and I-OLTC – piloted by Antonio Majorana, SISA's commercial director, and Commander Giuseppe Bertocco respectively, embarked on the last of a long series of proving flights. Carrying two members of the local press, both aircraft departed Portorose at 1130 hours. After an hour's flight Venice was reached for a refuelling stop at the WWI seaplane station Giuseppe Miraglia on Sant'Andrea Island. From there, the aircraft tracked along the Po River for a further halt at Pavia, where two more newspaper journalists were embarked for the final leg to Turin, which was reached at 1755 hours.

On 1 April 1926, a grand inaugural ceremony took place with the two Cant 10ter taking off at 1205 hours from Portorose, since the Molo Audace site in the San Giorgio basin at Trieste was rendered inoperable by the bora, a katabatic wind blowing off the Adriatic Sea with gusts of up to 70 km per hour. Portorose was protected from the strong winds by the surrounding hills. Another two Cant 10ter seaplanes started at the same time from Turin. Travelling from Portorose were I-OLTC, flown by Antonio Majorana, with on board the mechanic Vittorio Ferrari, Alderman Sulligoi-Silvani, the journalist Luciano Cavara from the *Corriera della Sera*, and 6 kg of mail

Cant 10ter I-OLTD on Sant'Andrea Island, Venice

Cant 10ter I-OLTE and I-OLTH moored by the Isabella Bridge in Turin

and packages, while I-OLTD was commanded by Count Ragazzi and had the mechanic Giannetti. General Alberto Bonzani, Undersecretary for Aviation, Dr Manlio Wolfese, Director of Civil Aviation, and Oscar Cosulich on board. Leaving Turin was I-OLTB, flown by Commander Bruno Pascaletto with mechanic Giovanni Casnaghi, and I-OLTE, commanded by Mario Cerone, with mechanic Inghingolo. Both had two passengers on board. To increase comfort, the passengers were provided with blankets, hot water bottles against the cold and drafts, and cotton wool balls to cushion the deafening noise of the engine. They were also told not to throw objects out of the window! It is interesting to note that at both Turin and Pavia, embarkation and disembarkation of passengers took place inside the hangar, with the seaplane winched to and from the river.

The flights arrived at Turin after three hours and 10 minutes to great acclaim. The four aircraft had rendezvoused at Pavia on the River Ticino, a left-bank tributary of the river Po, for an official ceremony attended by Benito Mussolini.

The director of the Italian Post Office announced the regular carriage of mail over the route. For this purpose, a special mailbox was positioned at Trieste's main post office, allowing postings to be made up to 90 minutes before departure. The service was also opened to the public, offering three departures each week in both directions, taking an average of 5 hours 10 minutes for the 480 km journey, for a one-way fare ITL (Italian lira) 350 (then USD 18.50). The Trieste-Pavia sector cost ITL 190, and Pavia-Turin was charged at ITL140. This was quite expensive, being equivalent to the first-class rail journey plus the sleeping car supplement. The service was put on a daily basis except

Sundays on 16 June. On 26 September, SISA constructed a new slipway near the base of the Molo Audace, with a 37 x 37 m floating hangar that could accommodate four Cant 10ter seaplanes.

A new flying-boat emerged from the Monfalcone workshops in early 1928. The Cant 22 was an unequal-span biplane, powered by three 150 kW (200 hp) Isotta-Fraschini Asso 200 engines and could accommodate up to 12 passengers in comparative luxury with improved leather seating, curtained windows, interior lighting and a small lavatory. The first examples, I-AABN, named *San Marco,* and I-AACJ *San Giorgio* were both registered to SISA in early 1929 and took over from the Cant 10ter used on the new circular route around the Adriatic Venice-Trieste-Ancona-Zara (now Zadar in Croatia)-Ancona-Trieste-Venice, which had been inaugurated in stages on 16 October, with the complete circuit flown from 15 December 1928. By the end of the year, SISA had flown 1,588 passengers on 575 flights in 1,589 hours, logging 238,262 km, with a remarkable regularity of 97 per cent. Also uplifted were 13,470 kg of freight and mail, and 12,946 kg of luggage.

Several months later, a metal-hulled version of the Cant 10ter was rolled out of the factory. The hull was of duralumin, the bows were redesigned, the cockpit had two side-by-side seats, and there were only two windows (instead of five) in each side of the passenger cabin, but the original designation was retained, although it has also been shown as the Cant 10ter II. It was powered by the 373 kW (500 hp) Isotta-Fraschini Asso 500 engine. Flown by First World War ace and Cant/SISA test pilot Mario Stoppani, one of the first two registered, I-AANM or I-AANN (probably the

Cant 22 I-AABN *San Marco*

Cant 22 I-AACJ *San Giorgio* at the Trieste seaplane base

The higher-capacity Cant 22R.1 I-ALFA *San Sergio*

Cant 22R.1 I-ADDA *San Vito* had a short life with SISA having sank near Grado after just one year of service

former), left Trieste on 19 May 1929 for Lake Bracciano, where it was inspected by Italo Balbo, then Head of the Regia Aeronautica. Thereafter, the aircraft proceeded to Genoa for a demonstration to the directors of another airline, Società Anonima di Navigazione Aerea (SANA). This gave rise to speculation that that the two companies would co-operate over a route linking Genoa with Milan, but nothing materialised. Instead, on 5 October 1929, a proving flight was undertaken covering Trieste-Venice-Pavia-Genoa-Marseille (France). The proving flight by Mario Stoppani in Cant 22 I-AACJ *San Giorgio*, with Guido Cosulich on board, did not proceed smoothly. A dense fog bank at the Faro del Piave lighthouse in Venice forced him to ditch and continue to Venice at a speed of 25 km/h while floating. After an improvement in the weather, the flight continued to Pavia and Genoa and, after another ditching at Toulon, finally reached Marseille. Although an agreement was signed with the government, nothing came of it.

In the meantime, the airline had taken delivery of more Cant 22, I-AACK *San Sergio*, and I-AACL *San Giusto*, before the end of 1929, with I-AACM, I-AACN, I-AAQX following in 1930, and I-ADDA *San Vito* and I-ALFA *San Sergio* in 1931. All of these were of the Cant 22R.1 variant, which was powered by one (510 hp) Asso 500 and two (250 hp) Asso 200 engines, and also differed in having wing tip floats. The Cant 22R.1 normally carried two crew and 10 passengers.

SISA facilities at Portorose with three-engined Cant 22 biplane flying-boats

SISA
OCIETA' ITALIANA
ERVIZI AEREI
BAGAGLIO PER
GRAFICHE MODIANO-TRIESTE
PORTOROSE

S.I.S.A.
SOCIETA' ITALIANA
SERVIZI AEREI
BAGAGLIO PER
VENEZIA

MILANO (PAVIA)
TORINO
VENEZIA
TRIESTE
PER BUDAPEST
GENOVA
ZARA
ANCONA
S.I.S.A.
SOCIETA' ITALIANA
SERVIZI AEREI
TRIESTE

IDROVOLANTE
TRIESTE - LUSSINPICCOLO IN 70 MINUTI
LINEA AEREA COMMERCIALE
S.I.S.A.
SOCIETÀ ITALIANA SERVIZI AEREI
TRIESTE
URBANWEAR

Re-organisation and expansion

On 6 January 1930, after several proving flights, the airline began flying between Trieste, Fiume (now Rijeka in Croatia) and Zara thrice weekly, initially operated by I-OLTD, later extended westwards to Venice, with the Cant 10ter I-OLTG and I-OLTH. The Free State of Fiume had been annexed by Italy on 22 February 1924, while the Zara enclave had become Italian territory as the Governate of Dalmatia after a treaty was signed with the Kingdom of the Serbs, Croats and Slovenes (later Yugoslavia) on 12 November 1920. On 14 April 1930, two further routes were opened, linking Trieste, Venice and Genoa thrice-weekly with a Cant 22, and Trieste, Brioni (now the Brijuni Islands in Croatia) with Venice daily. In July 1930, four examples of the all-metal Cant 10ter II, I-AASF *Aquila*, I-AASG *Falco*, I-AASH *Sparviero*, and I-AASI *Nibbio*, officially entered service.

That year proved to be a turning point for the company. The financial repercussions of the 1929 stock market crash in America were being felt worldwide, not least in Italy. Many private business owners were facing difficulties, including the Cosulich brothers, who were dangerously exposed to the banks and, as a result, were being drawn into the new era of Italy's growing nationalised industrial regime. The State-controlled Banca Commerciale Italiana had obtained a majority stake in the Monfalcone shipyard and in June 1930, the various subsidiaries, including SISA and the aeronautical workshops, were merged under the title of Cantiere Riuniti dell'Adriatico (CRDA). In the subsequent re-organisation, the aeronautical aspect became a separate division under the overall management of Augusto Cosulich, and was itself divided into two sections; one for the construction of seaplanes, the other concentrating on landplanes. Overall direction was in the hands of Ing Filippo Zappata, who would be responsible for many of the classic Cant aircraft of the 1930s. The first of these, the single-engined Cant Z.501 Gabbiano (Gull), was built in response to a request from the Regia Aeronautica and first flown by the CRDA test pilot, Mario Stoppani, on 7 February 1934. On 18 October that year, registered I-AZIL, it departed Trieste on a record-setting flight to Massawa in Italy's colony of Eritrea, covering the 4,130 km route in 26 hours 35 minutes.

Accidents were fairly common in the early days of commercial aviation, and SISA suffered its share, although very little has been recorded. Several Cant 10ter were lost, including I-AAAN in November 1929, I-OLTD on 19 June 1927, and I-OLTH, which crashed into the sea on 23 March 1928. Also destroyed in unknown circumstances and locations were I-OLTB and I-OLTE, both in March 1932, and I-OLTG in July that same year. For the Cosulich family, one accident was particularly tragic. Early on the morning of 20 August 1930, SISA's Cant 22 I-AACL *San Giusto* was heading towards Zara with 15 passengers aboard, including 10 year-old Emma, daughter of Oscar and Augusto's brother Guido, and her maternal grandmother. Over the island of San Pietro dei Nembi (now Sveti Petar in Croatia), the aircraft shed its port propeller, parts of which penetrated the cabin, killing young Emma and seriously injuring her grandmother. This was the second calamity to befall the family. In July 1926, Oscar Gosulich had drowned at Portorose while attempting to save his six-year-old son, who had fallen into the sea from a sailing vessel. Cant 22 I-AACK *San Sergio* crashed at Grado, Italy on 5 September 1929, and I-ADDA *San Vito* was also destroyed in October 1932, although the circumstances are unclear.

As a consequence of its financial difficulties, the year 1931 was a period of consolidation. The only new service was Fiume-Venice, with a stop at Pola (now Pula, Croatia) on the Istrian peninsula, which was inaugurated with the Cant 10ter on 18 January. On 5 October 1931, work began on the construction of a new and large, 80 x 35 m hangar at Trieste, capable of accommodating 12 aircraft, which was completed, after a serious accident, on 24 May 1933. On that day, it was officially inaugurated by the Duke Amedeo d'Acosta and was blessed by the Bishop of Trieste, Monsignore Luigi Fogar. The duke later acted a co-pilot, when the Cant 22, I-AACL *San Giusto*, made a trip to the Istrian coast and back.

At the end of 1931, SISA had a fleet of 12 seaplanes for line services – seven Cant 22, and five Cant 10ter – as well as nine Cant 7, 16 Cant 18, 10 Macchi M.18 and five SIAI S 16 for the flying school. However, SISA began downsizing its activities in 1932 and only operated services from Venice and Trieste down the Dalmatian cost, and the Ancona-Zara newspaper flights, primarily due to encroachment by other companies in its sphere of operation. Nevertheless, trial flights were conducted with a Cant 22 over the route Trieste-Lusin (now Lošinj in Croatia)-Zara-Lagosta (now Lastovo in Croatia)-Durazzo (now Durrës in Albania)-Brindisi. The flight training business was sold to the Regia Aeronautica on 14 October 1933. In 10 years, 4,210 pilots had qualified from the school. The decline of SISA was now irreversible and the moves towards a wholesale restructuring of civil aviation were now in full swing, with government-owned Società Aerea Mediterranea (SAM) taking over the private airlines. On 1 May 1934, in the presence of management and staff, the SISA flag was ceremoniously lowered, and on the next day was hoisted the SAM banner with its swallow symbol that had been inspired by a painting of the Venetian artist, Amelia Venturini, to which was soon added the Fascist *lictus* symbol. Four Cant 10ter and four Cant 22 were taken over by SAM with effect from 1 August.

In its short history, SISA had completed 12,093 flights in 28,330 hours in the air, and transported 59,021 passengers,

SANA's mainline fleet comprised a large number of Italian-built Dornier Wal Cabina flying-boats including I-AZDI

74,774 kg of mail and newspapers, 447,176 kg of freight and baggage, with a remarkable average regularity of 96.88 per cent on its scheduled services.

Italian-built Wal

SAICM was keen to start using its successful product, the Dornier Wal, which had been sold to a number of foreign companies, on Italian routes as well. Flying-boats were considered ideal due to Italy's long coastline in the Mediterranean, and its surrounding possessions in Libya (Libia Italiana) and later in the Horn of Africa. On 19 January, 1925, SAICM, together with the Banca Commerciale Italiana, formed the Società Anonima di Navigazione Aerea (SANA), which became the second Italian airline to take to the skies. The initial stock capital was ITL 1,000,000 divided into 10,000 shares, each worth Lire 100. A contract was signed in April 1925 with the Italian

Government for the concession of two air services: Genoa-Brindisi, and an international Genoa-Barcelona route, for a period of ten years. SANA could count on a subsidy for 640,000 kilometres per year. A second contract was signed on 20 November, 1925, which regulated the terms and conditions under which SANA could operate. The first air service scheduled to open would be from Genoa to Rome, Naples, and Palermo on the island of Sicily. A contract was placed for five Dornier Wal Cabina, the first two of which arrived on 27 February 1926. Registered I-DAUR and I-DEAR, the first was powered by two 268 kW (360 hp) Rolls-Royce Eagle IX engines, with the latter equipped with the Piaggio-built Bristol Jupiter IV engine, both in the type's distinctive tandem configuration. Financing of the fleet was accomplished with an ITL 3 million capital increase.

Developed from the Gs I and Gs II, the Do J Wal was a twin-engine, strut-braced monoplane with a two-step hull of

The Dornier Wal I-DAER was one of two that inaugurated the first SANA service from Genoa to Palermo via Rome and Naples in April 1926

Dornier Wal I-DAUR arriving at the Palermo Monte Pellegrino seaplane base

metal construction with a light alloy skin. It had a ten-seat cabin in the bows and, in early versions, an open two-seat cockpit under the leading edge. Its twin engines delivered a speed of 180 km/h and range was 800 km. On 2 March, Captains De Briganti and Antonio Locatelli in I-DAUR and Captains Tullio Crosio and Guilio Marsaglia in I-DEAR departed on a series of trial flights over the extended Line No.3   Genoa-Rome/Ostia-Naples/Angioino-Palermo/Santa Lucia. These flights lasted eleven days and enabled a smooth opening of the air service the following month. The first official service over the route, Italy's second air service, was inaugurated on 7 April 1926 with the same aircraft. The 1,070 km-long service was operated three times a week in both directions on alternate weekdays, and took some nine-and-a-half hours, compared to 46 hours by train. Flights left Genoa at 07:45 and arrived at Palermo at 17:15; while the service in the other direction departed Palermo at 07:00 and landed at Genoa at 16:15 hours. The initial one-way fare was set at ITL 450 (USD 23.70), as against ITL 750 (USD 39.50) by train. The cost of the ticket included bus transport from Piazza De Ferrari at Genoa to Passo Nuovo, near the seaplane base Vittorio Emmanuele III at the base of the Laterna. Within the year, fares had increased to ITL 800 for Genoa-Palermo, ITL 300 for Genoa-Rome, and ITL 500 for Genoa-Naples. Rome-Naples was charged at ITL200, Rome-Palermo at ITL 500, and Naples-Palermo at ITL 300. Higher fares were available for special luxury flights, as stated in the timetable, which included breakfast, but not wine and liquors! Baggage in excess of 10 kg also incurred a premium.

Just before the inaugural date, SANA had received the next two of its initial order, I-DOAR and I-DAER. The fifth flying boat, I-DAOK, was handed over on 8 November. All aircraft had different engines and were assigned a fleet number in Roman numerals:

- I-DAUR   I   Rolls-Royce Eagle IX
- I-DAER   II   Rolls-Royce Eagle IX
- I-DEAR   III   Piaggio Jupiter IV
- I-DOAR   IV   Piaggio Jupiter IV
- I-DAOK   V   Rolls-Royce Eagle IX

On 9 June, 1926, I-DEAR was involved in a serious accident near the island of Capri, when its rear engine lost its Reed propeller and substantially damaged the aft of the flying boat. A new hull was used on this aircraft and two new Piaggio Jupiter VIIIR engines were fitted. The aircraft did not re-enter service until 9 August, 1930. During the first year of operation (the service was operated until 31 December) the five aircraft had made 479 flights a total distance of 162,770 km, in 1,076 flying-hours. They carried 1,814 passengers, 213 kg of airmail, 9,931 kg of luggage and 4,638 kg of freight. Regularity was a disappointing 66 per cent.

The SANA fleet was extended in 1927 by another four Dornier Wal, one of which, I-AZDI, was the first to be assembled by Rinaldo Piaggio's eponymous company at Finalmarina, Piaggio having been a founding director of the airline. Piaggio went on to build a small number of aircraft, primarily to meet orders, which the CMASA production at Marina di Pisa could not accommodate. Piaggio also built the Bristol Jupiter IV engine under licence. The airline now operated nine flying boats, which enabled the line to be split into two at Rome, with the service on each sector scheduled to connect with the express trains to/from Paris, and to meet the steamships heading for Alexandria in Egypt from Naples. After the delivery of the new aircraft daily services were started on the route on 12 September. The increase in frequency and the size of the fleet had a positive effect on SANA's operating performance in the year, with 1,050 flights completed in 2,535 hours.

The four-engined Dornier Do R4 Super Wal enabled SANA to initiate its long-haul expansion. I-RUDO was one of six acquired

More flying-boats

Highlights of 1928 were the introduction of a new flying boat and the opening of a new air service. After the ending of the ban on German aircraft production in 1926, Dornier Metallbauten GmbH was able to start producing larger flying boats at its German plant at Friedrichshafen. One of the first civil products was the four-engined Dornier Do R4 Super Wal II, a larger and much improved development of the earlier Wal. This strut-braced high-wing monoplane of all metal design was powered by four 410 kW (550 hp) Gnome-Rhône-built 9Ak Jupiter VI radial engines arranged

in tandem pairs, and had a cruising speed of around 195 km/h and a range of up to 1,000km. On the port side just forward of the leading edge was a raised enclosed cockpit with side-by-side seats for two pilots, with a radio and navigation cabin in the hull to starboard. In normal configuration, the cabin forward of the crew station had seats for up to 11 passengers, with another cabin for eight passengers situated aft of the trailing edge of the wing. The first Dornier Super Wal made its maiden flight on 30 September, 1926.

Already in November 1926, SANA had placed a firm

Super Wal I-REOS taking off

I-ALTE was one of four Savoia-Marchetti S.66 twin-hulled flying-boats acquired in winter 1933/34

order for two, plus an option of four, which were firmed up in March 1927. The first two of the series were delivered in January 1928 and registered as I-RENE and I-RIDE and by the end of the year, the fleet of six was complete, also including I-RATA, I-REOS, I-RONY and I-RUDO. The new and improved aircraft enabled SANA to expand its horizons and, on 1 November 1928, a weekly service was opened over the 1,210 km route connecting Rome with Tripoli in Libya, via Syracuse on the east coast of Sicily. Malta was added to the schedule later. The opening of this service was given high priority, as it was the first link between mainland Italy and its dependencies of Cyrenaica and Tripolitania, which were taken from the Ottoman Empire in the Italo-Turkish War of 1911-1912. Both were combined into the unified colony of *Libia Italiana* in 1934 by then Governor-General, Italo Balbo, with Tripoli as the capital.

Four days after the inauguration of the Tripoli service, on 5 November, SANA used one of its Super Wal aircraft to add another major route, connecting three of the Mediterranean's major port cities – Barcelona, Marseille and Genoa – with Rome, slashing the surface-journey time by a massive 75 per cent. Negotiations over the Barcelona service had been started with the Spanish Government back in May 1925, but had foundered over Spanish demands for a 33 per cent stake in SANA. Agreement was finally reached after three years, but it is not known if this involved a financial interest by the Spanish Government. The SANA network now totalled 3,360 km. Between 1 January and 31 December, 1928, its aircraft flew 579,772 km, and carried 4,430 passengers, 1,850 kg of mail and 61,899 kg of freight. In the first two months of operation of the air service to Barcelona, the Dornier Super Wal had flown 10,800 km, carried 53 passengers, 56 kg of mail and 666 kg of freight and luggage, having made nine flights in each direction. Similar results were achieved on the route to Tripoli. Here,

6,160 km were flown, carrying 45 passengers, 45 kg of mail and 1,002 kg of freight and luggage. Emphasising the prestige of its services, SANA adopted fancy marketing titles for each route: *Freccia Rossa* (Red Arrow) for Rome-Tripoli, *Freccia Verde* (Green Arrow) for Genoa-Palermo, and *Freccia Mediterraneo* (Mediterranean Arrow) for Genoa-Marseille-Barcelona, the latter renamed later *Freccia Azzurra* (Blue Arrow).

Following a meeting in Turin in June 1929 between the French Aviation Minister, Laurent-Eynac and his Italian counterpart, Undersecretary of State for Air, Italo Balbo, a further concession was obtained from the French Government, allowing SANA to extend its Rome-Naples-Palermo route, which it had opened on 7 April 1929, onwards to Tunis, in exchange for the French gaining access to Naples and Rome on their regular services to the Orient. The first service to Tunis was operated on 19 December 1929.

Long-haul expansion

In the meantime, on 11 April 1929, SANA had embarked on yet another long-distance service, this time to Alexandria in Egypt. Originating at Genoa, the 2,895 km route, flown by the Super Wal, staged via Rome, Naples, Corfu, Athens, Rhodes and Tobruk. But it was short-lived and was closed down in 1930, having carried just 257 passengers during the course of 33 roundtrips, which represented an average per flight of only four passengers in an aircraft with 19 seats. Also transported were 3,952 kg of mail and newspapers and 36,731 kg of freight and luggage. In reality, this had been merely a political gesture, after a breakdown of talks with Britain's Imperial Airways Limited (IAL), which wanted to operate a through service from London to Alexandria via Italy. The Italian Government had demanded that SANA be allowed to operate a pool service with IAL, but when this was not granted, the Italian Government refused Imperial

SANA had intended to use Dornier's giant 12-engined Do X flying-boat on the Tripoli service, but I-AABN and I-REDI went instead into limited service with the Regia Aeronautica

Airways overflying rights over its territory, and Italian aircraft were banned from airfields in Sudan. Imperial was forced to reschedule its service from London to Basle, from where passengers and goods were transported overland by train to Genoa, before embarking the Short S.8 *Calcutta* flying-boats for the trip across the Mediterranean to Alexandria. The British continued after SANA exited from the route, and later, passengers, goods and mail had to travel by train the 1,530 km from Paris to Brindisi, for the onward flying-boat service to Egypt and beyond.

Having discontinued the air service to Alexandria, SANA concentrated on its surviving network. The Genoa-Rome sector (430 km, 3 hours flying time) was operated six times a week (except Sundays), as was the Rome-Naples-Palermo leg (640 km, 5½ hour flying time). At Palermo, Società Aerea Mediterranea (SAM), the new state-owned airline company, offered a connection to Tunis. The service to France and Spain was divided into two services: Rome-Genoa-Marseille (745 km, 7 hours flying time) and Genoa-Marseille-Barcelona (770 km, 7 hours flying time). Both services were flown three times a week on alternate days. With the train from Rome to Genoa and Marseille taking 24 hours, and that from Genoa to Barcelona 28 hours, the advantage of aviation over surface travel was clear to see. Even the fast steamer service to Barcelona was 21 hours at sea. SANA also continued the air service to Tripoli, but the stop at Syracuse was now made only on demand, but Malta had been added to the schedule.

The fleet underwent significant changes, forced on the airline in part by the loss of several airframes in accidents. I-DEAR was lost in January 1929, and on the night of

12/13 April, the Super Wal, I-RIDE, caught fire and burnt out completely. SANA took delivery of its tenth Wal, I-AZDZ, built by Piaggio, at the end of 1929 and, on 9 August 1930, the rebuilt Dornier Wal, I-DEAR was redelivered after its incident in June 1926 and received the same registration. It was a timely return, as SANA suffered two further losses during 1930. As early as 3 January, the Dornier Wal, I-DAER was lost at sea in unknown circumstances, followed by I-RENE at Cap d'Antibes on 28 May 1930. On 21 November, Dornier Super Wal, I-RONY, was destroyed in a crash. Further additions to the fleet were three more Wal, I-AEZA, I-AIZB and I-AEZC, in June 1930. I-AEZA and I-AEZB were powered by two 373 kW (500 hp) Piaggio Jupiter VIIIR engines, while I-AEZC was delivered with two Isotta-Fraschini Asso 500 R engines with similar power. The latter is said to have had a luxury cabin configuration, but no details have been found. A notable external difference from earlier examples were the round instead of square cabin windows, while the interior was fitted with improved seating.

The following results for the period April 1926 to June 1930 were published in the Annual Report:

- 2,701,754 km flown;
- 19,575 flying-hours
- 7,757 take-offs and as many landings
- 19,527 passengers carried
- 7,294,450 passengers/kilometres
- 347,385 kg freight, luggage and mail
- 84 % regularity
- 67 % average overall load factor

Nord Africa Aviazione (NAA) used six Caproni Ca.101bis high-wing trimotors including I-ABCC *Leptis* on network along the Libyan Coast

Improved performance

While SISA's operations were declining, SANA remained buoyant. It reported its best year ever in 1930 with regard to overall results. The aircraft had flown 1,268,881 km and transported 8,083 passengers, nearly double those of 1929; 28,874 kg mail and newspapers; and 122,758 kg goods and luggage. A few minor changes were implemented the following year. The service to Tripoli was now divided into two different services: Rome-Naples-Syracuse, and Syracuse-Malta-Tripoli. At Tripoli, SANA's service connected with the internal network of the Società Anonima Nord Africa Aviazione (NAA), created on 4 July 1931 at the behest of the Fascist Minister for Colonies, Emilio De Bono. It was headed by experienced former SISA pilot, Luigi Maria Ragazzi, and the technical director was Bruno Vellani, later to become a vital figure in the development of the post-war Alitalia. Services got under way on 26 December 1931, with Ragazzi carrying dignitaries, including Governor Badoglio and the consul Melchiori, and mail in a Caproni Ca 101 trimotor along the Libyan Coast between Benghazi,

Ajdabiya, Sirte and Tripoli. Initial operations were with two Ca 101 bis – I-ABCB *Cirene*, and I-ABCC *Leptis*, - but, with the addition of four more – I-ABCH, I-ABCI, I-ABCJ and I-ABCK – the Libyan coastal network was extended eastwards to Derna, Tobruk, Cyrene, Mersah Matruh and Alexandria in Egypt.

A fabric-covered high-wing strut-braced monoplane, the Ca 101bis was specially adapted for operations over the Libyan desert. Its three engines provided additional safety, their ample power reserve permitting flight with either the central engine or the two-wing-mounted engines, and boosted climb rate to avoid the frequent sandstorms. An extra wide and reinforced undercarriage eased landing on sand in case of an emergency. Most of the NAA aircraft were powered by a single 313 kW (420 hp) Alfa Romeo-built Jupiter engine in the nose, with two 150 kW (200 hp) Lynx engines, also built in Italy. Some aircraft were equipped with three Lynx engines. The cockpit for three crew was situated in the front of the fuselage, at the leading edge of the wings, separated from the passenger cabin by a firewall. The cabin was divided into a first-class section with six seats for European passengers, and a second-class section with a two-seat sofa for native passengers, and a lavatory on the right. Aft was the luggage and mail compartment. Two aircraft, I-ABCB *Cirene* and I-ABCH were lost in non-fatal accidents, but the other four passed to Ala Littoria, when NAA was incorporated into the new State airline on 1 August 1935. In its short history, the airline transported some 2,800 passengers, 10,000 kg of mail, 33,000 kg of baggage, and 17,000 kg of freight. Only five of the 280 scheduled flights were cancelled, attesting to a remarkably successful operation under difficult conditions.

Following a trial flight on 31 August 1931 by SANA pilot Luigi Bonotto with the Dornier Wal, I-AZED, a new service was inaugurated on 6 September extending the Barcelona service to Los Alcázares (for Cartagena) and Algeciras, a port on the Bay of Gibraltar in southern Spain. Here a link was made with three transatlantic steamships of the Italian shipping company, Lloyd Sabaudo, which connected Europe with the United States. Two weeks later the Gibraltar-based airline, Gibraltar Airways Ltd, began an experimental Gibraltar – Tangier service with its newly acquired Saunders-Roe *Windhover* amphibian, thus offering a connection with Morocco. This service was primarily for the transfer of mail, but passengers could also be accommodated.

The remaining Dornier Super Wal aircraft were only used if needed, and all services were flown with the twin-engined Wal, of which the airline had eventually acquired 19 in total. Having been very satisfied with the Wal, SANA now turned its attention to Dornier's giant Do X, powered by 12 Italian-built 433 kW (580 hp) water-cooled Fiat A.22R engines, and placed an order for two aircraft in 1931. The plan was to use these behemoths on the Tripoli service, with a view of extending this route further at some future stage. The first Do X2, I-REDI, christened *Umberto Maddalena* after a decorated Italian aviation officer and pilot, arrived in the Italian skies on 28 August 1931, with the second machine, the Do X I-ABBN, named *Alessandro Guidoni*, a general in the Regia Aeronautica, arriving on 13 May 1932. Between 16 September and 21 October 1931, I-REDI made a demonstration flight from Naples to Venice, touching down at Taranto, Ancona, Zara, Fiume, Pola and Trieste along the way. In the event, neither was delivered to SANA, instead being transferred to the Regia Aeronautica, the Italian Royal Air Force, where they were given the serials MM182 and MM208 respectively. The giant flying-boats found little use with the air force and were withdrawn from active service in 1935 and scrapped two years later.

SANA's operating results improved further in 1931, as well as in 1932, when the last available statistics indicated that the airline flew 1,330,000 km during the course of 8,797 flying hours and uplifted 9,990 passengers, 37,417 kg of mail, and 293,229 kg of freight, newspapers and baggage. Disappointing, however, was the decline of mail on the air services in connection with the express steamers to and from the USA. This figure dropped from 24,629 kg in 1931 to 7,252 kg in 1932. The reason for this decline is not clear. In the same year, SANA also received its last two Dornier Wal, I-AZDQ and I-CITO, both powered by two 448 kW (600 hp) Fiat A.22R engines, a great improvement over the early aircraft. I-AZDL, on its way from Tripoli to Malta, was forced to ditch into the sea due to engine trouble, shortly after taking off from Syracuse. Although a passing ship rescued the eighteen passengers and crew, the aircraft was lost during the tow. On a flight from Lisbon to Barcelona, the Super Wal, I-RATA, crashed near Playa Pinedo off Valencia, Spain, on 11 August 1933. One of the injured was the Chief of Staff of the Italian Air Force, General Julio Valle. General Valle was flying ahead of

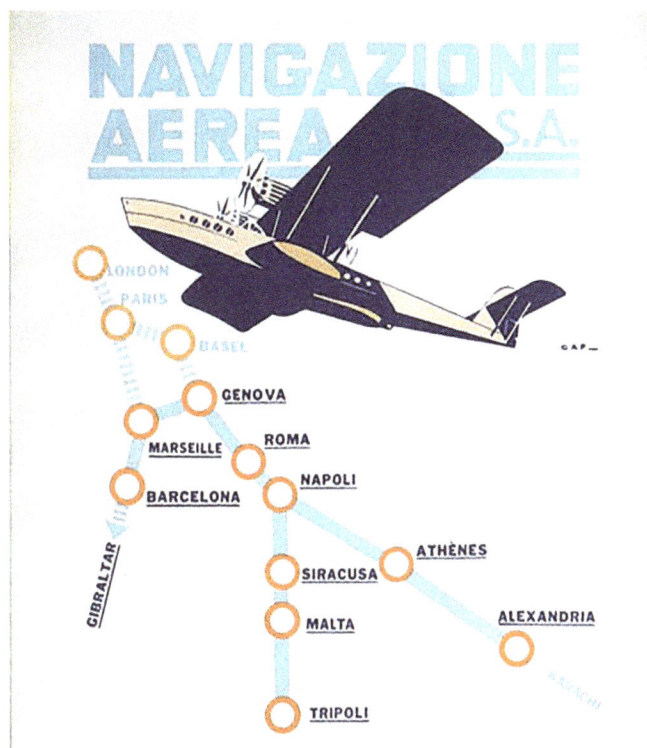

Libyan dignitaries in traditional dress posing by Caproni Ca.101bis I-ABCB

SITAR Savoia S.16 flying-boat I-AACH in San Remo Harbour

General Italo Balbo who was on the last leg of his round-trip to the US with 24 seaplanes. It is interesting to note that SANA was the biggest user of Dornier flying-boats in the world.

SANA's history was cut short in the State-sponsored re-organisation of Italian civil aviation. Thus, on 30 June, 1934, its shares were acquired by the Società Aerea Mediterranea (SAM) and all services were transferred to the State-owned carrier the next day. SAM also took over nine Dornier Wal and one Super Wal, but, for no clear reason two Wal, I-AZEA and I-CITO, were not acquired.

Smaller seaplanes could also be seen at Genoa for a few years, operated by Società Incremento Turismo Aereo Riviera (SITAR), which had its main base at San Remo, a growing tourist resort on the Mediterranean coast of Liguria. This company was established by local interests headed by Colonel Mario de Bernardi, a famous World War I fighter pilot and seaplane air racer, in 1928 and, as its name suggests, its main purpose was to develop the tourist market on the Italian Riviera. SITAR began operations with a motley collection of aircraft, including the Breda 15 and Macchi-Nieuport M.18, initially operating air-taxi services,

SITAR Breda 15 two-seat light aircraft I-AANX

sightseeing flights on Sundays, and occasional special services from in front of the Forte Santa Tecla in San Remo to Genoa and Avigliana near Turin. When the Hamburg America Line, a transatlantic shipping enterprise, offered an occasional stop at San Remo on its Genoa-Nice route, SITAR initiated a scheduled San Remo-Genoa service in July 1929 with its Savoia S.16 flying-boats, which included I-AACD, I-AACH, I-AACI, I-AAN, I-AANZ and I-ANOA. It would appear that the company folded in 1934 and the two World War One hangars of Pian di Nave, which housed the fleet in San Remo, were demolished two years later. De Bernardi had also intended to open a San Remo-Genoa-Munich line for the export of flowers, but this did not come to anything, nor did other plans for overland flights from a field at Arma di Taggia, which was already being used by airships.

Eastward bound

While SISA and SANA had been the prime movers in the development of Italy's early air services, two other companies also made significant contributions. One of these was Società Anonima Aero Espresso Italiana (AEI), also known as Aeroespresso del Levante, which too ventured beyond Italian shores. The company was established in Rome on 12 December 1923 with a capital of ITL 1 million, on the initiative of Giuseppe Volpi, 1st Count of Misurata, an eminent businessman and Governor of Tripolitania, and

was controlled by the Banca Commerciale Italiana. Playing an important part in the early days of the airline was Major Umberto Maddalena, given leave by the Regia Aeronautica to act as consultant to the airline for one year. A decorated First World War naval pilot, Maddalena would later be celebrated for leading the aerial expedition, which found Umberto Nobile's stranded party in the Arctic in 1928, following the downing of his airship *Italia* and, later, as a record-setting pilot on Balbo's long-distance flights.

Plans were drawn up, and in 1924, AEI reached a special agreement with the Deputy Commissioner for Aeronautics, that settled on a variation of Line No.4: Brindisi-Athens-Istanbul, the so-called *Linea Aerea Levante* with a subsidy of ITL 30 per km, an annual contribution for the maintenance of the fleet, and the free use of land, water, buildings and materials "necessary in Brindisi for the shelter of the aircraft and for servicing the line". This 10-year agreement was signed on 7 May 1924 and initially provided for a route Brindisi-Athens-Smyrna (Izmir), and, if not possible, for Brindisi-Athens-Thessaloniki-Istanbul. However, Turkey did not permit a route to Izmir, and Greece did not give permission for a stop at Thessaloniki. The contract was converted into law by Royal Decree No.1815 on 27 July 1924. AEI obtained the use of World War One hangars on the harbour of Fontanelle, which provided sheltered accommodation for 12 seaplanes, and the authorisation for a connecting office building and slipway. The service was intended to open in September 1925, but bureaucratic red tape by the Greek and Turkish Governments, and the lack of facilities in those countries for the operation of seaplanes, resulted in a one-year delay. Eventually, the Turkish government agreed to lease land at Büyükdere, some 25 km from the centre of Istanbul, where AEI built two hangars, a workshop, office, and a concrete ramp to pull the aircraft from the water.

Savoia-Marchetti S.55C I-ADIM together with I-AMES operated the first Brindisi-Istanbul service on 1 August 1926

I-ABOR was the first S.55C to be acquired by AEI

A fleet of five twin-hulled Savoia-Marchetti S.55C flying-boats was eventually obtained by AEI, enabling services to commence on Line No.4: Brindisi-Ithaka-Athens-Syros-Istanbul, a route of 1,437 km. After several proving flights, the inaugural service, flown by Maddalena in S.55C I-AMES, departed Brindisi after much ceremony and speeches by the Mayor of Brindisi, Serafino Gianelli, the representatives of the Greek and Turkish Governments, Dr Casalis and Dr Rifaat Bey, AEI's President Admiral Del Bono, and the Undersecretary of State for Aeronautics, General Alberto Bonzani, attesting to the importance given to this service. Passengers were taken by speedboat to the aircraft. The flight took off at 09:00 hours on 1 August 1926 and, after an uneventful flight, reached Athens/Palaio Faliro at 13:30 hours, with a refuelling stop at Ithaka. The final sector was completed with I-ADIM, piloted by Perucati, which departed Athens at 09:00 hours the same day, reaching Istanbul/Büyükdere, via Limnos, at 14:00

hours. The return service from Istanbul to Athens was flown by Mario de Bernardi with I-AFER. The intermediate stop at Limnos on the way to Istanbul was replaced by one at Mytilene on the island of Lesbos on 18 February 1930. If the weather at Athens was poor, the flight touched down at Porto Rafti (Limin Markopoulou), a seaside resort in East Attica.

A one-way fare of ITL 700 (USD 36.85), then a considerable sum, was never going to attract large numbers of passengers, and by the end of 1926, AEI had completed 40 flights and carried only 57 passengers, 138.1 kg of mail, and 5,002 kg of freight.

The S.55C was an unusual aircraft, the commercial version of which was developed from a torpedo-bomber monoplane, designed by Alessandro Marchetti. It had two wooden, single-step hulls, each with accommodation for four or five passengers. The tailplane, one-piece elevator, twin fins and triple rudders, were attached to each hull with

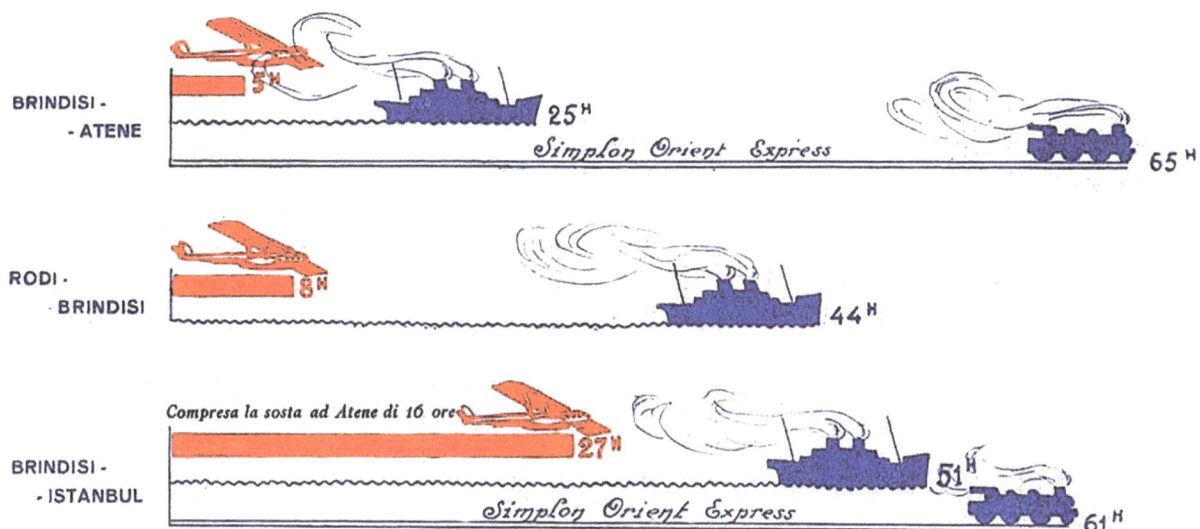

Comparisons of different travel modes between Brindisi and Istanbul

wire-braced booms. Mounted on struts above the wing were two 335 kW (450 hp) Isotta-Fraschini-built Lorraine-Dietrich water-cooled engines, providing a maximum speed of 207 km/h (128 mph). Range was up to 1,000 km (620 miles).

Following several serious mishaps with the S.55C, Maddalena determined that the prime cause was their under-powered Lorraine-Dietrich engines, and throughout 1927, they were gradually superseded by the Dornier Wal. The S.55C is best known for General Balbo's mass formation flights across both the North and South Atlantic. Also used on the trans-Mediterranean services by AEI was a single example of the Macchi M.24bis, I-BASE *Fra'Ginepro*, an unequal span biplane flying-boat. powered by two Isotta-Fraschini engines mounted in tandem between the wings. The main cabin had provided accommodation for six passengers in the bows, but there was another cabin aft for two more passengers. The pilots had to make do with an open two-seat cockpit.

On 29 December 1926, the new Greek Government, which succeeded the dictatorial government of General Pangalos, annulled all contracts signed between the government and foreign companies between 25 June 1925 and 22 August 1926. As a result, AEI was forced to suspend the service on 31 December 1926. However, the service resumed on 1 May 1927 on a twice-weekly basis. The optional stop at Ithaka on the way to Athens was replaced on 29 August 1929 by one at Patras.

Along with SANA, AEI also relied on the Italian-built Dornier DoJ Wal Cabina, taking delivery of the first six aircraft, I-AZAA, I-AZDA, I-AZDB, I-AZDC, I-AZDG and I-AZDH during 1927, with four more added over the following years. All were powered by the Isotta-Fraschini Asso engine. However, while the Wal was superior to the S.55C, the Aegean proved a watery grave for three aircraft, with another burnt out on the ground. On 25 January

Savoia S.16ter I-BAUV biplane flying-boat

Greek postage stamps referencing AEI's Italy-Greece-Turkey service

1929, I-AZDA was on a flight from Brindisi to Athens and was forced down onto the sea by a heavy thunderstorm, crashing into the rocky north-west coast of Corfu. The co-pilot and radio operator perished, the pilot was injured, and the mechanic and five passengers were unhurt. The pilot, Achille Rossi, and four crew members lost their life on 24 December 1929, during an emergency landing of I-AZDB near Agios Estratios Island in the Aegean Sea on a cargo flight from Istanbul to Athens. I-AZDH was destroyed by fire during engine start in the harbour of Mytilene, Lesbos on 10 June 1930, but none of the 12 occupants were hurt. The Aegean Sea also claimed I-AZEE on 18 July 1933. The aircraft left Athens for Rhodes, but soon after passing Makronisos Island, where it was observed by passing ships, all radio contact was lost. Greek warships and seaplanes mounted an extensive search, but failed to locate the crash site. Nothing was ever found of the aircraft, two crew including the pilot, Giorgio Pessi, four passengers and mail.

Aegean Italianisation

In 1923, Rhodes and the Dodecanese islands had been ceded to Italy by the Treaty of Lausanne, following their seizure from the Ottomans in the Italo-Turkish War of 1911-12. Italy named the islands *Isole Italiane dell'Egeo* (Italian Islands of the Aegean) and proceeded to initiate a broad programme of Italianisation under the administration of governors. It was natural and would be only a matter of time, before the islands were connected to the mainland by an air service, although it would take until 1930 for this to be achieved. In preparation, AEI undertook a proving flight between Athens, Syros and Rhodes on 28 February 1930. This was followed by an inaugural service over the route Rhodes-Athens-Brindisi and vice versa on 1 April 1930, on this occasion flown with the Dornier Wal. The flying-boats alighted in the front of the new luxury Grande Albergo dell Rose hotel, where passengers stayed overnight, with the cost of the hotel included in the ticket price. The stop at Syros on the way to Rhodes was initially on demand only, but became a permanent fixture in the timetable from

DORNIER-WAL
N25
DORNIER-WAL
ISTANBUL
ROMA
BRINDISI
RODI
ATENE
PATRASSO
A.E.I.
BRINDISI·ATENE·RODI
BRINDISI·ATENE·ISTANBUL
S.A. Aero Espresso Italiana

Dornier Wal I-AZDA was lost off Corfu in January 1929

Seven Dornier Wal including I-AZDM passed to the Ministero dell'Aeronautica in 1934

I-TUTO was one of three Savoia-Marchetti S.66 flying-boats, a larger and more powerful development of the S.55

Dornier Wal I-AZDC No.4 at Istanbul/Büyükdere seaplane base

1 July 1930. In August, mail was flown all the way from Athens to Venice, via a connection with Transadriatica at Brindisi. An addition to the fleet was a single 18-passenger Savoia-Marchetti S.66, I-AABF, a developed version of the S.55 with increased wingspan, greater operating weight and improved comfort and performance, which entered the fleet in 1934, and completed the Brindisi-Athens sector in just over 2 hours and 30 minutes.

To encourage travel to the Italian Aegean islands and Turkey, a series of 'package trips' was offered in 1933, which included air transport, hotel accommodation and discounted rail fares on connecting services. With costs varying from ITL 1000 for five days to ITL 2,000 for two weeks, organised by the three biggest travel agents in Italy - CIT, American Express and Wagon-Lits Cook - tourists could visit all the main attractions in the Eastern Mediterranean and Turkey and stay in luxury hotels. Approved by the Ministry of Aeronautics, the packages were offered on the Brindisi-Rhodes and Brindisi-Istanbul lines, both via Athens, and on the Rhodes-Istanbul line, all of which were flown by AEI. Tours in the other direction provided visits to Naples and Rome. The package tours proved popular and helped to boost AEI's passenger numbers.

AEI was acquired by Società Aerea Mediterranea (SAM) on 1 June 1934 but protracted negotiations in place between AEI and the governments of Greece and Turkey meant that it continued operating its Eastern Mediterranean services under its own name until 31 August 1935, when Ala Littoria took over all routes and services.

German ambitions

Since 1922, Junkers had nursed an ambition to extend its influence to Southern Europe and had discussions with financial institutions and private individuals with a view of establishing a manufacturing facility for its single-engined Junkers F 13, which would be used to initiate air services. Although plans were proposed for services between Genoa and Sardinia, from Naples to Palermo and Malta, and from Naples to the Isle of Capri in the Gulf of Naples, the last-named in co-operation with the Grand Hotel at Capri, none could be realised, in large part due to a general disinterest among the targeted companies. More promising were discussions with Karl (Carlo) Kupelwieser, son of an Austrian industrialist, who had purchased the Brioni Islands on the Adriatic coast (now part of Croatia and known as Brijuni). In 1924, Kupelwieser suggested to Junkers to operate regular flights and joyrides for the wealthy with a float-equipped F 13. Planned services were from Brioni to Trieste and Venice, as well as to popular summer and winter resort of Abbazia on the Gulf of Quarnero. Kupelwieser chartered a F 13, which was registered in Italy as I-POLA, the name of the city where it was to be stationed. Although several joyrides were made, as far as could be ascertained, no scheduled services were operated, but from 31 August 1925, he traded under the title of Triester Luftverkehrs-Gesellschaft.

Enter the Morandi Brothers, Bruno, Corado, Mario and Renato, who had expressed an interest in representing Junkers in Italy as far back as August 1922, when Junkers director Gotthard Sachsenberg made contact with the brothers in

Transadriatica 'terminal' at Venice/Lido (Nicelli) Airport

Karl Kupelwieser's Junkers F 13 I-POLA *Brioni*

Naples. However, Junkers concluded that aircraft production would be too expensive in Italy and abandoned that part of the plan, but on 29 August 1925, Renato Morandi, a young engineer from Ancona, his brother Mario, and attorney and former military pilot, Domenico Giuriati, founded the Società Anonima Italiana di Navigazione Transadriatica. Headquartered at Ancona, it had a modest starting capital of ITL 150,000, later increased in two tranches to ITL 1 million. To circumvent ownership restrictions, all shares were officially in the hands of the Morandi family, although the money was provided by Junkers, with only a gentleman's agreement in place between Renato Morandi and Gotthard Sachsenberg. As a young student in Naples, Renato had known members of the Junkers family and, as a result, was invited to the manufacturer's *Flugzeugwerke* in Dessau, where he worked as a volunteer learning the commercial and technical aspects of aviation. This in turn led to the hiring of German technical personnel to help establish the new airline. It had been anticipated that Transadriatica would join the Europa Union of Junkers-affiliated airlines, but the plan faltered after Junkers began to experience financial difficulties in 1926.

Junkers had continued to explore other opportunities before the establishment of Transadriatica, especially in the southern half of the country, an area where Benito Mussolini was keen to support industrial initiatives. This led to the formation of *Sindicato Aviazone Civile* (SAC) on 27 July 1925, at the instigation of William Knight, who fronted the Junkers efforts in Italy. SAC applied for a Milan-Brindisi route and wanted to use a float-equipped G 24, although the Italian Government had requested the use of the locally-built Caproni Ca.73bis. Nothing came of these plans.

Junkers F 13 I-BAVB was the former I-POLA

International outlook

Operations began in Ancona using a single Macchi-Nieuport M.18 flying-boat, I-BASA, between Venice and Rome, although this was only an irregular service. On 18 April 1926, the airline switched to the new Venice Lido (Nicelli) airport, which had been licensed for regular services on 31 January 1926. It was the first land airport in Italy, with an 850-m long flat grass runway. This came about as a result of the choice of six-passenger Junkers F 13 landplanes for Transadriatica, the first two of which, I-BATB and I-BATC, were delivered the following summer. Transadriatica launched its inaugural service on 18 August 1926 to great acclaim and in the presence of General Mario Bonzano, Undersecretary of the Regia Aeronautica, when I-BATB, commanded by chief pilot, Ricardo Pasquali, flew from Venice to Vienna/Aspern, via Klagenfurt, a variation of Line No.5. The service was initially flown three times a week, but frequency was soon increased to daily, except Sundays, in association with Austrian airline Österreichische Luftverkehrs AG (ÖLAG), which operated the service on alternate days. Technical stops were made at Ferrara and Klagenfurt, with Graz added as a stop from 1928. Three weekly services were operated non-stop between Venice and Vienna, cutting the journey time to three hours, compared to the 19 hours it took by train. It was also the first regular service across the Alps and was flown at an altitude of 13,000 ft (3,962 m). Up to 31 December 1926, Transadriatica had flown 66,434 km in 456 flying hours, carrying 917 passengers, 37 kg of mail, and 7,866 kg of freight and luggage on this service. A third F 13, the former I-POLA, was leased in November 1926 as I-BAVB, and a fourth aircraft, I-BBCA joined the Transadriatica fleet in December 1927. The little four-passenger F 13 was the world's first all-metal transport aircraft. At that time, it accounted for a large part of the European networks and was operated by many airlines, most sponsored by the manufacturer.

An extension to Rome/Monticello was added on 31 January 1927, flown with the three-engined G 24, I-BAUS, which had been registered to Transadriatica on 15 October 1926, also on a daily basis. The Rome terminal was changed to the new airport at Littorio in 1928. A second G 24, I-BAZI, followed on 20 April 1927. Both were acquired on lease from Junkers. Special permission was also given to use the 14-passenger G 24 on the Venice-Vienna route, but only three flights a week were allowed. The remaining flights were to be operated by the F 13 and the Caproni Ca.73bis. The subsidy for the G 24 was set at ITL 16 per flown kilometre.

The airline did much to ensure not only regularity, but also comfort for its passengers. It provided protective lagging to its fuel tanks and lines to prevent freezing at the low temperatures prevailing at the high altitudes of the Alps and

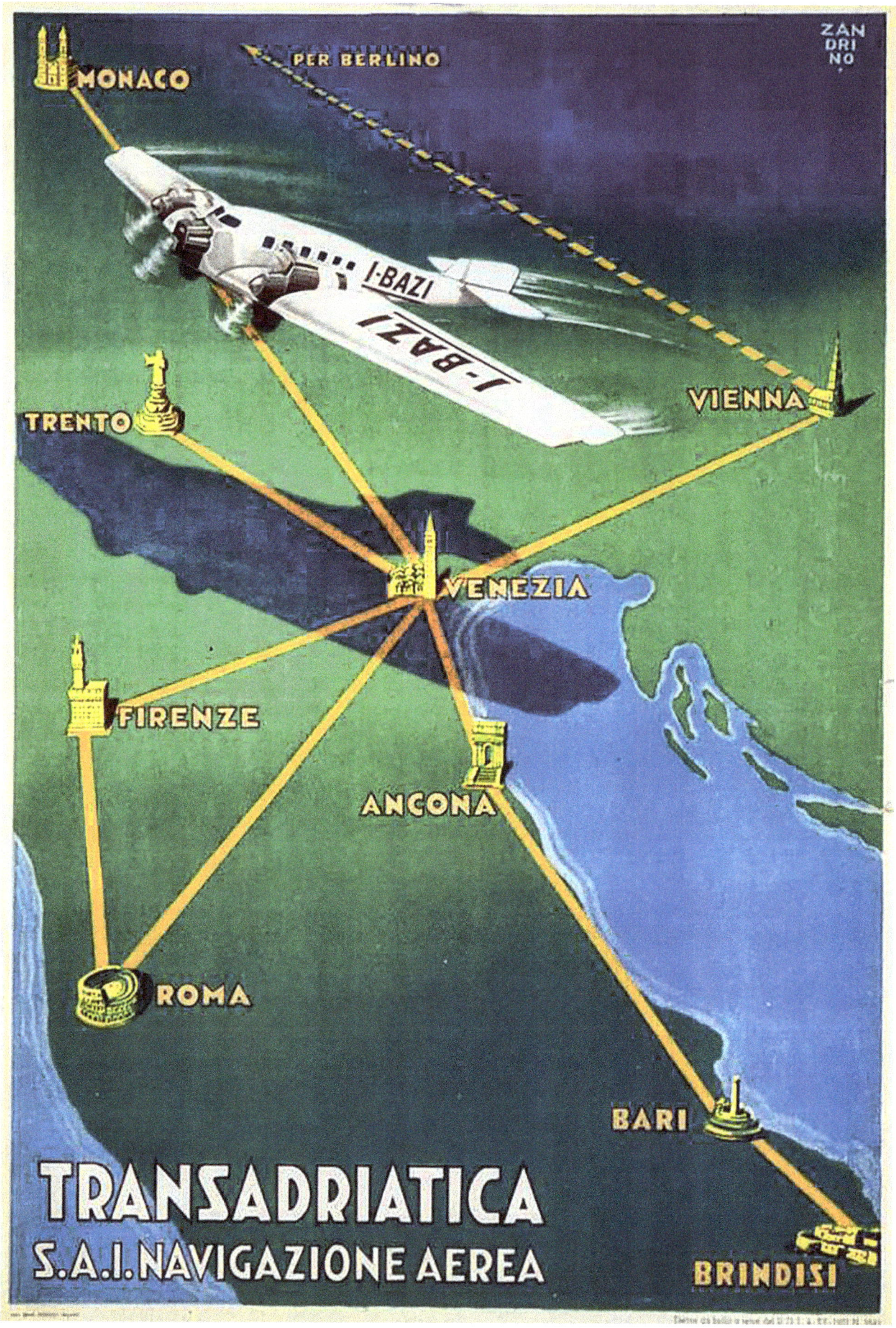
ZAN DRI NO
PER BERLINO
MONACO
TRENTO
I-BAZI
VIENNA
VENEZIA
FIRENZE
ANCONA
ROMA
BARI
TRANSADRIATICA
S.A.I. NAVIGAZIONE AEREA
BRINDISI

Junkers F 13 I-BBAS after having suffered a mishap

Junkers F 13 I-BATB at Venice Lido preparing for the first Venice-Vienna service

G 24 I-BAUS started its career in Sweden and was delivered to Italy in October 1926 (Roberto Gentilli)

Junkers G 24 being transported from the crash site. It was repaired and put back into service (Roberto Gentilli)

Cabin layout of Junkers G 24

Transadriatica's single Pratt & Whitney-powered Junkers W 33 b I-AAMA

Apennines overflown on its services, and a heating system in the cabin which was effective for outside temperatures down to 4.5 degrees centigrade. Its flights were timed to connect with fast trains from Rome to Naples, and by other airlines from Vienna to Berlin. As a result, it was possible to make the trip from Rome to Berlin in 11 hours, as against 39 hours by train. Transadriatica's aircraft were being maintained by German engineers. King Vittorio Emmanuele III came to Venice on 4 September 1928 and stayed for a long time at

Lido, visiting the Transadriatica facilities.

In June 1927, one of the G 24s was at Vienna-Aspern for a major overhaul, during which it had its two wing-mounted Junkers L 2 engines replaced by the more powerful L 5, for which Renato Morandi was prepared to pay RM 15,500 per engine. In November, a G 24 had to make an extraordinary landing, because the tube to the water pump had been incorrectly installed. In June 1929, I-BAZI was involved in an accident after take-off

The sole Hamilton Metalplane H-47 I-ROMA was an unusual addition to the fleet

Macchi-Nieuport M.18 biplane flying-boat I-BASA

from Venice. The port engine stalled and the heavily loaded aircraft (three crew members, seven passengers and luggage) crashed just outside the airport. The port wing hit the ground and was severely damaged, while the engines and doors fell off the aircraft. The pilot, Umberto Bianchini, the rest of the crew, and passengers were unhurt. The aircraft looked impossible to save, prompting a request to Junkers for a new G 24 on charter, but, surprisingly, it was rebuilt. I-BAZI had originally been delivered as a G 24 fe, but had its wings strengthened by January 1929, converting it into a G 24 ge. The centre engine was replaced by an Italian-built 373 kW (500 hp) Isotta-Fraschini Asso 500 in March 1930.

In the meantime, disagreements had surfaced between Junkers and the Morandi brothers. On 13 December 1927, Junkers suggested a 50/50 division of shares and was willing to set up a comprehensive workshop at Venice. But this was not acceptable to Renato Morandi, who wanted the family to retain a 80 per cent share and also indicated that he would want free use for Transadriatica of the proposed workshop. No agreement was reached and during an official visit of General Italo Balbo, Italy's Secretary of State for Air, to the Junkers works in Dessau,

Dr Kaumann and Fischer von Poturzyn informed the general about the differences between Junkers and Transadriatica. Following this meeting, the Air Ministry invited the involved parties to a meeting in Rome, where both Renato Morandi and Fischer von Poturzyn met with Gennaro Tedeschini from the Air Ministry. These talks led to the purchase by Transadriatica of the two G 24s and four Junkers F 13s at a total price of RM500,000.

Transadriatica's network continued to be strengthened. A line down the Adriatic coast from Venice to Ancona (Loreto), Bari and Brindisi was opened on 21 April 1928, which was flown three times a week, connecting with the flying-boat service of Aero Espresso Italiana (AEI) to Athens and Istanbul. On 15 May 1930, another route was established between Venice and Trento in northern Italy, while a second service between Rome and Venice was opened with a stop at Florence on 7 July. Experimental night flights were started in the spring of 1929 over the Venice-Mestre-Padua-Venice and Venice-San Dona di Piave-Treviso-Venice routes, but nothing is known of their effectiveness.

The fleet was boosted by a single Pratt & Whitney Hornet-powered W 43 b, I-AAMA, which had been

Statistics of Italian Air Services 1927

Routes	Length (km)	Passengers	Mail (kg)	Baggage (kg)	Goods (kg)
Turin-Pavia-Venice-Trieste	575	1,971	1,631	15,111	5,286
Trieste-Zara	252	1,302	562	9,025	740
Genoa-Rome-Naples-Palermo	1,070	3,387	2,456	26,207	18,146
Brindisi-Athens-Istanbul	1,437	470	1,212	17,499	5,196
Rome-Venice	500	1,197	430	14,192	2,466
Venice-Vienna	510	1,109	111	20,298	5,474
Albanian routes	320	321	295	-	-
Total	**4,664**	**9,757**	**6,697**	**102,332**	**37,308**

added in October 1928, and operated until coming to grief on 15 October 1930 during a test flight at Venice. Engineer G Ferrari was killed, but the pilot, Ricardo Pasquali, and one passenger survived with severe injuries. Another tragedy two weeks later halted the energetic expansion of Transadriatica. On 29 October 1930, Renato Morandi died when he was hit by a light aircraft, while taking photographs of the Junkers G 38, D-2000, at Rome's Littorio Airport. An unusual addition to the fleet was a single Hamilton Metalplane H-47, I-ROMA, a six-passenger all-metal high-wing monoplane, powered by one 391 kW (525 hp) Pratt & Whitney R-1690 Hornet air-cooled radial engine. It was registered on 7 August 1929, but was destroyed in November 1932

State interference

The Italian Government, which, through General Italo Balbo, Secretary of State for Air, had issued a decree that only Italian aircraft were to be operated, stated that if Transadriatica was to continue using Junkers aircraft, these had to be built in Italy. Documentary evidence is unclear if the company obtained the manufacturing rights, but two Junkers F 13 aircraft were assembled in its workshops in 1931, I-BAJA and I-BAJO, carrying construction numbers 1 and 2 respectively. Parts for the assembly of these aircraft came from Dessau. Both were powered by a 313 kW (420 hp) Fiat A.20 engine, although I-BAJO initially had a Pratt & Whitney Hornet when registered on 23 July 1931. On 1 May 1931, the

airline crossed the formidable Alps with a service to Munich via Trento, using its two Junkers G 24. It was flown three times a week until closed down for the season on 31 August 1931. The service was maintained during the other months by Deutsche Luft Hansa (DLH). The airline again became a target of General Balbo, who was determined to reform and consolidate the Italian airline business, while also providing encouragement to local aircraft manufacturers. As a result, Transadriatica was purchased on 23 December 1931 by the *Ministero dell'Aeronautica* for merging it immediately with state-owned Societa Aerea Mediterranea (SAM). All this, combined with a considerable increase of SAM's capital stock, as signed in an agreement with SAM's president Umberto Klinger on 22 December 1931, was approved by Royal Decree on 10 March 1932. Mario Morandi was elected to the Board of Directors of SAM.

Eight aircraft, I-AEDO, I-AFFA, I-BATB, I-BATC, I-BAJA, I-BAJO, I-BAVB and I-BBAS passed to SAM on take-over, but I-BATC, I-BAJO and I-BAVB were destroyed by fire at Venice aerodrome on 4 November 1932. The two G 24, I-BAUS and I-BAZI, were also taken over immediately. Although initially purchased by the *Ministero dell'Aeronautica,* both were officially registered to SAM in July and March 1932 respectively. But the formation of SAM had been only the first step in the further consolidation of Italy's airlines.

Italo Balbo – in cruise control

Italo Balbo was born on 6 June 1896 at Ferrara, north of Bologna. As a young man he served in WWI initially as a junior officer in the 8th Alpine Regiment before volunteering for flight training in October 1917. Before this could happen, he was recalled to the front when Austro-Hungarian forces broke through Italian lines during the battles of Caporetto and Vittorio Veneto. By the time that war ended, Balbo had been awarded several medals for military valour and attained the rank of Captain. Returning to his interrupted studies at the university in Florence, Balbo gained a law degree and as a fervent anti-Communist and Republican sympathiser, joined the fast-growing Partito Nazionale Fascista (National Fascist Party), soon becoming a prominent organiser of Blackshirt squads and ultimately, one of the four principal co-ordinators of the 'March on Rome' in October 1922 that propelled Mussolini to power.

Balbo had developed an early interest in aviation and in May 1922 had attempted to form a Blackshirt flying squadron in his home town. His reward was appointment as Under-Secretary for Air in November 1926, despite having little actual practical experience of aviation. To remedy this, he took a crash course in flying and emerged as a competent, if unexceptional pilot. Recognising his limitations, he took on Stefano Cagna, a brilliant lieutenant from the Seaplane Experimental Centre, as his own personal co-pilot. Balbo quickly embraced his new role and set about building-up the Regia Aeronautica (RA) into a modern air arm, independent from the influence and control of the army and navy, which nevertheless continued to receive the lion's share of increased state budgets.

When Balbo took over, he faced a dire situation, just 35 squadrons with an abysmally low number of serviceable aircraft, lack of spares, poor airfields, recruitment and training, riddled with bureaucracy and above all, very low morale. But with characteristic vigour and enthusiasm, Balbo turned things around and by the time of his departure after seven years, he had turned the RA into a professional force comparable with other European air arms, boasting around 2,000 aircraft and above all, a sense of mission and pride. He was also responsible for civil aviation, which consumed 5-10% of his total aviation budget, but soon formed the opinion that the industry was never going to survive without heavy government subsidy and formulated plans to combine all of the independent airlines into a single state-controlled carrier, leading to the formation of SAM, and subsequently, Ala Littoria.

Italo Balbo 1896-1940
A towering figure in Italy's prewar aviation

With his innate sense of showmanship, early in 1928 Balbo conceived the idea of 'aerial cruises', mass formations of flying-boats that would stage from port to port, rather in the manner the navies of the great maritime nations 'showed the flag'. The first of these was planned to cover the Western Mediterranean and would provide valuable operational training for the crews and support personnel. To organise this mammoth exercise, Balbo relied heavily on pioneering long-distance pilot, Francisco de Pinedo, who had made a return flight between Rome, Australia and Japan in a SIAI S.15ter flying-boat Gennariello between April and October 1925. He topped this achievement with his 'Four Continents' flight in 1927, which took him to South America, the Caribbean, the USA and Canada. for which he was decorated both by Mussolini and the Americans.

The Western Mediterranean cruise began on 26 May 1928, when a total of 61 aircraft (51 SIAI S.59bis and ten S.55P) spectacularly departed en-masse from Orbetello, north of Rome, heading for Elmas on Sardinia. Under the command of de Pinedo, the aerial armada then proceeded over the next seven days to

Pollensa (Majorca), Los Alcazares and Puerto Alfaques in Spain and Berre l'Étang, near Istres, France, before returning home on June 2. Each location had been chosen for a substantial sheltered harbour capable of housing the large fleet and be no more than 500 km or three to four hours flying time from the next destination. Apart from some damage incurred during a storm while moored at Los Alcazares, the cruise went off without a hitch and in recognition, Balbo was promoted to reserve general, while Pinedo received the title of marquis.

Balbo was soon airborne again on a cruise of European capitals, this time employing twelve landplanes, including six Ansaldo A.120 reconnaissance aircraft. Departing on June 28, the ultimate destination was the annual RAF Hendon Annual display for which Balbo's formation flew into RAF Hornchurch, accompanied by a flight of Armstrong-Whitworth Siskins from No.111 Squadron.

Encouraged by the success of his first cruises, Balbo was soon concentrating on his next expedition, this time to the Eastern Mediterranean. It was originally planned to visit Smyrna, Alexandretta (Iskenderun, Turkey) and Beirut, but the ruling Turkish authorities refused permission, so the round trip would instead take in Athens, Istanbul, Varna, Constanţa and Odessa. A reduced fleet of 35 machines (32 SM.55, two S.59bis and one Cant 22) left Taranto on 5 June 1929, reaching Odessa a few days later. Despite his well-known opposition to communism, Balbo was warmly greeted by the Soviets. Again, Balbo had relied heavily on Pinedo, but increasing disagreements and perceived rivalry led to a falling out, causing Pinedo to resign his post.

Not content to rest on his laurels, Balbo conceived an even more ambitious project - a crossing of the South Atlantic. He replaced Pinedo as leader with Lt-Col Umberto Maddalena, a highly decorated aviator with a series of record breaking and long-distance flights behind him. After months of intense training, twelve twin-engined SM.55A with two reserves led by Balbo in I-BALB and Maddalena in I-MADD, departed on 17 December 1931 on the first non-stop leg to Los Alcazares. Encountering a violent storm, Balbo and five aircraft were forced to take shelter in the Balearic Islands. They were all reunited two days later and, on 21 December, set off to work their way down the West African coast to Bolama in Portuguese Guinea (now Guinea-Bissau), their departure point for the hazardous 3,000 km ocean crossing. Lifting off from Bolama at 01.30 on 5 January 1932, one aircraft, I-RECI, failed to get airborne and crashed with the loss of five crewmen;

two, I-BAIS and I-DONA, came down in the ocean with engines overheating, both rescued by support ships, but one sank while under tow. The rest arrived safely at Natal, Brazil before making a grand entry to Rio de Janeiro's harbour at 16.30 on 15 January, greeted by a 48-gun salute and an equally exuberant reception from the Italian immigrant community. Returning home by sea after a three-week stay in Brazil, Balbo arrived to a tumultuous reception and was bestowed with the nation's gold medal for military valour and the International Federation of Aviators gold medal.

However, the flight that would consolidate Balbo's worldwide fame and acclaim was the Crociera Aerea del Decenale, marking the tenth anniversary of Mussolini's rise to power. An even more costly and logistically challenging aerial armada that would cross the North Atlantic to attend the Century of Progress Fair in Chicago. Balbo had envisaged a round-the-world flight, but the Sino-Japanese war precluded this aspiration. After months of intense preparation, the eight flights of three aircraft apiece (plus one reserve) crossed the Alps on 1 July 1933 heading for the first stop at Amsterdam, where one aircraft was lost during an alighting accident. The machine chosen was the improved SM.55X equipped with specialised instrumentation and up-rated 560 kW (750 hp) Fiat A.24R engines giving a cruising speed of 225 km/h over a range of 4,000 km. After a halt at Londonderry (Northern Ireland) the armada headed for Reykjavik where six days were spent waiting for a suitable weather window, before heading out on the gruelling 2,400 km flight to Cartwright, Labrador. Chicago was finally reached on 15 July via Montreal, having flown 9,766 km in a little under 49 hours at an average speed of 202 km/h. Rapturous crowds greeted the majestic formation over Lake Michigan and the city's mayor declared 'Balbo Day" and renamed a thoroughfare in his honour; Balbo himself was declared as 'Chief Flying Eagle' by the Sioux tribe, complete with ceremonial headdress. Following four days of lavish celebrations, the cruise continued to New York where a ticker-tape parade awaited them, while Balbo lunched with President Roosevelt, met fellow aviator Wiley Post and was awarded America's Distinguished Flying Cross. Returning home via Ponta Delgada, Azores, where I-RANI came to grief fatally, and Lisbon, they arrived in Rome on August to an ecstatic crowd.

Despite greeting Balbo warmly in public and making him air marshal, Mussolini, in the xenophobic manner of all dictators, resented Balbo's celebrity regardless of the propaganda kudos his exploits had brought to the country and Italian aviation. Seeing Balbo not only as a rival, but even a potential successor, in 1935 he consigned him to the outer reaches of the empire, designating him Governor-General of Italian Libya. Although disappointed by his treatment from Mussolini and his cadre, Balbo characteristically threw himself into turning this backward desert land into a viable colony that would attract Italian immigrants.

While having serious misgivings about Italy's growing leanings towards Germany and being heartily opposed to their policy towards the Jews, Balbo, nevertheless, remained loyal to Il Duce and the fascist regime. But when Mussolini took Italy to war on the German side, Balbo was reported as accusing Mussolini of "licking Hitler's boots" and predicted, correctly, that the alliance would lead to Italy's downfall. Balbo assumed military leadership in Italian Libya, but the forces at his disposal were poorly trained and equipped with obsolete equipment, having been under-resourced by Mussolini's 'adventure' in Ethiopia and support for Franco in the Spanish Civil War, Resigned to making the best of a bad job and with his customary hands-on approach, Balbo set off on a morale building tour of inspection on June 28, 1940.

At 17.00 Balbo's SM.79 bomber, registered I-MANU after his wife, departed from Derna's El Feteyat airfield for Tobruk, 168 km distant or about 25 minutes flying time. He was accompanied in a second SM.79 piloted by General Felice Porro, head of the RA in Libya. Shortly before his arrival, Tobruk's T-2 airfield had been attacked by six RAF Bristol Blenheims and defences were on full alert. Balbo had failed to carry out arrival identification manoeuvres and elected to land straight-in out of the sun. Although the airfield was aware of his imminent arrival, one nervous Italian gunner fired a short burst believing the two Italian bombers to be Blenheims returning for another pass. This, in turn, prompted shore batteries and ships in the harbour, who had not been advised, to open up. Balbo, whose aircraft lacked R/T radio equipment, could not be warned and descending rapidly to 200 m with the undercarriage down, flew into this fusillade. A stray shell struck the fuel tanks and Balbo's aircraft crashed in flames and burnt for several hours.

While condolences and plaudits were forthcoming from Göring, Hitler and even the RAF, Mussolini remained silent about his faithful ally's demise. But the RAF had the last word, nicknaming large formations of enemy aircraft as 'Balbos'.

Charismatic, yet sometimes contradictory, Italo Balbo was undoubtedly one of the most significant figures of Italian pre-war aviation.

SAM Savoia-Marchetti S.55P at Cagliari, Sardinia (Archivio SIAI Marchetti)

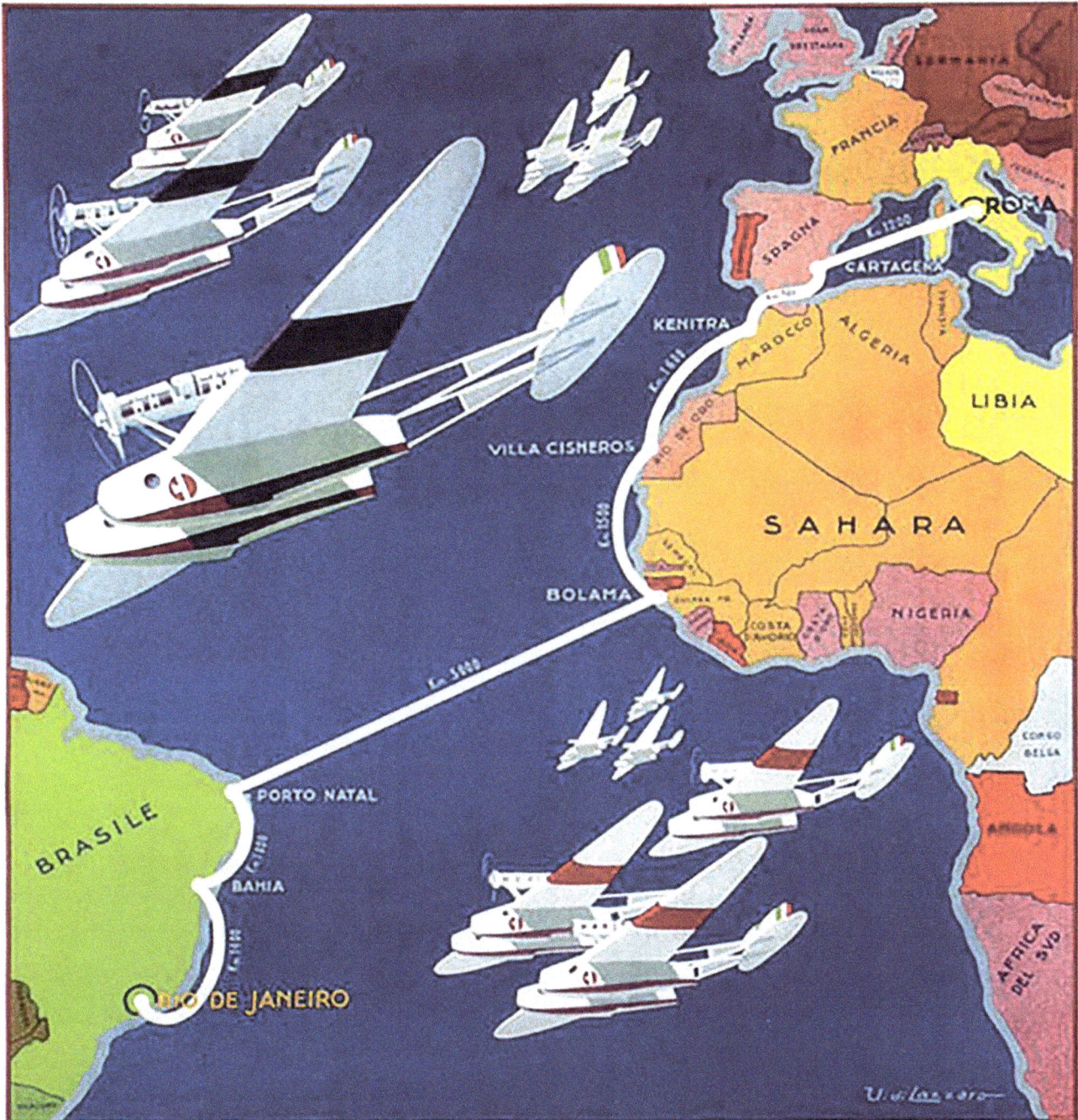

First consolidation

Founded on 27 March 1926, with government capital and contributions from aircraft manufacturer Savoia-Marchetti and Isotta-Fraschini, which built aero-engines and automobiles, the *Societa Aerea Mediterranea* (SAM) was initially headed by the Marchese Francesco de Pinedo, one of Italy's most distinguished aviators, famous for his series of long-distance flights. Starting capital was ITL 7.8 million, provided mostly by the State and industrial concerns. The first SAM service took place on 21 April 1928, when an S.55P, I-AABE, piloted by Rigoberto Salminci with five passengers in board, flew from Rome to Palermo, Sicily, via Olbia on Sardinia. A Rome-Cagliari route was also inaugurated on the same day. On 26 May, Benito Mussolini and Italo Balbo were photographed disembarking from a S.55P at Orbetello (Grosseto) in Tuscany. SAM was the only one of the main airlines to operate the single-engine S.59bis, a biplane flying-boat with an enclosed cabin forward of the wing for two crew and three or four passengers. On 20 November 1929, SAM lost S.55P, I-TACO, due to unusual circumstances. It crashed on landing at Terranova Pausania, Olbia, when the calm waters apparently created an optical illusion, causing an erroneous altitude assessment by the pilots. One person of the twelve aboard lost his life.

Pending the full integration of the four independent airlines, SAM proceeded to develop its own network. On 18 and 20 July 1929, successful trial flights were made between Rome and Tunis, one flight operating direct, and the other via Cagliari, which led to an extension of the Rome-Cagliari

Umberto Klinger and Italo Balbo

route on 10 December 1929, with some flights serving Tunis directly from Rome. A Rome-Tirana service was added on 1 July 1931, followed by Rome-Brindisi on 6 July. In 1929, following a series of disagreements with Balbo, de Pinedo ceded the management of SAM to Umberto Klinger, a decorated war pilot and latterly head of the Regia Aeronautica's main wartime transport unit. Klinger set

Eight-passenger twin-hulled flying-boats I-SILI and I-STRO outside the SAM hangar

about putting SAM on a firm footing. Passenger numbers increased from 5,253 in the first year of operations, to 7,801, although there was a slight reduction to 7.563 in 1930, probably as a result of the growing economic depression. After a deficit of ITL 80,127 in 1928, SAM recorded a profit the following year of ITL 13,902 and managed to stay in the black for the next four years.

In 1930, its capital was increased to ITL 12 million, with a further increase to ITL 18 million fully paid-up capital authorised by the State on 10 December 1931, consisting almost entirely of equipment, engines, inventories, workshop materials and spare parts. The capital increase was a reflection of the increased operation with the take-over of Transadriatica, whose entire network passed to SAM on 23 December 1931. The network was divided into three distinct areas: *Adriatic*, based around Venice, *Tyrrhenian*, centred on Ostia (Rome), and *Levante*, radiating from Tirana. The Adriatic network comprised the routes Rome-Florence-Venice, Rome-Venice-Vienna, Venice-Munich, and Venice-Ancona-Bari-Brindisi. The Tyrrhenian network was made up of the Ostia-Cagliari, Ostia-Tunis, and Palermo-Tunis routes, while the Levante network was headed by Rome-Bari-Brindisi-Tirana, Tirana-Thessaloniki-Sofia, and the Albanian domestic lines from Tirana to Coritza (Korçë), Shkodra (Shkodër),

Valona (Vlorë) and Gjirokaster. Passengers carried in the 1931/32 financial year were 11,240. The fleet had also grown and now comprised 10 S.55P seaplanes and eight landplanes, including 13 Junkers F 13, two G 24 and three Savoia-Marchetti S.71, a light transport for eight passengers. The Ostia and Venice workshops were improved and enlarged for the maintenance and overhaul of aircraft and aero-engines.

Albanian concession

Civil aviation also came late to the Balkan state of Albania, which had regained its independence in 1914 and was declared a republic in 1925 after the rebellion under the leadership of Ahmed Bey Zogu who, in 1928, proclaimed himself King Zog I. The country had long depended on Italian support, but under its new leader, Albania became a virtual Italian protectorate. An Italian company, Società Transporturi Aerei Internazionali, of Milan had proposed services from Italy and within Albania as early as 1919. These were intended to connect Antivari, Shkodër, San Giovanni, Durazzo, Vlorë, Santo Quaranta and Corfu, and Rome with Vlorë, but were never opened. It was not until the political situation had stabilised in 1925 that German interests, through Deutscher Aero Lloyd (DAL), established the Società Adria Aero Lloyd in the capital

Savoia-Marchetti S.55P advertising the Rome-Cagliari link

Tirana on 1 February 1925, with a starting capital of 200,000 Goldfrancs, of which DAL provided 55 per cent. Adria Aero Lloyd obtained a 10-year concession from the government for the transportation of passengers and all mail and freight to and within Albania. As the largely mountainous country along the Aegean possessed no rail system and roads were poor, travel by air offered a good chance of success. Air services were started the following month from Tirana to Shkodër, Vlorë and Korçë with two AEG K aircraft supplied by DAL. In August, Adria Aero Lloyd made a trial flight to Thessalonica, which was to be the start of a regular service to Greece, but this was never implemented. During the first year, the airline flew some 36,000 km and carried 800 passengers. After its establishment on 6 January 1926, Deutsche Luft Hansa (DLH) took over the shares of the Albanian company, but did not operate any air services there until 1 February 1927,

which was reflected in statistics, which showed that only 158 passengers were carried in the year.

A further change of ownership was completed on 7 July 1927 when DLH sold its shares to SAM, which renamed its Albanian subsidiary Società Anonima Adria Aero Lloyd (Italiana). After the take-over, the airline underwent something of a renaissance and it was later that year that the Junkers F 13 was first introduced on the network. In October 1927, Adria Aero Lloyd took over one of the aircraft allocated to the Italian Government and used by the Regia Aeronautica, having been given the civil registration I-LUMT. Another F 13, I-TALO, had been acquired from Junkers in July by the *Ufficio Aviazione Civile Italiana* and then handed over to SAM. Both aircraft were used on the domestic network linking Tirana to Korçë, Shkodër and Vlorë. Passenger traffic increased to 321 in 1927.

SAM Junkers F 13 I-ABAA outside the Aerolloyd hangar in Albania

A SAM Junkers F 13 taking off

Junkers G 24 I-BAZI on Rome-Vienna service

Savoia-Marchetti S.66 I-AABF at the Ostia seaplane base in March 1934

Albanian postage stamps overprinted with Vlorë-Brindisi route inaugurated on 21 April 1928

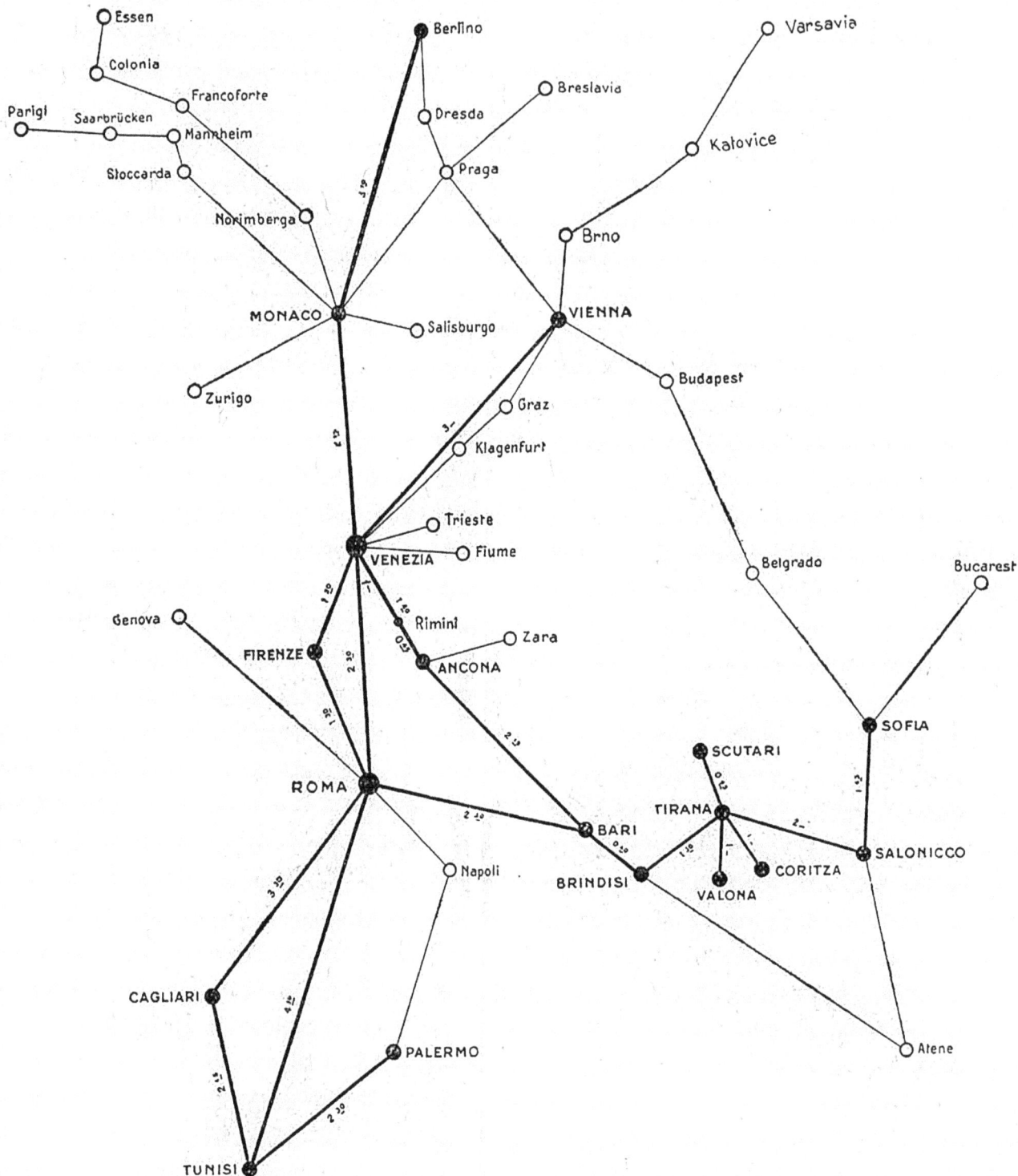

SAM routes and connections to other parts of Europe

Another domestic service was added in 1928 from Vlorë to Gjirokaster, close to the Greek border, while the first international service connected Vlorë twice a week with Brindisi in Italy from 21 April that year, made possible by the addition of a third F 13 to the fleet, I-ABAA, on 28 October 1928. In this way, the Italian Government provided three aircraft to Adria Aero Lloyd, presumably free of charge. One can safely assume that there were political reasons behind this generosity, as Albania was one of the regions where the Fascist Government in Italy strove to increase its influence.

By 1930, passenger numbers had increased to 3,140 and mail, freight and luggage to 37,720kg. With 139,576

Savoia-Marchetti S.71 I-AAYP operated on the Rome-Brindisi connection

The sole six-passenger Caproni Ca.97 I-ABCA in the SAM fleet

km flown, these results were the best ever achieved on the Albanian network prior to World War Two. All its services were subsidised by the Albanian and Italian governments. However, the economic crisis after 1929 hit the country hard and results declined. The Gjirocaster route was discontinued on 30 April 1931 and replaced on 1 May by a new line from Vlorë to Santo Quaranta, which connected with the Brindisi route operated by SAM. The first major international air route crossing Albania was opened by SAM in 1932, when the company rerouted its Rome–Bari–Brindisi service to Rome-Brindisi–Tirana–Thessalonica–Sofia, giving Albania's capital direct connections to Italy,

Greece and Bulgaria. SAM now had two F 13s stationed at Brindisi that were possibly used on the Brindisi– Vlorë service, as well as on the domestic network in Albania. Sofia was dropped from the schedule and, also in 1933, Adria Aero Lloyd opened a domestic Tirana-Peskopeja-Kukes link. As at 1 June that year, SAM now had three different F 13s stationed in Tirana, including I-ABBI, I-BBCA and I-AFFA. On 20 March 1935, after the formation of Ala Littoria as successor to SAM, Adria Aero Lloyd ceased to exist and was dissolved in 1936.

Junkers G 24 I-BAUS photographed at Foligno Airport in Umbria

Momentous change

The last financial year 1933/34, when a decision had already been taken by the Ministries of Aeronautics and Finance about the takeover of the independent airlines, was characterised by an emphasis on preparatory work for this momentous change, rather than seeking further developments. The Venice-Ancona-Bari-Brindisi and Venice-Florence-Rome routes were discontinued, as was the Rome-Tunis line. On the other hand, between 1 July and 15 September 1933, an experimental tourist line, Rome-L'Aquila-Chieti-Pescara, was inaugurated, in order to establish if such routes could be operated profitably without subsidy, or at least with modest contribution from local authorities. Even though these flights were operated with unsuitable equipment, a total of 89 flights were made, carrying 277 passengers at an average load factor of 63.9 per cent. What was more remarkable was that the operational performance exceeded forecasts and a break-even situation was achieved. While this generated interest from many provinces for local air services, SAM's paymasters had other priorities. Attention was also paid and plans made for bringing Trieste into the network, with a direct service to Rome, and further afield to the Balkans and the Near East. This was another project put on the back burner. In recognition of acquiring the fleets of the independent airlines, all single-engine aircraft were removed from scheduled services on 1 January 1934. The financial year to 30 June 1934 ended with improved figures, in spite of the reduction in the network. A total of 23,012 passengers were transported, of which only 277 were freeloaders. Freight amounted to 71,056 kg, baggage to 333,115 kg, mail to 13,504 kg and newspapers to 17,746 kg. A profit of ITL 570,245 was well above that of all previous years.

The final integration began on 1 May 1934 with the purchase of the shares in Società Italiana Servizi Aerei (SISA), although full integration did not take place until 1 August. This was followed on 1 June 1934 by the acquisition of Società Anonima Aero Espresso Italiana (AEI), although AEI continued operating under its own name until 31 August 1935. The final step came on 1 July with the integration of Società Anonima di Navigazione Aerea (SANA). SAM prided itself on the fact that the integration was achieved with such a precision that all scheduled services continued operating without disruption, with not a single service either suspended, postponed or delayed. The fleet, which, at 30 June 1934, had comprised nine twin-engine Savoia-Marchetti S.55P (six powered by the Fiat A 24.R engines, and three with the Isotta-Fraschini Asso 500 R), three three-engined S.66, five three-engine S.71 (three with Walter Castor engines and two with the Piaggio Stella 7), two single-engine Junkers F 13 and two three-engine Junkers G 24, was now swelled to a great extent, leaving SAM with a motley collection of eight different types. In addition, two further S.66 were under construction, and an order had been placed for two high-wing S.74 aircraft equipped with four Piaggio Stella N engines, with accommodation for 24 passengers, which made its first flight on 16 November 1934.

Powered by three 560 kW (750 hp) Fiat A 24.R engines, the S.66 twin-hulled flying-boats with accommodation for 16 passengers in greater comfort, better flight characteristics and increased speed, were considered better to meet the needs of intense traffic and had the added advantage of being able to maintain level flight with only two engines operating. The G 24 was used on the longer routes, including Rome-Venice-Vienna, Rome-Florence-Venice and Venice-Munich and Berlin. I-BAUS had its centre engine replaced in 1933 by a 373 kW (500 hp) Isotta-Fraschini Asso 500 and converted into a G 24 gy. Both aircraft were now flying with Italian-built centre engines.

On 28 October 1934, on the twelfth anniversary of the Fascist March on Rome, SAM became Ala Littoria Società Anonima.

AEI (Società Anonima Aero Espresso Italiana) Fleet 1927-1934

CMASA/Piaggio Dornier Wal Cabina 1927-1934 (11)

19-passenger strut-braced high-wing monoplane (seaplane), powered by four tandem 386 kW (525 hp) Siemens-Piaggio/Bristol Jupiter VI engines, generating a cruising speed of 190 lm/h (118 mph)

I-AZAA	52/72	20.04.27-14.08.34	to Ministero dell'Aeronautica
I-AZDA	53/73	27.04.27-25.01.29	lost off Corfu, Greece
I-AZDB	59/79	10.05.27-24.12.29	crashed in the Aegean Sea near Andros
I-AZDC	60/80	30.05.27-14.08.34	to Ministero dell'Aeronautica
I-AZDG	64/84	23.08.27-14.08.34	to Ministero dell'Aeronautica
I-AZDH	65/85	09.09.27-10.06.30	destroyed by fire in Mytilene Harbour, Lesbos
I-AZDM	83/103	27.02.28-14.08.34	to Ministero dell'Aeronautica
I-AZDN	84/104	27.02.28-14.08.34	to Ministero dell'Aeronautica
I-AZDO	105/125	12.11.31-14.08.34	to Ministero dell'Aeronautica
I-AZEE	127/147	06.01.32-16.07.33	lost in the Aegean Sea en route Piraeus-Rhodes
I-AZEG	129/149	14.06.32-14.09.34	to Ministero dell'Aeronautica

Macchi M.24bis 1930 (1)

Six-passenger biplane flying-boat, powered by two 373 kW (500 hp) Isotta-Fraschini Asso engines, generating a maximum speed of 185 km/h (115 mph)

I-BASE	*Fra'Ginepro*	00.00.30-	

Savoia S.16ter 1926-1934 (2)

Two-passenger biplane flying-boat, powered by one 298 kW (400 hp) Lorraine-Dietrich 12Db V engine, generating a maximum speed of 194 km/h (120 mph)

I-BAUT	5148	07.12.26-00.08.34	destroyed
I-BAUV	5149	07.12.26-00.00.34	

Savoia-Marchetti S.55C 1925-1934 (7)

Eight-passenger cantilever wing twin-hull monoplane flying-boat powered by two tandem 335 kW (450 hp) Lorraine-Dietrich 12Db V in-line engines, generating a cruising speed of 170 km/h (106 mph)

I-ABOR	10501	14.08.25-00.09.27	sank in Sea of Marmara (Black Sea)
I-ACNO	10502	28.08.25-00.12.27	destroyed
I-ADIM	10503	24.07.26-00.11.26	destroyed near Athens, Greece
I-AFER	10504	20.03.26-00.11.26	destroyed near Athens, Greece
I-AGRO	10505	00.10.27-00.08.34	ex SISA; destroyed
I-ALTA	10506	00.10.27-00.08.29	wfu
I-AMES	10507	20.03.26-00.12.27	destroyed

Savoia-Marchetti S.59bis 1928 (1)

Four-passenger biplane flying-boat, powered by a single 373 kW (500 hp) Isotta-Fraschini Asso 500 engine, generating a maximum speed of 210 km/h (130 pmh)

I-AACO	9566	00.09.28-	to Società Aerea Mediterranea (SAM)

Savoia-Marchetti S.66 1934-1936 (3)

18-22 passenger cantilever wing, twin-hull monoplane flying-boat, powered by three 515 kW (700 hp) Fiat A.24R engines, generating at cruising speed of 222 km/h (138 mph)

I-AABF	15006	08.10.34-31.08.35	ex Società Aerea Mediterranea (SAM); to Ala Littoria
I-ONIO	15009	04.07.34-31.08.35	ex Società Aerea Mediterranea (SAM); to Ala Littoria
I-TUTO	15003	13.07.34-31.08.35	ex Società Aerea Mediterranea (SAM); to Ala Littoria

NAA (Nord-Africa Aviazione Società Anonima) Fleet 1931-1935

Caproni Ca 101 1931-1935 (6)

Eight-passenger strut-braced monoplane, powered by three 149 kW (200 hp) Armstrong-Siddely Lynx engines, generating a cruising speed of 166 km/h (103 mph)

I-ABCB	*Cirene*	3251	15.12.31-00.03.34	destroyed
I-ABCC	*Leptis*		15.12.31-08.08.35	to Ministero dell'Aeronautica
I-ABCH		3337	02.05.32-00.07.32	destroyed
I-ABCI		3349	05.08.32-08.08.35	to Ministero dell'Aeronautica
I-ABCJ		3350	24.09.32-08.08.35	to Ministero dell'Aeronautica
I-ABCK		3351	29.05.34-08.08.35	to Ministero dell'Aeronautica

SAM (Società Aerea Mediterranea) Fleet 1928-1934

Cant 10ter 1934 (4)

Four-passenger biplane flying-boat, powered by one 298 kW (400 hp) Lorraine-Dietrich engine, generating a cruising speed of 150 km/h (93 mph)

I-AASF	203	01.08.34-	ex SISA;
I-AASG	204	01.08.34-	ex SISA;
I-AASH	206	01.08.34-2810.34	ex SISA; to Ala Littoria
I-AASI		01.08.34-00.10.34	ex SISA;

Cant 22 1934-1936 (6)

Eight-passenger biplane flying-boat, powered by three Isotta-Fraschini Asso 200 in-line engines, generating a cruising speed of 140 km/h (87 mph)

I-AABN	5	01.08.34-28.10.34	ex SISA; to Ala Littoria
I-AACJ	64	01.08.34-28.10.34	ex SISA; to Ala Littoria
I-AACL	159	01.08.34-28.10.34	ex SISA; to Ala Littoria

I-AACM	160	01.08.34-28.10.34	ex SISA; to Ala Littoria
I-AAQX	162	01.08.34-28.10.34	ex SISA; to Ala Littoria
I-ALFA	230	01.08.34-28.10.34	ex SISA; to Ala Littoria

Caproni Ca 97 1934 (1)

Six-passenger, strut-braced high wing monoplane, powered by three 108 kW (145 hp) Walter Mars radial engine, generating a maximum speed of
192 km/h (119 mph)

| I-ABCA | 3079 | 17.09.34-10.34 | new ex Caproni, to Ala Littoria |

Fokker F.VIIb-3m (2)

Eight-passenger high-wing monoplane, powered by three 272 kW (365 hp) Gnome-Rhône Titan Major engines, generating a maximum speed of 222 km/h (138 mph)

| I-BBEC | 4982 | 12.09.33-29.01.34 | leased from Avio Linee Italiane (ALI) |
| I-BBED | 5059 | 03.11.33-30.04.34 | leased from Avio Linee Italiane (ALI) |

Junkers F 13 1931-1934 (12)

Four-passenger, cantilever wing monoplane, powered by one 136 kW (182 hp) BMW IIIa in-line engine, developing a cruising speed of
170 km/h (105 mph)

I-ABBA	2027	01.06.28-28.10.34	to Ala Littoria
I-ABBI	762	10.09.30-.00.07.34	traded in to Junkers, later D-OQEX
I-AEDO	2022	23.12.31-00.06.34	ex Transadriatica; to Deutsche Lufthansa as D-ODEN *Kohlmeise*
I-AFFA	623	23.12.31-00.05.34	ex Transadriatica; to Deutsche Luftahansa as D-OTAL *Blaumeise*
I-BAJA	2071/1	23.12.31-04.11.32	ex Transadriatica; destroyed by fire at Venice/San Nicolò Airport
I-BAJO	2070/2	23.12.31-04.11.32	ex Transadriatica; destroyed by fire at Venice/San Nicolò Airport
I-BATB	778	23.12.31-00.04.34	ex Transadriatica; cancelled as broken up
I-BATC	759	23.12.31-04.11.32	ex Transadriatica; destroyed by fire at Venice/San Nicolò Airport
I-BAVB	762	23.12.31-04.11.32	ex Transadriatica; destroyed by fire at Venice/San Nicolò Airport
I-BBAS	2008	23.12.31-16.11.33	ex Transadriatica; traded in to Junkers, later D-OMAS
I-LUMT	621	26.05.29-11.10.34	ex Adria Aero Lloyd; to Junkers for lengthy repairs and to Deutsche Verkehrsfliegerschule as D-OHIR 05.35
I-TALO	2010	23.08.28-00.11.32	ex Ufficio Aviazione Civile Italiane; cancelled as destroyed

Junkers G 24 ge (2)

14-passenger cantilever wing monoplane, powered by three 231 kW (310 hp) Junkers L-5 engines, generating a cruising speed of
170 km/h (110 mph)

| I-BAUS | 924 | 23.12.31-28.10.34 | ex Transadriatica; to Ala Littoria |
| I-BAZI | 947 | 23.12.31-28.10.34 | ex Transadriatica; to Ala Littoria |

Savoia-Marchetti S.55P 1928-1934 (13)

Eight-passenger cantilever wing, twin-hull monoplane flying-boat powered by two tandem 373 kW (500 hp) Isotta-Fraschini Asso 500 engines, generating a cruising speed of 170 km/h (106 mph)

I-AABE	10509	19.04.28-00.07.28	ex MM45018; returned Regia Aeronautica
I-AABF	10506	16.06.28-00.09.33	ex MM97; wfu time expired
I-AABG		02.07.28-00.11.31	ex MM98; destroyed
I-BICO	10524	26.05.30-28.10.34	to Ala Littoria
I-MERO	10515	07.05.29-28.10.34	to Ala Littoria
I-NACO	10516	03.06.29-28.10.34	to Ala Littoria
I-NDRA	10513	16.03.29-28.10.34	to Ala Littoria
I-OLAO	10526	07.01.31-28.10.34	to Ala Littoria
I-OLCO		05.10.29-00.02.30	ex MM119; destroyed
I-RZIO	10522	07.11.29-28.10.34	to Ala Littoria
I-SILI	10518	29.07.29-28.10.34	to Ala Littoria
I-STRO	10523	19.12.29-28.10.34	to Ala Littoria
I-TRIA	10525	07.04.30-	

Savoia-Marchetti S.59bis (2)

Four-passenger biplane flying-boat, powered by a single 373 kW (500 hp) Isotta-Fraschini Asso 500 engine, generating a maximum speed of 210 km/h (130 pmh)

I-AACO	9566		ex-AEI;
I-ABBE	3633	03.04.30-	ex MM40145; to Società Incremento Turismo Aereo Italiane (SITA)

Savoia-Marchetti S.62 1928 (1)

Four-passenger biplane flying-boat, powered by one 373 kW (500 hp) Isotta-Fraschini Asso 500 engine, generating a maximum speed fo 200 km/h (124 mph)

I-BBBY	6202	02.01.28-	to American Aeronautical Corporation as NC9146

Savoia-Marchetti S.66 1933-1934 (9)

18-22 passenger twin-hull cantilever monoplane flying-boat, powered by three 515 kW (700 hp) Fiat A.24R engines, generating a cruising speed of 222 km/h (138 mph)

I-AABF	15006	30.11.33-08.10.34	to Aero Espresso Italiana (AEI)
I-ALTE	15005	30.06.34-28.10.34	ex SANA; to Ala Littoria
I-BLEO	15010	07.07.34-28.10.34	to Ala Littoria
I-EGEO	15011	09.10.34-28.10.34	to Ala Littoria
I-FBAA	15008	11.03.34-28.10.34	to Ala Littoria
I-ONIO	15009	30.05.34-04.07.34	to Aero Espresso Italiana (AEI)
I-REDI	15004	30.06.34-28.10.34	ex SANA, to Ala Littoria
I-TUTO	15003	30.06.34-13.07.34	ex SANA; to Aero Expresso Italiane (AEI)

| I-VALE | 15007 | 30.06.34-28.10.34 | ex SANA; to Ala Littoria |

Savoia-Marchetti S.71 1931-1934 (2)

Eight-passenger high wing cantilever monolane, powered by three 179 kW (240 hp) Walter Castor radial engines, generating a cruising speed of 180 km/h (112 mph)

| I-AAYP | 7101 | 27.01.31-28.10.34 | to Ala Littoria |
| I-SIAI | 7102 | 19.01.32-00.07.34 | destroyed in forced landing |

SANA (Società Anonima di Navigazione Aerea) Fleet 1926-1934

CMASA/Piaggio/Marina Fiat Dornier Wal Cabina 1926-1934 (18)

19-passenger strut-braced high-wing monoplane (seaplane), powered by four tandem 386 kW (525 hp) Siemens-Piaggio/Bristol Jupiter VI engines, generating a cruising speed of 190 km/h (118 mph)

I-AYZY	48/68	03.03.27-30.06.34	to Ministero dell'Aeronautica
I-AYZZ	50/70	01.04.27-00.09.28	destroyed by fire
I-AZDI	81/101	07.11.27-30.07.34	to Ministero dell'Aeronautica
I-AZDL	82/102	25.10.27-03.11.32	crashed into sea en route Sicily-Tripoli
I-AZDZ	91/111	29.01.30-30.06.34	to Ministero dell'Aeronautica
I-AZEA	92/112	01.03.30-16.02.32	crashed after engine failure on take-off at Malta
I-AZEB	93/113	07.06.30-30.06.34	to Ministero dell'Aeronautica
I-AZEC	94/114	10.07.30-30.06.34	to Ministero dell'Aeronautica
I-AZED	96/126	14.01.30-30.06.34	to Ministero dell'Aeronautica
I-AZEG	129/249	13.06.32-14.08.34	to Ministero dell'Aeronautica
I-AZER	/256	25.09.33-30.06.34	to Ministero dell'Aeronautica
I-CITO	/146	21.05.32-25.05.33	crashed on take-off at Etang de Berre, Marseille, France
I-DAER	29/48	03.04.26-00.07.28	destroyed
I-DAOK	38/58	03.01.27-12.10.34	to Ministero dell'Aeronautica
I-DAUR	28/47	24.07.26-	
I-DEAR (1)	30/49	24.07.26-30.01.30	damaged into the sea off Capri; rebuilt as I-DEAR (2)
I-DEAR (2)	124/144	00.08.30-30.06.34	to Ministero dell'Aeronautica
I-DOAR	31/50	01.04.26-23.05.34	destroyed

Dornier Do R4 Super Wal 1928-1934 (6)

19-passenger strut-braced high-wing monoplane (seaplane), powered by four tandem 386 kW (525 hp) Siemens/Bristol Jupiter VI engines, generating a cruising speed of 190 lm/h (118 mph)

I-RATA	145	06.08.28-11.08.33	crashed off Valencia, Spain
I-RENE	141	27.10.28-00.06.30	wfu
I-REOS	144	27.10.28-21.04.34	destroyed at La Spezia
I-RIDE	142	07.01.29-12.04.29	destroyed by fire at Naples

| I-RONY | | 170 | 02.05.29-21.11.30 | damaged en route Barcelona-Madrid, but reported to be in service in 1931 |
| I-RUDO | | 171 | 19.07.29-30.06.34 | to Ministero dell'Aeronautica |

Dornier Do X 1931 (2)

66-100-passenger strut-braced high-wing monoplane flying-boat, powered by twelve 425 kW (570 hp) Fiat A22R engines ounted in tandem pairs, generating a cruising speed of 175 km/h (109 mph)

| I-REDI | *Umberto Maddalena* | 3 | 28.08.31- | not taken up; to Regia Aeronautica as MM182 |
| I-ABBN | *Alessandro Guidoni* | 3 | 13.05.32- | not taken up; to Regia Aeronautica as MM208 |

Savoia-Marchetti S.66 1933-1934 (4)

18-22 passenger twin-hulled cantilever monoplane flying-boat, powered by three 515 kW (700 hp) Fiat A.24R engines, generating a cruising speed of 222 km/h (138 mph)

I-ALTE	15005	15.01.34-30.06.34	to Società Aerea Mediterranea (SAM)
I-REDI	15004	30.11.33-30.06.34	to Società Aerea Mediterranea (SAM)
I-TUTO	15003	07.12.33-30.06.34	to Società Aerea Mediterranea (SAM)
I-VALE	15007	30.01.34-30.06.34	to Società Aerea Mediterranea (SAM)

SISA (Società Italiana Servizi Aerei) Fleet 1926-1934

Cant 10ter 1926-1932 (9)

Four-passenger biplane flying-boat, powered by one 298 kW (400 hp) Lorraine-Dietrich engine, generating a cruising speed of 150 km/h (93 mph)

I-OLTB	002	12.01.26-05.04.30	
I-OLTC	003	12.01.26-01.05.28	destroyed by fire
I-OLTD	004	22.03.26-01.05.27	destroyed in accident
I-OLTE	005	22.03.36-00.03.32	destroyed in accident
I-OLTF	006	22.03.26-04.05.28	destroyed by fire at Portorose
I-OLTG	007	03.08.26-01.07.32	destroyed
I-OLTH	008	03.08.26-23.03.28	crashed into the sea in unknown circumstances
I-OLTI	009	11.08.26-01.11.28	to Taxi Aéreo, Argentina as R-ACVX
I-OLTL	010	01.12.26-00.03.28	toTaxi Aéreo, Argentina as R-ACVW

Cant 10ter-II 1929-1934 (5)

Four-passenger biplane flying-boat, powered by one 368 kW (500 hp) Isotta-Fraschini Asso V in-line engine, generating a cruising speed of 160 km/h (100 mph)

| I-AANN | | 165 | 06.09.29-21.07.29 | destroyed in accident at Calendaso (Piacenza) |
| I-AASF | *Aquila* | 203 | 12.04.30-31.07.34 | to Società Aerea Mediterranea (SAM) |

I-AASG	*Falco*	204	14.06.30-31.07.34	to Società Aerea Mediterranea (SAM)
I-AASH	*Sparviero*	206	22.12.30-31.07.34	to Società Aerea Mediterranea (SAM)
I-AASI	*Nibbio*		09.09.30-31.07.34	to Società Aerea Mediterranea (SAM)

Cant 22 1928-1934 (3)

Eight-passenger biplane flying-boat, powered by three Isotta-Fraschini Asso 200 in-line engines, generating a cruising speed of 140 km/h (87 mph)

I-AABM	*San Giusto*	004	18.07.28-01.12.31	destroyed in accident
I-AABN	*San Marco*	005	12.12.28-31.07.34	to Società Aerea Mediterranea (SAM)
I-AACJ	*San Giorgio*	064	22,04.29-31.07.34	to Società Aerea Mediterranea (SAM)

Cant 22R.1 1929-1934 (7)

10-passenger biplane flying-boat, powered by one centre 375 kW (510 hp) Isotta-Fraschini Asso 500 V12 and two outer 184 kW (250hp) Semi-Asso in-line engines, generating a cruising speed of 140 km/h (87 mph)

I-AACK	*San Sergio*	158	17.05.29-05.09.29	crashed into the Marano-Grado Lagoon, Friuli-Venezia Giulia
I-AACL	*San Guido*	159	05.11.29-31.07.34	to Societa Aerea Mediterranea (SAM)
I-AACM	*San Carlo*	160	21.03.30-31.07.34	to Società Aerea Mediterranea (SAM)
I-AACN	*San Vito*	161	19.04.30.08.08.30	crashed on take-off at Trieste
I-AAQX	*San Sebastiano*	162	19.07.30-31.07.34	to Società Aerea Mediterranea (SAM)
I-ADDA	*San Vito*	231	04.08.31-26.09.32	sank near Grado
I-ALFA	*San Sergio*	230	11.06.31-31.07.34	to Società Aerea Mediterranea (SAM)

Savoia-Marchetti S.55C 1926-1927 (2)

Eight-passenger cantilever wing, twin-hull monoplane flying-boat powered by two tandem Lorraine-Dietrich 12Db in-line engines, generating a cruising speed of 170 km/h (106 mph)

| I-ALTA | | 10506 | 20.03.26-00.10.27 | to Aero Espresso Italiana (AEI) |
| I-AGRO | | 10505 | 20.03.26-00.10.27 | to Aero Espresso Italiana (AEI) |

SITAR (Società Incremento Turismo Aereo Riviera) Fleet 1928-1934

Breda 15 1929 (2)

One-passenger high-wing braced float-equipped monoplane, powered by a single 82 kW (110 hp) Walter Venus radial piston engine, generating a maximum speed of 200 km/h (124 mph)

| I-AANX | | 1411 | 07.09.29- | |
| I-AANY | | 1407 | 07.09.29- | |

Fiat AS.1 1929 (1)

One-passenger parasol wing monoplane, powered by a single 67 kW (90 hp) Fiat A.50 engine, generating a speed of 158 km/h (98 mph)

I-AANV	17	20.08.29-	to Aero Club d'Italie Scuola Aero Turismo Milano

Macchi M.24bis 1930 (4)

Six-passenger biplane flying-boat, powered by two 373 kW (500hp) Isotta-Fraschini Asso engines, generating a maximum speed of 185 km/h (115 mph)

I-BBAM	3607	00.00.30	
I-BBAN	3608	00.00.30-	
I-BBAO	3609	16.09.30-00.06.32	destroyed
I-BBAP	3610	00.00.30-	

Macchi-Nieuport M.18 1928-1933 (4)

Three-passenger biplane flying-boat, powered by a single186 kW (250 hp) Isotta-Fraschini V6 engine, generating a maximum speed of 170 km/h (105 mph)

I-AACE		08.11.28-	
I-AACF	3303	30.07.29-	
I-AALB		29.11.28-00.00.29	broken up
I-AALC		29.11.28-oo.06.33	destroyed

Savoia S.16ter 1928 (6)

Two-passenger biplane flying-boat, powered by one 298 kW (400 hp) Lorraine-Dietrich 12Db V engine, generating a maximum speed of 194 km/h (120 mph)

I-AACD*		21.08.28-
I-AACH*		06.11.28-
I-AACI*	10	17.07.29-
I-AANW	5239	09.09.30-
I-AANZ	5187	25.11.30-
I-AAOA**	4004	28.10.29-

* Savoia S.16bis with reinforced hull and greater fuel capacity; ** S.16R with Fiat 300 engine

Savoia-Marchetti S.57 1928 (1)

One-passenger biplane flying-boat, powered by a single 186 kW (250 hp) Isotta-Fraschini V6 engine, generating a maximum speed of 215 km/h (134 mph)

I-AACG	1	21.08.28-

Transadriatica (Società Anonima di Navigazione Aerea Transadriatica) Fleet 1926-1931

Hamilton H-47 1929-1931 (1)

Six-passenger semi-cantilever monoplane, powered by one 391 kW (525 hp) Pratt & Whitney R-1690 radial engine, generating a cruising speed of 201 km/h (145 mph)

I-ROMA	57	07.08.29-23.12.31	to Società Aerea Mediterranea (SAM)

Junkers F 13 1926-1931 (9)

Four-passenger, cantilever wing monoplane, powered by one 136 kW (182 hp) BMW IIIa in-line engine, developing a cruising speed of 170 km/h (105 mph)

I-AEDO	2022	05.07.28-23.12.31	ex D-1374; to Società Aerea Mediterranea (SAM)
I-AFFA	623	13.10.31-23.12.31	to Società Aerea Mediterranea (SAM)
I-BAJA	2071/1	27.02.31-23.12.31	to Società Aerea Mediterranea (SAM)
I-BAJO	2070/2	23.07.31-23.12.31	to Società Aerea Mediterranea (SAM)
I-BATB	778	16.08.26-23.12.31	ex D 83; to Società Aerea Mediterranea (SAM)
I-BATC	759	13.09.26-23.12.31	ex D 507; to Società Aerea Mediterranea (SAM)
I-BAVB	762	09.11.26-23.12.31	ex I-POLA; to Società Aerea Mediterranea (SAM)
I-BBAS	2008	07.02.29-23.12.31	ex D-1182; to Società Aerea Mediterranea (SAM)
I-BBCA	632	09.12.27-24.07.31	ex D 216; lsd from Junkers; to Hungary as D-6, later HA-JAD *Sío* of Malért

Junkers W 34 b 1928-1930 (1)

Six-passenger cantilever wing monoplane, powered by one 373 kW (500 hp) Gnome-Rhône 9A Jupiter engine, generating a cruising speed of 233 km/h (145 mph)

I-AAMA	2605	18.10.28-15.10.30	crashed on test flight at Venice/San Nicolò Airport

Junkers G 24 ge 1926-1931 (2)

14-passenger cantilever wing monoplane, powered by three 231 kW (310 hp) Junkers L-5 engines, generating a cruising speed of 170 km/h (110 mph)

I-BAUS	924	15.10.26-23.12.31	ex S-AABC; to Società Aerea Mediterranea (SAM)
I-BAZI	947	200.4.27-23.12.31	ex D 963; to Società Aerea Mediterranea (SAM)

Macchi-Nieuport M.18 (1)

Three-passenger biplane flying-boat, powered by one 184 kW (250 hp) Isotta-Fraschini V.6 engine, generating a cruising speed of 145 km/h (90 mph)

I-BASA		16.9.26-	

Fiat defiance

While Balbo's vision for a single state carrier came to fruition with the establishment of Ala Littoria, one carrier that would completely escape the clutches of the State was Avio Linee Italiane (ALI), backed by the might of the Fiat industrial empire, with a strong business in the manufacture of aircraft and aero-engines. Established on 13 November 1926 by Giovanni Agnelli, head of Fiat, ALI had elected to concentrate primarily on international routes. Services were inaugurated on 23 May 1928 with a Milan-Trento-Bolzano-Klagenfurt-Munich route, flown with a Fokker F.VIIb-3m, either I-BBEC or I-BBED, in conjunction with Austrian airline Österreichische Luftverkehrs AG (ÖLAG). An extension from Milan to Rome was added on 9 October, by which time, two more, I-BBEE and I-BBEF, had been delivered. A Turin-Rome service followed on 1 September 1929 and, by 1934, these had been developed into separate Milan-Turin and Milan-Rome services. ALI was also operating to Rimini, and from Rome to Berlin via Trento, Bolzano, Munich, Nuremberg and Leipzig. The latter service was inaugurated on 1 April 1931.

The Fokker F.VIIb-3m was one of the outstanding transport aircraft of the pre-war era. A high-wing cantilever monoplane of wooden construction, the aircraft delivered to ALI were powered by three 158 kW (215 hp) Alfa Romeo Lynx engines and had accommodation for two crew and eight passengers. The range with full tanks was some 1,200 km. Three more aircraft, I-AAXY, I-AAXZ and I-FERO, were built under licence for ALI in 1930/31 by Officino Ferroviarie Meridionale Romeo under the designation Ro 10. Regrettably, I-AAXZ, on a scheduled passenger flight from Turin to Milan, crashed some 30 km from Turin on 15 April 1936, although the circumstances are unknown. All seven occupants lost their lives.

An unusual addition to the fleet in 1934 was a Fiat G.2, appropriately registered I-FIAT. Designed by Ing Giuseppe Gabrielli, this low-wing all-metal aircraft was first flown on 4 July 1932 and was intended to replace the airline's Fokker aircraft but proved unsuitable and only a single example was built. It accommodated the pilot and seven passengers and was initially powered by three 119 kW (160 hp) Fiat A.60 engines, but was re-engined several times while in service. Similarly unsuccessful was the APR.2, a sleek 12-passenger monoplane, of which only the prototype, I-VEGA, entered service with ALI. Gabrielli had more luck with his third design, the G.18, a twin-engine low-wing all-metal cantilever monoplane for 18 passengers not dissimilar to the Douglas DC-2, of which ALI already operated a single aircraft, I-EROS. ALI took delivery of the prototype and two production models, I-ELIO, I-ETNA

Licence-built Ro 10 (Fokker F.VIIb-3m) I-AAXY and I-AAXZ

The Fiat G.2 proved unsuitable as a replacement for the Fokker aircraft and only this example was built

and I-ETRA, but with its performance proving inadequate, the G.18 was re-engined with the more powerful 746 kW (1,000 hp) Fiat A.80 RC.41, gaining the designation G.18V (V for *veloce*), generating a maximum speed of 400 km/h and a range of 1,675 km. ALI acquired five of the improved model, registered I-EION, I-ELCE, I-ENEA, I-ERME and I-EURO, all during 1937. In that same year, Ali further boosted the fleet with six 18-passenger, three-engined Savoia-Marchetti S.73 aircraft, registered I-SAMO, I-SAUL, I-SETI, I-SITA, I-SUTO, and I-STAR. All were transferred to the Regia Aeronautica in 1940.

With the new fleet, ALI was able to expand its network, which soon included services from Venice to Milan, Turin and Paris from 7 April 1937, extended to London on 1 June 1938, and a Milan-Frankfurt-Cologne-Rotterdam-Amsterdam route, flown daily except on Sundays. Between 1 June and 31 August 1939, a seasonal service was flown from Turin to Cannes and Marseille, and other pool services had been added to Budapest, Warsaw and Gdynia with Malért and LOT, and from Venice to Zagreb and Belgrade in pool with Aeroput. At Belgrade, connections were available to Bucharest and Constanta by Romanian airline LARES. On 16 March 1940, ALI suffered its second fatal accident on a scheduled service when the Savoia-Marchetti S.73 I-SUTO crashed into Mount Stromboli on Stromboli, a small island off the north coast of Sicily, with the loss of all five crew and nine passengers. The aircraft was on a flight from Tripoli to Rome via Naples and encountered severe weather conditions.

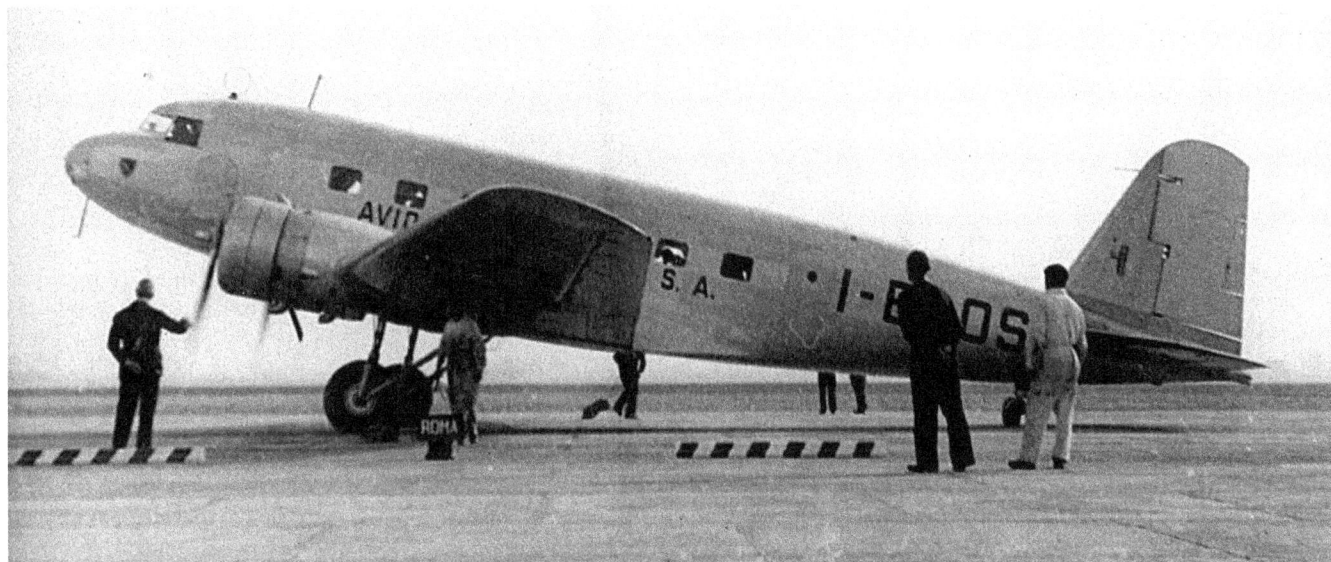

Avio Linee Italiane (ALI) operated a single Douglas DC-2 registered I-EROS

ALI operated a mixed fleet including this Caproni Ca.97 I-AANM

The sleek 12-passenger Fiat APR.2 proved unsuccessful and only I-VEGA was built

Fiat had more success with the 18-passenger G.18. I-ELIO was one of three of the type in the fleet

The G.18V was an improved model with greater speed

The Savoia-Marchetti S.73 enabled ALi to expand its network. I-SETI was one of six acquired by the airline

was ITL18 million (then USD 910,000) and, while state subsidisation was maintained at previous rates, the creation of a single airline saved the treasury an estimated ILT 12.8 million, having reduced from the ITL 62.498 million to all the companies in the year 1933/34, to ITL 49.696 million in Ala Littoria's first year. This government support would reduce further by around 25 per cent over time owing to increased efficiencies. The establishment of Ala Littoria was greatly stimulated by political motives and served as a prestige instrument of the increasingly more aggressive Mussolini regime, showing the Italian flag and the prowess of its manufacturing industry in the capitals of Europe.

The integration process continued in 1935, and was completed with the induction of NAA on 31 July, AEI (which had been allowed to continue its own operation for a few months), and Adria Aero Lloyd on 20 March, the latter allowing the consolidation of Adriatic services by September. New services were added to Budapest on 1 April 1935, and to Paris via Marseille on 29 July. The existing Munich service was extended to Berlin. Negotiations were also concluded with Air France, Deutsche Lufthansa and KLM Royal Dutch Airlines for continuation and extension of pool services to Frankfurt, Amsterdam, Paris and London, the latter two inaugurated in July with Savoia-Marchetti's new S.74, of which the airline had acquired three, I-URBE, I-ALPE and I-ROMA. The S.74 provided accommodation for eight passengers in reclinable seats on the port side, and 16 on the starboard side. I-URBE and I-ALPE were powered by four 522 kW (700 hp) Piaggio Stella X.RC air-cooled radial engines, while I-ROMA had the 630 kW (845 hp) Alfa Romeo Pegasus III engines. All three later passed to the Regia Aeronautica.

As the network expanded rapidly, there was an urgent need for further fleet renewal. SAM had inherited a fleet of 76 aircraft, comprising 46 seaplanes and 30 landplanes, but the majority were largely obsolete and inadequate for a

Fascist control

On the formation of Ala Littoria, the fascist symbol had been firmly stamped onto Italy's civil aviation sector. Even the name was significant and provided a constant reminder that the airline was not simply an air transport company, but an instrument of the State designed to further the regime's political ambitions abroad. It was named after the *lictor fasces*, the symbol of Mussolini's fascist party, represented by a bunch of reeds bound around an axe head, signifying equality under the State. *Ala* means wing, the whole name appropriately translating into 'fascist wing'. With Umberto Klinger remaining at the helm, the new national carrier initially focused on integrating the diverse constituent companies and upgrading the nation's airport infrastructure, largely operated by private interests. The airline's capital

Savoia-Marchetti S.74 I-URBE and two others enabled Ala Littoria to expand services to Paris and London

I-ORIO was one of four six-passenger twin-engined Breda 44 biplanes used in Albania

rapidly growing network. In August 1935, 25 examples of the new three-engine Z.506 seaplane by Cantieri Reuniti dell'Adriatico, formerly Cantieri Navale Triestino, were ordered, with deliveries commencing the following year. Designed by Ing Filippo Zapata, the Z.506 was a low-wing cantilever monoplane with twin floats and a large single rudder. The whole structure was divided into a number of watertight compartments. Power was provided by three cowled Wright Cyclone GR-1820-F52 engines, but the next batch of Z.506C aircraft had Alfa Romeo engines, both types rated at 560 kW (750 hp). The enclosed crew compartment had side-by-side pilots' seats and a radio operator's position, while passenger accommodation was in two cabins, providing accommodation for up to 16 passengers. The Cant Z.506 is believed to have entered service in 1936 on the Rome-Benghazi route, and later

also served the Rome-Palma-Melilla-Cadiz, Rome-Genoa-Marseille, and Trieste-Brindisi routes.

Fleet build-up

Also added to the fleet in 1936 was a batch of Savoia-Marchetti S.73 landplanes and Macchi C.94 flying-boats. Ala Littoria took delivery of its first S.73, I-PISA, towards the end of 1935 and, while this was powered by three 522 kW (700 hp) Piaggio Stella X.RC engines, subsequent aircraft, which eventually totalled 22 units, also had 567 kW (760 hp) Wright GR-1820 Cyclone engines. An attractive and fast low-wing cantilever monoplane designed by Engineer Mario Castoldi, the S.73 normally comprised two pilots, radio operator, engineer and steward, with the passenger accommodation divided into two sections, with a four-seat cabin above the spars, and a 14-seat main cabin at a slightly

Ala Littoria acquired the complete production of the high-wing twin-engined Macchi C.94 flying-boat

The fast three-engined Savoia-Marchetti S.73 landplane enabled the airline to expand and modernise its fleet

lower level. The cabins were heated, provided oxygen for high altitudes, and had toilet facilities. The Macchi C.94 was a high-wing aircraft with the engines mounted above the wing on faired steel struts. Half of the production had two 575 kW (770 hp) Wright Cyclone SGR-1820-F52 engines, while the other half was powered by the 597 kW (800 hp) Alfa Romeo 126 RC,10 radials. Twelve passengers were accommodated in three cabins, each with his/her own large circular window, reading light and air vent. Seats were

upholstered in leather. Ala Littoria acquired the prototype of the C.94, I-NEPI, and all eleven production models, for use on the Adriatic services, the first being introduced in July.

Upon its establishment, Ala Littoria had taken over eight single-engine Junkers F 13 and two three-engined G 24 aircraft, but these were never used. Instead, they were traded in to the *Reichsluftfahrtministerium* (RLM), the German air transport ministry, in part payment for three Junkers Ju 52/3m airliners, an order for which was placed

The three-engined S.66 was the latest development of Savoia-Marchetti's twin-hulled flying-boats. I-AABF and I-ONDA were two of them

Junkers Ju 52/3m I-BAUS was delivered in 1935 but crashed four years later

on 9 November 1934. The three aircraft, I-BAUS, I-BEZI and I-BIZI, were delivered already in January/February 1935. The 17-seat trimotor was powered by the more powerful 522 kW (700 hp) Piaggio P.X.R engine, which was considered more suitable for the trans-Alpine route and was given the designation Ju 52/3m lu. The new Junkers aircraft were put on the long-established Venice-Munich-Berlin service, flown jointly with Deutsche Lufthansa, with the two German cities also later linked to Rome. The Venice-Rome connection was operated by Ala Littoria's S.73.

It was on the Berlin schedule that I-BAUS came to grief on 4 December 1939. Having taken off in stormy weather and icy conditions from Munich, the aircraft struck a hillside in the Bavarian Forest near Bayerisch Eisenstein, Germany, at an altitude of about 1,000 meters during the final leg of a flight from Munich to Berlin and crashed, killing four of the 13 passengers. The crew of Captain Leonida

Schiona, co-pilots Ugo Boscola and Luigi Bruzzoni, and radio operator Umberto Settimelli were injured and two passengers escaped unhurt. Seven passengers received minor injuries. Lufthansa provided a replacement aircraft, I-BALI, which was leased for the period from 30 January to 25 May 1940. I-BEZI had been written off on 30 March 1938 during a training flight off Venice Lido Airport. During the descent, the student pilot executed a sharp turn and the aircraft impacted the water at full power. There were no injuries but the aircraft was heavily damaged by the corrosive effect of seawater and eventually had to be scrapped. A BMW-powered replacement aircraft, I-ABJZ was temporarily leased from Lufthansa between November 1938 and March 1939.

With a great mixture of different seaplanes and landplanes, which totalled some 123 in 1939/40, still relatively primitive navigational and communication

Junkers Ju 52/3m I-ABJZ was temporarily leased as replacement for I-BEZI which was destroyed on a training flight

Ali Littoria acquired several eight-passenger Fokker F.VIIa-3m from Swissair including I-ADUA

facilities, minimal infrastructure, and varying weather conditions along its routes, especially in the Mediterranean and North and East Africa, it was not unexpected that Ala Littoria would suffer more accidents. On 22 June 1935, the S.66 I-NAVE struck the sea on landing at Marsaxlokk Bay, Malta at night after falling from a height of 16 m, either after a stall or after encountering an air pocket. There were no casualties. Another S.66, I-VOLO, crashed into the Mediterranean Sea off Terranova, Sardinia, on 14 July 1938, with the loss of 20 lives. It was on a flight from Cagliari to Rome and the circumstances have not been reported. On 2 August 1937, the S.73, I-SUSA, on a flight from Asmara to Rome, stalled for unknown reasons and crashed short of the runway on a night-time approach to Wadi Halfa. All three crew and six passengers died in the crash. Fokker F.VIIb-3m, I-AFRO, was damaged beyond repair at Bologna on 6 March 1939, as was F.VIIa-3m,

I-BBEE, in July 1937. The Cant Z.506C, I-DENO, was destroyed by fire at Melilla on 7 September 1938.

The Imperial Line

The Italian colonial territories in the Horn of Africa included Italian Somaliland and Italian Eritrea, but Mussolini's long-range expansionist programme led to the invasion and victory over neighbouring Abyssinia (now Ethiopia and Eritrea), with Italian forces entering the capital city Addis Ababa on 5 May 1936. Using the thinly disguised excuse of a border dispute with Italian Somaliland, Italian forces had invaded on 3 October 1935, followed by seven months of fighting. The three territories were combined on 1 June 1936 into *Africa Orientale Italiana* (Italian East Africa). This foreign policy triumph temporarily increased Mussolini's standing both at home and abroad and encouraged him to further advance his Fascist system.

Up to 16 passengers could be accommodated in two comfortable cabins in the twin-float Cant Z.506 seaplane

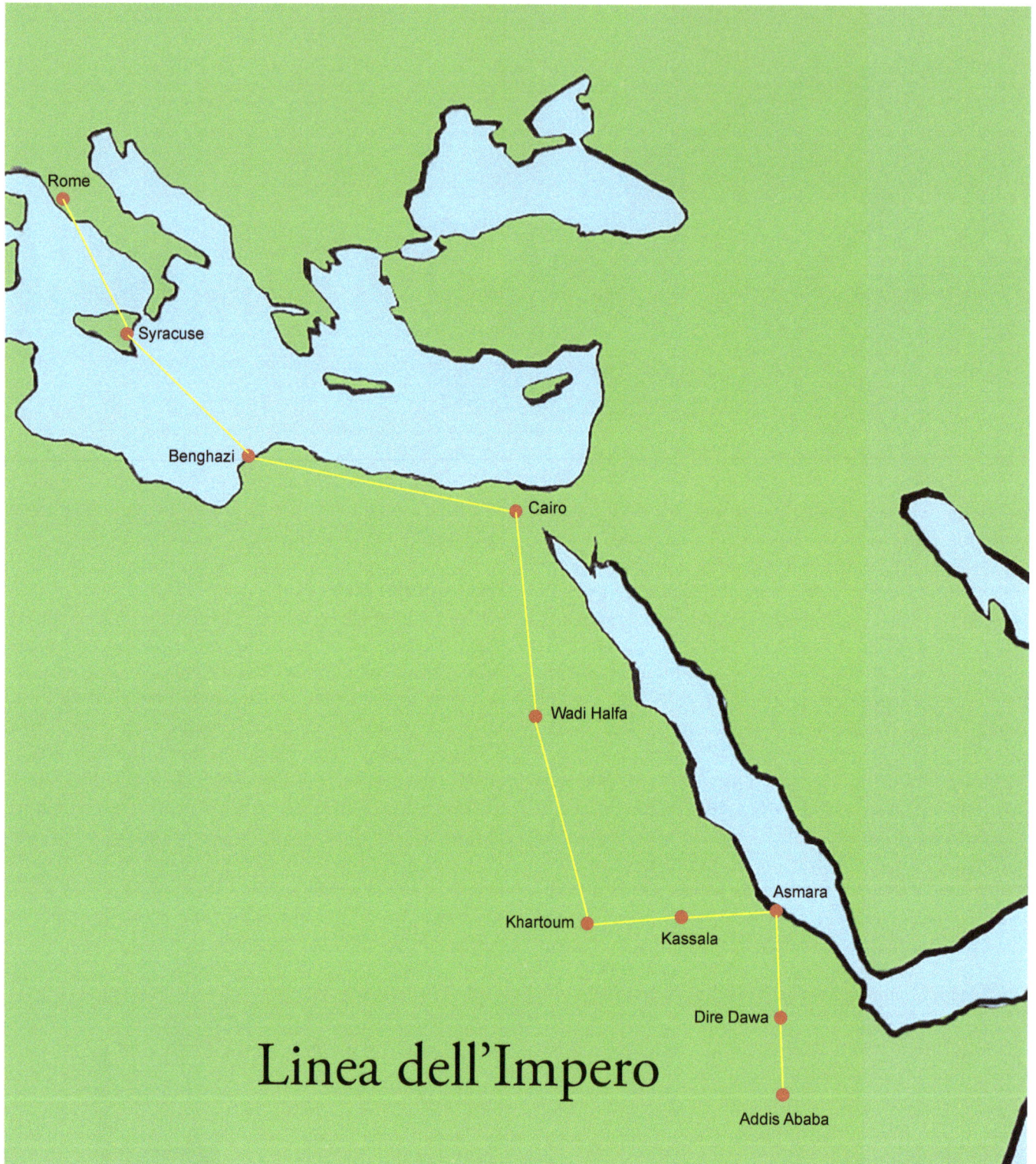

Linea dell'Impero

It was now crucial to maintain transport and communications links between the mainland and its satellites, a task that was entrusted to Ala Littoria. An air service to East Africa was first considered in 1929 and 1930, together with possible extensions beyond the colonies from Asmara to Khartoum and from Mogadishu to Nairobi, but financial consideration and the need to establish and assimilate the European network put this in cold storage for a while.

Nevertheless, already in November 1934, First War ace, Major Carlo Francis Lombardi and Vittoria Suster, SAM's chief pilot for Northern and Central Europe, had undertaken a proving flight in the Savoia-Marchetti S.71, I-ALPI, between Rome and Mogadishu in Italian Somaliland (now Somalia). Staging via Tobruk in Libya and Massawa in Italian Eritrea, they covered the 6,200 km route in 35 hours and 35 minutes, establishing a new record, although one which was held only briefly.

The high-wing Savoia-Marchetti S.71 was powered by three Walter Castor radial engines

However, the commencement of a regular service was constrained by a lack of suitable long-range aircraft. A temporary solution was found by means of an agreement, signed with Britain's Imperial Airways Ltd on 7 July 1935, to transport Air Littoria passengers from Brindisi in southern Italy to Khartoum in Sudan by flying-boat, operating as part of IAL's colonial route to South Africa. But the tensions between Britain and Italy remained, not only related to overflying rights, but also encompassed suspicions of espionage. Imperial Airways flying-boats were banned from landing at Lake Bracciano, near Rome, because of several incidents during which the British airline's aircraft had flown at low altitude over nearby military installations in restricted airspace. For example, an Imperial Airways flying-boat was reported to have flown over the Vigna di Valle experimental aviation centre at an altitude of 250 m,

en route to Marseille, and ten days later, the same aircraft flew at low altitude over the Furbara military area.

Nevertheless, on 22 July 1935, Ala Littoria was able to open a stop-gap service via Khartoum to Italy's colonies. The route split into two lines, one to Asmara and Massawa in Eritrea via Kassala in Sudan, and the other via French Somaliland (Djibouti) to Mogadishu. Taking four days end-to-end, the service had an initial frequency of three or four per month, operated in the interim period with six Fokker F.VIIa-3m trimotors bought from various sources, and seven twin-engine, low-wing Caproni Bergamaschi Ca.308 Borea (North Wind) – I-DRIA, I-LIBI, I-MERA, I-MOLA, I-NTRA, I-SPRA and I-VREA - a small cantilever monoplane with accommodation for seven passengers. The latter aircraft were put onto postal services on 15 December 1935, covering the Tripoli-Kassala-Asmara sector of the

Caproni Bergamaschi Ca.308 Borea being loaded with mail bags at Benghazi

The 16-passenger Caproni Ca.133 was used on an internal network in Italian East Africa

Brindisi-Khartoum route, replacing Imperial Airways, largely due to the worsening relations with Great Britain. All, except L-LINI and I-NTRA, were withdrawn from use and broken up in February 1938.

With the deliveries of its new aircraft, Ala Littoria was finally ready to fly all the way from Italy to Asmara and Mogadishu under its own steam. But first the route was extended on 11 November 1935 between Eritrea and Italian Somaliland, with the route from Asmara following the coast to Djibouti in French Somaliland, before striking across Abyssinia to reach Mogadishu, also stopping at Berbera (British Somaliland) and Bura Galadi (British Kenya). The first outward proving flight from Rome took place on 19 December 1935, carrying around 200,000 letters. The return flight back to Rome departed Mogadishu on New Year's Day 1936. A regular service was opened shortly afterwards, building up to four times a week. The Rome/Lake Bracciano-Syracuse-Benghazi-Cairo sector was flown with the Cant Z.506 seaplanes, before the service continued on to Wadi Halfa and Asmara with the Savoia-Marchetti S.73, but flown only during daylight hours.

Emphasising the prestigious new service, the title *Linea dell'Impero* (Imperial Line) was adopted. A service to Addis Ababa commenced on 15 October 1936, following the same route as far as Asmara, before turning south to the Abyssinian capital via Assab and Dire Dawa. The route to Addis Ababa had a total length of 6,379 km, of which 4,966 km was over African territory. One unusual feature of the timetable was that, apart from a 1015 departure from Rome, the rest of the timings were just given as 'dawn', 'afternoon', or 'evening', reflecting the unpredictability of conditions and lack of mainline support along the route. By March 1937, Gorrahei (Abyssinia) and Beledweyne in Italian Somaliland had been added to the service. Along the Imperial Line, maintenance bases were established at Rome,

Brindisi, Benghazi and Asmara.

The one-way fare was a high ITL 6,000, keeping passenger numbers, mainly comprising government officials, at a level considerably lower than on the rest of the network. Nevertheless, much of the airline's revenue was derived from the East African sector, with mail providing the biggest share. This was not surprising since a distinctive feature of Ala Littoria's service was the significant numbers of public and military officials who enjoyed free transport on its routes, subject to a payment of only 10 per cent of the ticket price to cover insurance costs. Free air passes were given regularly to high-ranking officials: Mussolini himself was assigned private aircraft and crews, as well as regular free passes, not only on Ala Littoria, but also on ALI. Free travel was also assigned to colonial officials, including Rodolfo Graziani, viceroy for Italian East Africa; Ruggero Santini, the governor of Somaliland, and Alfredo Guzzoni, governor of Eritrea. The award of free travel to public officials on national airlines was not unheard of, but it did show that the airline was a key player in the region's attempt to maintain effective control and communications in its colonial possessions.

To maintain essential civil and military administration and ensure effective communications throughout the colony, it became necessary to establish an internal network quickly and, by the outbreak of the Second World War, 14 towns and cities were being served, centred on Addis Ababa, and including Djibouti in French Somaliland, most flown several times each week. The internal service was maintained with a fleet of Caproni C.133 trimotors, of which Ala Littoria had at least twelve. A direct development of the Ca.101 and very similar in appearance, the Ca.133 was powered by three 343 kW (460 hp) Piaggio Stella VII.C 16 air-cooled radials and provided accommodation for 16 passengers. All those operated in East Africa were fully equipped for night flying.

The massive 26-passenger Macchi MC.100 served between Rome and Tripoli after Italy entered the war

Another small company, ATSA-Avio Trasporti Società Anonima was established in 1938 to operate cargo services within East Africa from its base at Assab in Eritrea, with six Caproni Ca 148, a further development of the Ca.133 with three 343 kW (460 hp) Piaggio Stella VII engines and a strengthened undercarriage, designed for colonial operation. The six aircraft, delivered between September 1938 and February 1939, were registered I-ETIO, I-GOGG, I-LANG, I-NEGH, I-SOMA and. I-TESS. Services were begun on 28 October 1938 with services from Assab and Massawa to Addis Ababa, but were. rolled into Ala Littoria in March 1940, and the operational base was switched to Asmara. In June, the six aircraft received the military marks of MM60477-MM60482.

The Italian occupation of Abyssinia was not without political consequences. The League of Nations imposed

ATSA operated several three-engined Caproni Ca.148 high-wing monoplanes on cargo services in East Africa

The Savoia-Marchetti SM.75 retained the general configuration of the S.73 but was faster and could operate from shorter runways

economic sanctions on Italy, which could have affected the airline's substantial reliance on foreign-manufactured aero-engines to power its aircraft; more than half of its stock was from the UK, USA and Czechoslovakia. There were also difficulties with overflight rights through British-controlled Egypt and Sudan. In the event, these sanctions were implemented somewhat half-heartedly and were never fully applied and Italy withdrew from the League in December 1937.

Keen to forge links with other European right-wing leaders, Mussolini had come to the aid of Generalissimo Francisco Franco in Spain's Civil War with support of military troops, vehicles and large quantities of arms and munition. Italy's flag-carrier saw the benefit from this new-found 'friendship' by opening a service from Rome to Cadiz via Palma de Mallorca on 7 December 1936. By April 1937, this had developed into a thrice-weekly run over the route Rome-Palma-Melilla-Cadiz, flown with the Cant Z.506. The Spanish services were further extended in early 1938, also taking in Malaga and Seville, from where a multi-stop connection was eventually made to Lisbon in Portugal, all flown with the S.73. Ala Littoria also linked Melilla with Tetuán in Spanish Morocco. Barcelona was added in 1939, latterly employing the new 26-passenger Macchi C.100 flying-boat, a larger version of the C.94 with three engines and twin-fins and rudders. With the revival of the Iberia name in 1937, Ala Littoria took a 12.5 per cent stake, providing three Junkers Ju 52/3m through DLH in lieu of capital, to get the airline off the ground.

Away from satisfying the new demands in East Africa, Ala Littoria continued to expand its European network in association with various European airlines and, although it was still the smallest of Europe's main airlines, by 1937, its network reached far and wide. Services were operated between Venice and Budapest, via Klagenfurt, Graz and Vienna, opened on 4 October 1937, flown with ÖLAG

and Malért; Venice-Trieste-Klagenfurt-Bratislava- Prague with ČSA, inaugurated on 15 May 1937; a Rome-Belgrade-Bucharest line with Lares; a thrice-weekly route from Rome to Warsaw with Polish airline LOT; and Lufthansa operated part of the route from Rome to Berlin, with intermediate stops at Venice and Munich. While such collaboration extended the airline's reach, the fact that all airlines had to carry mail at the same price created some temporary difficulties. Ala Littoria also served Haifa, then in British-mandated territory, from 7 April 1937 on a weekly frequency, as an extension to the thrice-weekly Rome-Brindisi-Athens-Rhodes service. This was continued to Baghdad and Basra on 13 April 1939. Ala Littoria's domestic network, centred on Rome, connected Italy's major cities inland and on the coasts, and it also exclusively operated all domestic routes in Albania, serving seven cities with 43 weekly direct flights from the capital Tirana. The fleet was further increased in 1938 with the delivery of a large number of the Savoia-Marchetti SM.75, starting with I-TACO, I-TIMO and I-TITO.

The SM.75 made its first flight on 6 November 1937. It was the last design of Alessandro Marchetti and the largest of the manufacturer's three-engined civil transports. The result of a requirement by Ala Littoria for a fast middle-to-long-range airliner to replace the earlier S.73, it retained the general configuration of the S.73, but introduced a retractable main landing gear to minimise aerodynamic drag. Other features were short take-off and landing runs, which enabled its operation from smaller airports. The SM.75 was capable of carrying 24 passengers a distance of 1,500 km (930 miles). On January 10, 1939, the windowless I-TALO piloted by Giuseppe Bertocco succeeded in transporting 10,000 kg of cargo a distance of 2,000 km, at an average speed of 330 km/h and, on July 30 of the same year and in the same aircraft, Angelo Tondi beat the previous flight distance record by flying for 12,900 km in 57 hours and 35 minutes.

The Savoia-Marchetti SM.79 was a transport version of a medium bomber, but only two were used by Ala Littoria

Across the South Atlantic

The Italian diaspora between 1880 and 1920a saw the migration of several million people from the home country to Argentina and Brazil. The attraction of maintaining good relations and communications with those nations and its expatriate citizens, as well as challenging the dominance of Air France and Deutsche Lufthansa over South American routes, led Italy towards creating an air link across the South Atlantic. But Mussolini's adventures in East Africa and Spain had drained resources, delaying any serious efforts in that direction.

Although several flights were made between Italy and Brazil, most notably by Francesco de Pinedo and Major Carlo Del Prete in a Savoia-Marchetti S.55 *Santa Maria* on 13 February 1927 and by Arturo Ferrarin and Del Prete on 3 July 1928 in a single-engined Savoia-Marchetti S.64, covering the 7,188 km between Rome/Guidonia Montecelio to Touros, a coastal city in North-East Brazil, in a record time of 49 hours and 19 minutes, as well as Balbo's formation flight to Rio de Janeiro in January 1931, it was not until 28 December 1937, that any earnest moves were made. On that date, Cant Z.506B I-LAMA, commanded by test pilot Mario Stoppani and Enrico Comani, together with radio operator Demetrio Iaria and engineer Renato Pogliani , made a record 7,013 km crossing between Cadiz in Spain and Caravelas in Brazil in 26 hours 25 minutes, at an average speed of 265 km/h (165 mph). Unfortunately, the aircraft was lost on the return flight on 2 February 1938 when it caught fire and crashed into the sea off Natal. Mario Stoppani was rescued, but the five other occupants – pilots Mario Viola, Oscar Molinari and Enrico Comani, radio operator Iaria and engineer Pogliani, perished in the crash.

Concerted efforts to prove the route had already begun on 25 January 1938, when three Savoia-Marchetti SM.79T Sparviero three-engined bombers – I-BISE (ex I-BIMU), I-BRUN (ex I-FILU) and I-MONI (ex I-CUPA) – had left Rome's Guidonia military airfield for Dakar in French West Africa (now the capital of Senegal) and thence to Rio de Janeiro, which was reached in 13 hours 35 minutes from Dakar, a record for the 5,350 km flight. Their crews, which included Mussolini's younger son, Bruno, Colonel Attilio Biseo, and Captains Antonio Moscatelli, Renato Mancinelli and Amedeo Paradisi, were all officers of the *12° Stormo Bombardemento Terrestre,* known as the *Sorci Verde* (12th Bomb Wing, 'Green Mice'), which had previously achieved fame by winning the Istres-Damascus-Paris race in the same type of aircraft on 20-21 August 1937. It had been planned to continue the flight on to Argentina, but unlike in Brazil, a distinct anti-fascist sentiment prevailed there and it was deemed unwise to proceed. Instead, as a gesture of goodwill, the three SM.79 low-wing monoplanes were donated to the Brazilian Army Air Service and the Italian crews returned home by sea to an enthusiastic reception.

On 21 March that same year, Ala Littoria despatched Cant Z.506C I-ALAL from Cagliari/Elmas on a survey to Buenos Aires via Bathurst (now Banjul in The Gambia), Bahia and Santos (Brazil). On board of this flight, commanded by Carlo Tonini, was Umberto Klinger, who inspected all the intended stops to be used on a planned mail service, Aldo Grillo and Marshal Guido Fertonani. The return journey was made on 7 April via Rio de Janeiro, Natal, Dakar, and Mellila, arriving at Rome/Ostia on 13 April. Mussolini approved the project two months later, leading to the creation of the *Direzione Centrale Linee Atlantiche.* However, bitter differences soon arose between the management of Ala Littoria and the men of *Sorci Verde,* whom Mussolini favoured to lead the new division, regarding the choice of equipment – seaplanes or landplanes.

A Savoia-Marchetti SM.79T Sparviero bomber of the Sorci Verde pictured on the route proving flight to Rio de Janeiro in January 1938

The matter was ultimately resolved in favour of the latter, and, starting in late 1938, deliveries commenced of 12 Savoia-Marchetti SM.83 trimotors, developed from the S.79 bomber and supplied in two versions, T (*Terrestre*) and A (*Atlantiche*) respectively for overland and oceanic sectors. Closely resembling the S.73 and SM.75, it was the smallest of the manufacturer's three-engine low-wing monoplanes. Powered by the 560 kW (750 hp) Alfa Romeo 126 RC.34 air-cooled radial engine, the SM.83 was designed to carry 10 passengers, but on the South Atlantic run fuel capacity was increased and passenger capacity was limited to six, plus 700 kg of mail and baggage. The service was intended purely for postal transport, but revenue passengers were occasionally carried, although permission had to be sought from the Ministry of Aeronautics. Also, Ala Littoria's management did not encourage passenger transport as it considered the service unsuitable to provide adequate comfort during these long flights. An SM.83 undertook a route-proving flight 4-12 February 1939, flown by Attilio Biseo and Valentino Pivetti, formerly of Transadriatica. It suffered numerous setbacks *en route*, however, mainly due to overheating of the spark-plugs. The following month, on 16 March, tropical trials were undertaken in another SM.83, I-ATTE, with a crew headed by Bruno Mussolini, and also including

Aldo Moggi, Angelo Trezzini, Aldo Boveri, Arimondo Palanco and Dr Giorgi, to Tripoli, the Kufra Oasis, Asmara, Massawa, Gura and Agordat.

A year was spent establishing bases and infrastructure along the route that was intended to run from Rome to Seville/Malaga, Melilla, Casablanca, Dakar, the archipelago of Fernando de Noronha, Natal and Rio de Janeiro. Operating agreements were concluded with Air France for transit through French-administered territories, and by spring 1939, all preparations had been completed. However, in a climate of deteriorating relations, the French Government suddenly rescinded overflight permission for Morocco and its West African colonies, and withdrew approval of the agreements forged with Air France. This was undoubtedly a reaction to Mussolini's alliance with Germany and his aggressive stance over Corsica, Tunis, the port of Djibouti and the Suez Canal in Egypt, all of which were within France's sphere of influence. This setback delayed the projected start-up by six months, as it was necessary to adopt a completely new route staging entirely through neutral territory, with Casablanca and Dakar replaced by Villa Cisneros in Spanish Sahara (now Dakhla) and Ilha do Sal in the Portuguese Cape Verde archipelago. At the latter, where no infrastructure of any kind existed,

The Cant Z.506C I-ALAL was used on a survey flight to Buenos Aires

a complete airfield had to be hacked out of barren rock, with all supplies and specialist workers brought in by sea. Accommodation was built for the 50 personnel who were to be stationed on the island, together with two hangars, workshops to carry out repairs and overhauls of the aircraft, a power plant, and two radio stations. Two ships were also stationed in the South Atlantic as floating wireless and weather stations, one, the *Alato*, some 480 km south of Ilha do Sal, the other, *Librato*, 480 km north of Fernando de Noronha. Nothing was left to chance. Other bases were on the Brazilian island of Fernando de Noronha, Recife and Bahia.

The airline's ambitions were not limited to South America. Plans were being made for a service from Rome to Tokyo in Japan for strategic and propaganda reasons, and across the North Atlantic to the United States, but neither came to fruition, in part due to a lack of suitable four-engined aircraft, and a funding shortfall. By 1937, Ala Littoria was spending ITL 99.8 million per annum, but received state funding of only ITL 70.8 million. The Ministry of Aeronautics funded the ITL 29 million deficit by allocating costs to public interests that were receiving direct benefits from the airline's services. By far the largest contributor was the Ministry of Italian Africa with ITL 21 million, with ITL 4.8 million provided by the Libyan administration, and ITL 3 million by Italian cities, mainly Milan and Turin. However, this still left a deficit of ITL 1 million, which Ala Littoria tried to solve by reducing some services. Yet, expansion was still very much on the horizon, which was expected to cost ITL 231 million up to 1941. Records show that the airline remained underfunded throughout its short history.

Cabin of the Cant Z.506C

Savoia-Marchetti SM.83 I-ARIS flying over Lago Maggiore

Corporación Sudamericana de Servicios Aéreos, a joint venture between Italy and Argentina, operated three Macchi C.94 flying-boats including LV-MAB, the former I-NEVA

The birth of LATI

As time went on, irreconcilable tensions grew between the management of Ala Littoria, which was funding the project unsupported, and the *de facto* Green Mice leaders of the Atlantic Division. By autumn of 1939 it became apparent that the two organisations would have to forge separate paths, and thus, on 11 September that year, the *Direzione Centrale Linee Atlantiche* became Linee Aeree Transcontinentali Italiane Società Anonima (LATI), with a capital of ITL 40 million. A fixed grant of ITL 5 million for five years was awarded, in addition to the usual subsidy per kilometre flown. Its president was Raffaele Ricciardi, but he was soon replaced by General Aurelio Liotta, latterly commander of the Italian East African Air Force, while Bruno Mussolini and Attilio Biseo, both accomplished long-distance military pilots, were appointed as joint director generals. Biseo, a decorated veteran of Balbo's mass formation flights and co-commander of the Green Mice, survived the Second World War and continued his aviation career with Itavia, a major domestic airline.

Even before LATI was established, Italy had sought to widen its influence and had participated with Argentina in the formation of Corporación Sudamericana de Servicios Aéreos to extend services beyond Argentina and feed its South Atlantic services. Founded with a capital of ARS (Argentine peso) 500,000 in May 1937 by Mauro Herlitska and Dr Mario Pastega, and equipped with a small fleet of Macchi C.94 flying-boats – I-ANIO, I-NEVA and I-LATO (reregistered respectively LV-LAB, LV-MAB and LV-NAB) - flown initially by Italian crews, the company started operations on 6 February 1939, connecting Buenos Aires with Montevideo, Uruguay. On 6 March, the Argentine Government granted permission to Ala Littoria to operate from Buenos Aires to Europe, but it was some time before Buenos Aires was incorporated into the long-haul network. Corporación Sudamericana added a service from Buenos Aires to Rosario on 15 May but this lasted only for three months. Three SM.75s with 783 kW (1,050 hp) Pratt & Whitney SC3G engines were ordered, but these were never delivered. The airline expanded its activities on 25 March 1941 with a service to Asunción, capital of Paraguay, via Rosario, Santa Fe, Barranqueras and Formosa, but pressures to restrict supplies to Axis nations and their overseas interests intensified, and when the United States entered the war on 11 December that year, Corporación Sudamericana ceased operations.

On 11 November 1939, the SM.83 I-AZUR left Guidonia on a test flight to Villa Cisneros, Western Sahara, via Seville and Cabo Juby. On 14 November, the flight continued to Ilha do Sal, having covered a total distance of 4,914 km (3,052 miles). The flight was commanded by Gori Castellani and Amedeo Paradisi, with radio operator

SM.83 I-AMER was tasked with the service between Recife and Rio de Janeiro, later briefly extended to Buenos Aires

SM.83 I-AZUR on the Brazilian island of Fernando de Noronha

Aldo Boveri and engineer Angelo Trezzini completing the crew. On board as passenger was LATI's joint director general Bruno Mussolini.

Following these experimental flights to Ilha do Sal, LATI's first timetable gave details of a weekly roundtrip to Villa Cisneros, taking two days in each direction, as a prelude to the full service. This was divided into three sections, with each section allocated three or four Savoia-Marchetti SM.83 plus crews.

Initial distribution of Savoia-Marchetti SM.83 aircraft and crew

Section 1: Europe-Africa (Rome-Seville-Lisbon-Seville-Villa Cisneros-Ilha do Sal)

I-AREM   Commanders Umberto Carelli and Francesco Ficara, radio operator Francesco Verdosci, engineer Piacentini
I-ARIS   reserve, replacement for I-ARPA
I-ARPA   Commanders Antonio Rapp and Franco Pascucci, radio operator Carlo Zunino, engineer Gaddo Bugni
I-ASTA   Commanders Vittorio Suster and Daniele Baldini, radio operator Giovanni Messina, engineer Polli

Section 2: Atlantic (Ilha do Sal-Fernando de Noronha-Recife)

I-ARCA   Commanders Antonio Moscatelli and Vincenzo Baldini, radio operator Ezio Vaschetto, engineer Vittorio Trovi
I-ASSO   Commanders Bruno Satti and Luigi Baletti, radio operator Mario Parodi, engineer Giulio Cattomar
I-ATOS   Commanders Amedeo Paradisi and Aldo Moggi, radio operator Guido Fertonani, engineer Ubaldo Ardù
I-AZUR   Commanders Gori Castellani and Ireneo Moretti, radio operator Aldo Boveri, engineer Angelo Trezzini

Section 3: Americas (Recife-Bahia-Rio de Janeiro, later extended to Buenos Aires)

I-ANDE   Commanders Primo Ferioli and Alfredo Pastore, radio operator Greco, engineer Francesco Antonicelli
I-AMER   Commanders Pavia and Giuseppe Baratelli, radio operator Felice Cadognotto
I-ARMA   Commanders Igino Mencarelli and William Lisardi, radio operator Giovanni Cubeddu, engineer Eugenio Matriciano

I-ALAN

On 7 December I-ARMA, I-ATOS and I-AZUR were positioned at Recife. The same day, I-ASTA operated a regular service Rome-Seville-Lisbon-Villa Cisneros, I-ARCA flew to Ilha do Sal on 11 December, and I-ASSO was stationed on Cape Verde. With all the necessary elements now in place, the inaugural transoceanic flight, carrying 500 kg of mail, departed Rome/Guidonia on 21 December 1939, arriving in Rio de Janeiro two-and-a-half days later. Mail was guaranteed to be delivered within 10 days from posting. The first sector from Rome/Guidonia to Seville was flown by I-AREM under the command of Umberto Carelli, with Lisbon-Seville-Ilha do Sal by I-ARPA, flown by Antonio Rapp, and Ilha do Sal-Recife by I-ARCA, piloted by Antonio Moscatelli. The final sector from Recife to Rio de Janeiro was in the hands of Igino Mencarelly in I-ARMA. The simultaneous first flight in the opposite direction unfortunately came to grief on 24 December when I-ARPA, out of Villa Cisneros, crashed during a storm while attempting to make an emergency landing at Dar el Caid Allal Bou Fenzi, south-east of Essaouira (Mogador) in Morocco. The four crew members, including Commander Antonio Rapp, and three journalists lost their lives. The charred mail was recovered.

Regular LATI flights departed from Guidonia on Thursday morning and arrived in Seville that same morning (a distance of 1,734 kilometres). A Seville-Lisbon shuttle brought mail from Portugal and carried mail to Lisbon to connect with the Pan Am Atlantic flights to North America. The LATI route continued with a departure on Friday morning for Villa Cisneros on the Spanish Sahara coast (2,052 kilometres), arriving in the afternoon and departing that same afternoon on the first leg of the transoceanic crossing for a late afternoon arrival at Ilha do Sal (1,134 kilometres). The route continued with a Saturday morning departure from Sal to Recife (Pernambuco), where it arrived that afternoon (3,089 kilometres). The final leg to Rio departed early Sunday morning, with arrival in the afternoon (2,457 kilometres). From Rio connections were available to Buenos Aires and countries throughout South, Central, and North America via the various airlines that had been developed over the previous years. The return route followed the same route departing Friday mornings from Rio and arriving at Guidonia on Monday afternoon. On average, each trip took 28 hours flying time end-to-end over the course of two-and-a-half days, as opposed to an 18-day journey by sea. It should be noted that on the return flights to Rome, flights departed Brazil from Natal, as the runway at Recife was too short to accommodate the more heavily loaded aircraft.

New aircraft

By the time Italy entered the war on 10 June 1940, a total of 59 crossing had been completed, which included 15 by I-AZUR, 14 each by I-ARCO, I-ASSO and I-ATOS, and one each by I-ANDE and I-ARMA. The service was temporarily suspended but resumed on 22 June. Aircraft of Ala Littoria, Avio Linee Italiana (ALI) and the SM.83 of LATI were commandeered by the Regia Aeronautica, forcing LATI's new chief, Ing Carlo Pezzani, who had taken over from Liotta, to acquire new aircraft. On 23 August 1940, he ordered five of the new SM.76, essentially an SM.75 with 671 kW (900 hp) Pratt & Whitney Twin Wasp engines and improved payload and performance, but, owing

The 10-passenger Savoia-Marchetti SM.82 I-BACH was one of eight in the LATI fleet

LATI Savoia-Marchetti SM.82 I-BRAZ at Rio's Santos Dumont Airport

SM.82 I-BOLI landing at Natal, Brazil

to the exigencies of war, only one example was delivered on 16 October 1941, I-CILE, previously registered I-AZIS and I-LUEN, which was equipped with an autopilot, a rapid fuel unloading system, and two passenger cabins fitted with six reclining bunks in each.

Instead of the ordered S.76s, at least seven Savoia-Marchetti SM.75 and five of its military development, the SM.82 Marsupiale, were delivered for the South American route. Both types were powered by three 560 kW (750 hp) Alfa Romeo 126 RC.34 engines. On 21 September 1940, LATI received the first SM.75, I-TELA, from Ala Littoria, which was modified with increased fuel, the rapid fuel unloading system incorporated in the S.76, and strengthened undercarriage to take account of the increase of the weight from 15,550 kg to 17.500 kg (38,580 lb) At the same time, the Alfa Romeo 126 engines were fitted with constant-speed propellers. The modified aircraft was then reregistered I-BAYR. Unfortunately, on 15 January 1941,

during the 104th South Atlantic trip, I-BAYR was lost in the Atlantic between Natal and Ilha do Sal with eight crew and two passengers on board after being forced to ditch in the sea when No.2 engine lost power. The search was suspended on 22 January, neither aircraft, occupants, or mail was recovered. The loss of Vincenzo Baldini, Premio Ferioli, Guido Fertonani, Giuseepe Baratelli, Oscar Pinelli, Giovanni Angelo Bezzi, Duino Scorceletti, and Giovanni Cubeddu, as well as Alberto Cantoni of the LATI technical department, and German diplomatic courier Alexander Safarovski, was a heavy blow to the airline. It was suggested that the aircraft was heavily overloaded with special materials and diamonds that were needed for military industrial production in Italy.

Already on 12 August 1940, General Francesco Pricolo had authorised the use of the SM.82 Marsupiale, the first of which, I-BAIA/MM60291, was delivered on 1 September, followed at regular intervals by I-BRAZ/MM60309 (17

I-BAIA was the first Savoia-Marchetti SM.82 Atlantico to be put onto the South American route

October), I-BOLI/MM60317 (27 December), I-BENI/MM60326 (10 February 1941, and I-BATO/MM60333 (6 March 1941). These were special versions, designated SM.82 Atlantico, which were adapted to suit the crossing of the South Atlantic. Two additional fuel tanks of 653 litres each in the fuselage brought the take-off weight to 19,000 kg, and other changes from the standard Marsupial were the installation of the Salmoiraghi autopilot, passenger toilet and increased number of oxygen systems, and the elimination of some 350 kg of military equipment. On 14 October 1940, the 85th crossing (from Sal Island to Recife), was operated for the first time by a SM.82, with I-BAIA completing the journey in 11 hours 15 minutes, commanded by Primo Ferioli, Umberto Carelli and Renato Vigliar, with radio operator Guido Fertonani and engineer Oscar Pinelli also on board. I-BRAZ entered the route on 10 November. However, both aircraft soon suffered misfortunes. In a night landing at Villa Cisneros on 21 December, I-BAIA hit a herd of camels and the damage to the aircraft was deemed beyond repair. I-BRAZ was lost on 9 June 1942, when it crashed due to engine malfunction after take-off from Benghazi, Libya.

On 20 July 1941, the South American line was extended from Rio to the Argentine capital Buenos Aires, via Porto Alegre, on a biweekly frequency, but had to be suspended already on 9 August, because of LATI's failure to observe its contract to employ Argentine pilots on this final sector.

Suspicion of espionage

No sooner had Italy entered the war, LATI came under suspicion of being engaged in espionage and regular reconnaissance off the coast of Brazil to locate British naval vessels and guide Axis ships through the British blockade. It was also said to carry diplomatic bags, couriers and agents, as well as mica, quartz crystals and industrial diamonds, which were abundant in Brazil and necessary for Italy's war effort. The American Ambassador in Uruguay cabled President Roosevelt, warning that unless the United States acted effectively, countries in South America could very well fall under Nazi domination. This suspicion was heightened in June and July 1941 when LATI suddenly increased its flights, which coincided with an intense German submarine campaign against British shipping in the South Atlantic, and it was reasonable to believe that Axis submarines were being guided by LATI aircraft. In an effort to stop what it believed a direct menace to the British war effort, the United States put LATI on its 17 July 1941 blacklist of Latin American firms with which American companies were forbidden to trade. However, with new aircraft and an apparently plentiful supply of spare parts, this move had little immediate effect on the operation of the airline. It was not until October that Brazil, at the urging of the United States, moved towards taking over LATI, but this was not carried out as Brazil's Minister of External Relations, Oswaldo Aranha was reluctant to close the operation, which provided the only direct link with Brazilian missions in Europe, until an alternate service was put in its place. As yet, a replacement service that matched LATI was still out of reach of the Americans.

An earlier letter from the US ambassador to the State Department had put further pressure on the embattled airline. The latter stated that "in violation of our neutrality laws and without authorisation, LATI made a 7-hour 15-minute flight along the coast between Natal and Recife under the pretext of testing the gasoline consumption of an airplane that had already been extensively tested.

Linhas Aereas para Europa e demais Continentes

LATI is currently fined 20 contos and notified that its authorisation to fly in Brazil will be cancelled in the recurrence of such an event". Fuel supplies were restricted at the express instruction of Secretary of State, Cordell Hull, to a maximum of 30 days. When the US Army Air Force's Ferrying Command commenced operations across the South Atlantic in November, the continued operation by hostile airlines of airport ground facilities, radio communications and meteorological services, became unacceptable. After the US entered the war following the Japanese attack on Pearl Harbor on 7 December 1941, Standard Oil do Brasil stopped supplying fuel to the airline, but that was not yet sufficient to eliminate it, as LATI had reserves for at least four months.

The US had also engaged in an elaborate subterfuge, which finally heralded the end of LATI. A letter was fabricated purporting to have come from the head of LATI to the airline's general manager in Brazil. A genuine letter had been obtained and an Olivetti typewriter was rebuilt to conform to the exact imperfections evident in the original letter. To ensure further authenticity, the latter was produced using the straw pulp normally only found in Europe. The letter was smuggled into Rio and leaked to Brazilian President Getulio Vargas. A passage read "There can be no doubt the little fat man [Vargas] is falling into the pocket of the Americans, and that only violent action on the part of the green gentlemen [Germans] can save the country. I understand such action has been arranged for by our respected collaborators in Berlin". An incensed Vargas cancelled LATI's landing rights and ordered the arrest of the LATI general manager in Brazil.

Four aircraft were confiscated at Recife and attempts by the Italian ambassador, Ugo Sola, to negotiate their return to Rome, citing an agreement that commercial aircraft could not be seized, proved fruitless. The final crossing was made on 19 December 1941 by the SM.82, I-BOLI, which was then seized by the authorities. LATI was formally terminated on 27 December 1941. Its five aircraft, then in hangars at Rio, Recife and Natal, were immediately confiscated by the Brazilian Government and purchased in January 1942 by the US Defense Supply Corporation (DSC), as was all LATI equipment in Brazil, for USD 350,000. The aircraft were the Savoia-Marchetti SM.75 I-BUEN and I-BLAN, Savoia-Marchetti S.76 I-CILE, Savoia-Marchetti SM.82C I-BOLI, and Savoia-Marchetti SM.83 I-ATOS. All eventually found their way to Fiat Argentina

In the two years, LATI had made 211 transatlantic flights and failed to complete only one. 132 flights were carried out by the SM.83. Statistics show that LATI carried 1,784 passengers, 120,808 kg of mail, and 143,414 kg of goods on the 211 crossings. The service can be regarded as a success and LATI benefited greatly when Deutsche Lufthansa had ceased its service on the outbreak of war, and Air France also stopped its service later, leaving LATI the only operator across the South Atlantic.

After being forced off the South Atlantic, LATI redirected its operations to Europe and between Europe and North Africa. It started flying on 1 January 1942 between Rome, Seville and Lisbon; from Rome to Tunis and Algiers, via the intermediate port of Castelvetrano until 3 November 1942; from Rome to Tripoli until 13 April; Lecce-Benghazi until 31 May; Lecce-Derna until 6 November; and Lecce-Athens-Tatoi-Marsa Matruh until 26 October.

Airlines at war

The outbreak of the war following Germany's invasion of Poland in September 1939 halted the progress of all Italian airlines in Europe, although Mussolini's plan to create a new Roman Empire in the Mediterranean, the *Mare Nostrum*, was still very much alive. As a result of its ideological closeness to the Nazi regime in Germany, Ala Littoria acquired three more Ju 52/3m the following year, I-BERO, I-BIOS and I-BOAN, all of which were assigned to war duties following Italy's entry into the war on Germany's side

Savoia-Marchetti SM.75C I-BUTI in wartime markings

The LATI Fiat G.12LGA I-FELI ditched in the Mediterranean between Tobruk and Athens

on 10 June 1940. Anticipating only a short conflict, the nation was not ready for a long engagement either militarily or strategically. Italy's armed forces were ill-prepared and ill-equipped for any prolonged conflict, not least the Regia Aeronautica. On paper it had a strength of some 3,300 aircraft, but only around 1,800 were combat ready; the vast majority of its front-line fighters being outdated Fiat CR32/42 biplanes. One of the major problems was going to be lack of spare parts with much of the capacity having been absorbed by earlier military adventures in East Africa and support for General Franco in the Spanish Civil War. Another significant factor was that a large proportion of Italy's aircraft production had been exported in a drive to gain much needed foreign exchange to bolster an ailing

ALI Fiat G.18V I-ELFO/MM60430

economy. Moreover, following successes through the 1930s, Italian designers seemed to rest on their laurels, especially in the field of engine development. In 1933, the Air Ministry had decided to halt development of liquid-cooled in-line engines to concentrate on air-cooled radial engines, leaving it reliant on the likes of Daimler-Benz in Germany for the supply of engines to power its later improved fighters, such as the Macchi MC.202 and the Reggiane 2000 series.

With the Mediterranean becoming increasingly dangerous for shipping, there was an urgent need to substitute the traditional maritime transportation of troops and materials to North and East Africa, the Aegean and Balkans by some other more rapid means. Responding to the challenge, the Regia Aeronautica High Command, under General Francesco Pricolo, quickly created the *Commando Servizi Aerei Speciali* (SAS), whose role was to maintain air links within Italy, and between Italy and neutral and allied countries, while also taking responsibility for military transport and communications duties. One of the first acts of its operations division, known as SUPERAEREO, was to order accelerated production of the Savoia-Marchetti SM.82 bomber/transport, powered by three 641 kW (860 hp) Alfa Romeo 128 RC.18 radial engines, giving a cruising speed of 250 km/h over a range of 2100 km, carrying up to 40 troops. A number of variants were built, including

one with a modified fuselage to accommodate a complete CR.42 fighter.

Military mobilisation

On 24 May 1940, under Law No. 4611, the country's three airlines, Ala Littoria, ALI and LATI, and their personnel were mobilised. They would become an integral part of the SAS organisation, divided into the communication groups *(Nuclei di Comunicazione)*, tasked with the transport of commercial goods, and the T transport groups *(Reparti Trasporto T)*, whose role was military communications and personnel transport. Under the command of Lt Gen Aurelio Liotta and later Lt Col Umberto Klinger, three independent (T) transport groups were created, each with three or four squadrons based at Rome/Littorio, Reggio Calabria and Naples/Capodichino. Two additional independent squadrons were established at Guidonia-Montecelio airbase and Rome/Littorio, all equipped with a mixture of Savoia-Marchetti S.73, SM.75 and SM.83 aircraft.

Ala Littoria was activated at Rome/Littorio on 6 June 1940 under command of Lt Col Enrico Venturi, an engineer and director from the airline. Operationally, it was split into two sections. One was based at Rome/Littorio with initially two SM.71, six SM.75, one each DC-2 and DC-3 (I-EMOS, formerly OO-AUH with SABENA), Ro.10

Although designed as a civil aircraft, the Fiat G.12 served largely on military missions during the war

Ala Littoria's Savoia-Marchetti S.73 coded 605-4 in military camouflage

(Fokker F.VII/3m) and four Ju52/3m (I-BIZI/MM60410, I-BERO/MM60411, I-BIOS/MM60412, and I-BOAN/MM60413), and a seaplane unit based at Rome/Ostia Lido equipped with four Cant Z.506, six Macchi MC.94 and four Macchi MC.100. Additional locations were also established at Venice/San Nicolo, Trieste and Brindisi.

Four days later the ALI and LATI units were activated. ALI was based at Milan/Linate headed by its managing director Gen. Antonini Biondi, employing three Fiat G.12V, six G.18, one each Fiat APR.2, DC-2 and SM.73. Initial personnel comprised nine pilot commanders, twelve each wireless operators and engineers. The airline's remit was to maintain existing lines to neutral and friendly countries, especially in the Aegean and Balkan regions and maintain a daily service to Tirana. Under the leadership of Col Carlo Pezzani, the company's technical director, LATI operated from Guidonia with 13 SM.83, to which were later added two SM.75 and two SM.82. Its crew complement initially comprised 40 pilots and 15 each wireless operators and flight engineers. As well as maintaining its services to South America, LATI also flew military transport missions to North and East Africa.

One of the early problems was the ambiguous position of the airline crews, now undertaking essentially military operations, while still retaining civilian status. After much prevarication, this was finally resolved in April 1941, after intervention by the secretary of the airline trade union, when all *Nuclei* personnel were given military ranks. This anomalous situation had earlier proved very useful, when in September 1940, a former Ala Littoria SM.75, I-TINA, now in conspicuous military markings, was forced to land at Athens with engine trouble and faced being impounded. The aircraft's commander had transmitted a distress message *en route* under its Ala Littoria callsign and upon arrival insisted that the aircraft and its crew belonged to the airline,

despite lacking any civilian documentation. Fortunately, the Greek authorities did not delve too deeply into this and after repairs, the aircraft was allowed on its way. Later in October all three airlines were called upon to support Mussolini's ill-considered invasion of Greece and became involved in ferrying troops and munitions between Brindisi and Albania.

Supply missions to East Africa

Lt Col Umberto Klinger, now briefly in charge of SAS, began organising an air-bridge to supply Italy's forces in East Africa and at the end of June 1940, a fleet of SM.75 of Ala Littoria and LATI carried out seven missions starting from Benghazi. Unable to overfly Egypt, crews were forced to make a long hazardous detour south over the unfamiliar territory of the Libyan desert and across southern Sudan, relying solely on dead-reckoning navigation during a twelve-hour flight. No sooner had Italy entered the war, General Francesco Pricolo commandeered 11 of Ala Littoria's SM.75s and assigned them to the *147th Gruppo Trasporto* (Transport Group). Already on 30 June, Umberto Klinger piloted the SM.75 '601-6' on a flight from Rome to Asmara via Benghazi, carrying some 1,100 kg of mail, medicines and ammunitions, but only nine days later, on 9 July, this aircraft was destroyed during an English aerial attack on the Eritrean port of Gura.

Starting at the beginning of 1941, a fleet of SM.75Cs was again put on the supply lines from Benghazi to Gura, Gondar, Addis Ababa and Gimma, all a long way from Benghazi, resulting in an unacceptable reduction in payload. To improve the situation, the SM.75s were stripped of all unnecessary items and had additional fuel tanks installed in the cabin. After Benghazi fell to the English on 6 February, and until retaken by Rommel's German/Italian forces on 4 April, flights had to use emergency airstrips in Libya.

Cant Z.506 I-BUIE powered by three Wright Cyclone engines

The twin-float Savoia-Marchetti SM.87, one of four operated. Three were seized by Germany in September 1943

On 4 June, Leonardo Bonzi flew I-LUNO from Benghazi to Gimma, loaded with mail and medicines, but after Gimma had fallen on 21 June, all flights were routed to the stronghold of Gondar, starting on 30 June, again with I-LUNO. After landing in Gondar, he carried on to French Somalia (Djibouti) to refuel, where he was forced to remain until 6 August due to engine failure. On 16 August, the French decreed that to continue to ensure fuel supplies, all aircraft had to apply International Red Cross markings.

In the meantime, the situation inside Gondar, defended by the troops of General Guglielmo Nasi, had deteriorated drastically. Medicines and ammunition were fast running out and the pilots of the SM.75s were asked for further effort. On 18 September, Giovanni Balletti, in a SM.75 with Red Cross markings, flew 1,200 kg of provisions to Gondar and took on board six civilian passengers, all women, and returned to Libya via Djibouti. On 6 October, I-LUNO,

piloted by Max Peroli, succeeded once more in supplying Gondar, but was shot at by a Curtiss P40 of the British Royal Air Force while standing at Djibouti and destroyed. It was Peroli's sixth relief flight to the area. Another SM.75, commanded by Giuseppe Orlandini, was sent to rescue Peroli and his crew and, having successfully avoided the P40s, returned to Rome unscathed. The Italian pilots demonstrated exceptional courage running the gauntlet of the enemy on the long 12,000 km trip from Rome to Benghazi, Gondar and Djibouti unescorted and unarmed.

Another effort to support the besieged Italian troops was made on 9 November. The SM.75, I-LAME, took off from Rome under the command of Guido Bertolini, loaded with about 100 kg of medicines, cigarettes and food. Bad weather prevented him from landing at Gondar and forced him to fly on to Djibouti, where he landed on 11 November. The next day, he set off for Gondar. After about an hour of flight, he encountered a violent storm and poor visibility, and the aircraft crashed near the summit of the Debra Tabor Massif. The entire crew, which also included the second pilot Lt Fernando Battezatti, the wireless operator Lt Carlo Profumo, and the engineer Lt Giacomo Timolina, perished in this disaster. This also signalled the end of SM.75 operation to East Africa, although Savoia-Marchetti were trying to fit I-LINI with four 413-litre fuel tanks and a Samoiraghi autopilot for night flying. It was all too late, Nazi's troops surrendered Gondar, Italy's last bastion in East Africa, on 27 November 1941.

Northward bound

In autumn 1940, Ju 52/3m I-BIZI/MM60410, piloted by Riccardo Pasquali, supported the Italian air force, which relocated to Belgium to contribute to the German air offensive against Britain. The aircraft collected Fiat BR.20 and CR.42 pilots and technicians, who were stationed along the route between Italy and Belgium. Thereafter, it operated three weekly flights from Rome or Venice to Brussels to deliver mail and newspapers. The mission concluded with the completion of 91 return flights, totalling 127 flying hours. The other Ju 52/3m continued to serve the trans-Alpine routes, making 194 flights between June and December. On 1 October 1941, a SM.75 flown by Captain Carlo Pivetti, was forced to make an emergency landing close to Stradella in the Province of Piacenza. On board were four important generals: Francesco Pricolo, the commander in chief of the Regia Aeronautica; Mario Bernasconi, inspector-general of the Regia Aeronautica; Simon Pietro Mattei of the aerial brigade; and Maximilian Ritter von Pohl, commanding general of the Luftwaffe in Mid-Italy, who, because of poor weather conditions, collectively decided it prudent to continue to Munich by train. However, Captain Pietro Caggiano was alerted to the mishap, and was dispatched from Venice in Ju 52/3m I-BOAN/MM60413 to fly the generals to Berlin and onwards to Insterburg. Although the generals opted for other aircraft to fly them to the Russian Front, Budapest, Athens, and back to Italy, I-BOAN continued to escort the mission, which returned on 8 October.

Italian aggression

Following Italy's disastrous invasion of Egypt between 13 and 16 September 1940, designed to capture the Suez Canal, the British counter-offensive soon began pushing the Italian forces back westwards. With the Allies now attacking through Cyrenaica along the North Libyan coast, it became imperative to evacuate Italian civilians from the region. Both Ala Littoria's seaplane unit and LATI were tasked with repatriating women and children back to Italy. Unarmed and lacking escorts, their lumbering aircraft were at the mercy of Allied fighters. On 10 January 1941, the LATI SM.83, I-AREM, disappeared over the Mediterranean an hour out from Benghazi near the island of Lampedusa. Amongst all aboard who lost their lives was Captain Vittorio Suster, veteran of Transadriatica and the South American route, who was posthumously awarded the Gold Medal for Aeronautical Valour. With Italy facing imminent defeat by British and Commonwealth forces in East Africa (*Africa Orientale Italiana-AOI*), SAS ordered the evacuation of aircrews and key specialist personnel. On 3 April 1941, three Ala Littoria SM.75 left Addis Ababa, but were forced to head eastwards and, after an unplanned landing in the desert due to mechanical problems, they managed to reach Jeddah in Saudi Arabia. Following lengthy negotiations, the aircraft were finally allowed to depart for Benghazi on May 3.

Following major setbacks in the Greek campaign,

Junkers Ju 52/3m I-BERO, seen here possibly after its taxiing accident at Brindisi in September 1940 (Roberto Gentilli)

Ala Littoria Savoia-Marchetti SM.75C I-LIAN (Archivio SIAI-Savoia-Marchetti)

Wehrmacht units were drafted in to prop-up the beleaguered Italian army. No doubt grateful and wishing to show solidarity when Germany launched Operation Barbarossa against Russia, Mussolini sent an Italian expeditionary contingent in July 1941 to help out, initially in southern Ukraine. Aircraft of Ala Littoria participated in 14 supply flights over the route Rome-Milan-Venice-Pula-Bucharest-Traspol-Galaţi-Zaporizhzhia. SAS crews were instructed to communicate any sightings of enemy shipping via encrypted wireless message, but unknown at the time, their codes had already been broken by the British. In early October 1941, SM.83, I-AMER, flying between Catania and Benghazi, sighted a British naval formation and relayed this information as ordered. Unfortunately, this was not passed to SM.73, I-SAMO, carrying women and child evacuees, which unwittingly overflew the column triggering fire from the ships anti-aircraft batteries. A fighter launched from the carrier escort intercepted and attacked the unarmed Italian aircraft. which fortunately managed to escape, although its pilot was mortally wounded. This failure of inter-service communication and co-ordination occurred not infrequently and had been a contributory factor in the downing of Air Marshal Balbo's plane and his death in June 1940.

In October 1942, the number of aircraft available to *Nuclei* units stood at 56 and since the beginning of the war, Ala Littoria had completed 37,132 flight hours with 152,746 passengers. 2,845 tonnes of luggage, 1,396 tonnes of war material, 441 tonnes of newspapers and 2,503 tonnes of mail; LATI flew 10,733 hours transporting 8,445 passengers, 232 tonnes of luggage, 246 tonnes of material and 495 tonnes of mail; ALI was primarily concerned with maintaining the four lines to Tirana, Belgrade, Bucharest/Baneasa and Sofia, but at the peak of the Greek campaign it also became involved in an airlift carrying 4,316 troops, 90

Flight to the land of the rising sun

In May 1942, the General Staff decided to try and establish a regular link to Tokyo and tasked SAS to undertake this assignment. For this purpose, two SM.75GA, I-BUBA/MM60539 and I-TAMO/MM60543, were specially adapted and designated SM.75RT (Rome-Tokyo) to be flown by LATI crews, headed by Colonel Amaedeo Paradisi. Unfortunately, Paradisi was badly injured, losing a leg, when his aircraft, MM60537, crashed on take-off from Guidonia to Ciampino after all three engines failed on 11 May, after having returned from a gruelling 'symbolic' leaflet-dropping mission over Asmara two days earlier. Therefore, command passed to another seasoned LATI pilot, Lt Col Antonio Moscatelli. Departing Guidonia on 29 June 1942, I-BUBA/MM60539, crewed by Moscatelli, Captain Mario Cutro, Captain Dr Publio Magini, radio operator Ernesto Mazzotti, and engineer Ernesto Leone, staged via the Italian-held airfield of Zaporizhzhia in the Ukraine, where a refuelling and radio base had been established, and, having survived Soviet anti-aircraft shelling, touched down at Pao-Tow-Chen in Japanese occupied Inner Mongolia on 1 July. Tokyo (Tachikawa air force base) was reached on 3 July, having covered a total distance of 9,859 km. Mussolini himself was present when the aircraft returned to Guidonia on 20 July. Further flights were planned over a southerly route via Rangoon (now Yangon), but foundered due to lack of Japanese co-operation in establishing a radio beacon and other facilities at Rangoon. The next flight scheduled for August 1942, using I-TAMO/MM60543, was cancelled.

Cant Z.506B I-LAMA was lost when it crashed into the sea off Natal after an engine fire

tonnes of war material and munitions and 30 tonnes of mail during the course of 204 flight hours. At this stage, LATI had at its disposal 13 aircraft (three SM.82, nine SM.83 and one SM.75) and eight crews, and was flying around 75,000 km per month over regular lines linking Rome with Tripoli, Algiers and Tunis.

SAS was often called upon to perform unusual missions, but one assigned to LATI early in November 1942 would have unforeseen tragic consequences. The Ala Littoria S.73, I-DOUL (ex I-ARCO), which had been languishing at Rome/Ciampino after having escaped from Addis Ababa, was patched-up for a flight to Algiers to collect sensitive documents. After an enforced stop at Trapani with an engine problem and a burst tyre, the aircraft proceeded to Tunis for refuelling, before eventually reaching Algiers/Maison Blanche on 6 November. Its arrival unfortunately coincided with the American landings under Operation Torch and the aircraft and its crew fell into enemy hands. The sealed packages were seized and turned out to contain lists of agents and informants operating in French North Africa, who were later rounded-up and mostly shot by the Free French for having committed acts of high treason.

Severe losses
In North Africa, the Italians had been struggling to hold back a westward push by British forces, at least until General Rommel's Afrika Korps started arriving in North Africa from February 1941 to begin temporarily reversing British advances. Rommel's successes continued until late in 1942 when the tables were turned significantly and the German and Italian armies began retreating towards Tunisia. The failure to capture the strategic island of Malta now allowed the British Navy to severely disrupt Axis supply lines to North

Africa and growing Allied air superiority only compounded the problem. This was brought home when on 10 April 1943, two SM.75, I-MAST of Ala Littoria and I-BONI of LATI, joined an aerial convoy of 18 SAS SM.82 carrying battle ready troops and fuel drums to reinforce Tunis, now all but surrounded by the Allies. But approaching Cape Bon in the Gulf of Tunis, the formation was attacked by Allied fighters and all were shot down. One lucky crew, commanded by Lt Renato Vigliar, having been delayed for a spark plug change, arrived independently over the area to witness the sea littered with wreckage and many dead. They managed to land at Tunis, which was under air attack, but their aircraft was severely damaged by an incendiary bomb. After a few minutes wandering round the airfield, the flight engineer chanced upon an abandoned SM.82, which seemed airworthy and still had fuel. Vigliar managed to take-off and arrived back safely at Sciacca, Sicily after a two-hour flight. Flying out of Sicily had now become a game of Russian roulette and nine days later, another convoy comprising 15 SAS aircraft, including Ala Littoria SM.75 I-MONC, escorted by 12 Macchi fighters out of Sciacca, met a similar fate. Two were attacked by Beaufighters near Pantelleria and the remainder encountered heavy fire from five Spitfires near Cape Bon, again with most shot down or forced to ditch.

Things were not going to well on the Russian Front either with German forces surrounded at Stalingrad. Deployed SAS units were struggling to keep operational in the severe winter temperatures. Particularly, the castor oil engine lubricant froze necessitating pre-heating of the powerplants. Nevertheless, the crews contrived to carry out their endeavours under the harshest of conditions; one such SM.81 sortie attempting to supply a besieged

German garrison and evacuate its wounded failed to return to base. Among those on board was Gen. B A Pezzi, Italian Air Commander of the Russian Front. Surviving units were withdrawn in March and May 1943. At the end of 1942, SAS airworthy aircraft comprised 119 machines, 40 of which belonged to the *Nuclei*. Statistics for 1942 show 22,832 missions during 81,008 flight hours uplifting 313,689 passengers, 15,000 tonnes of various material, 430 tonnes of armaments, 500 torpedoes, 454 engines, 321 tonnes of newspapers and 2,333 tonnes of mail. An outstanding feat bearing in mind the limitations and dangerous conditions under which SAS crews and aircraft operated. But losses were now increasing at an alarming rate and by the beginning of 1943 the aircraft available to *Nuclei* units was down to only 35 machines.

SAS was now struggling to keep up with the demands of the retreating Axis armies, which by early February had fallen back to the Tunisian border and it had become so dangerous that operations were switched to night flights only. Up until the surrender in Tunisia on May 13, 1943, since January SAS had flown over almost 24,000 hours during over 12,300 war-related missions, but anticipating Allied landings was now looking to re-group for the defence of Sicily and Sardinia. With almost all Italian airfields in range of Allied aircraft and its armies poised to launch an assault on Sicily, losses continued to mount, especially without the benefit of fighter escorts, which were in very short supply; since January overall SAS had lost over 80 aircraft, around 10 of which belonged to the *Nuclei* units.

The day after Allied troops entered Tunis on 7 May 1943, one of the last Italian aircraft out of the city's El Aouina airport (now Tunis/Carthage International) was SM.75 I-MASO, which got airborne with a heavy load of passengers. While two other crews, who had set out from Sicily on 5 May, became stranded at Tunis while attempting repairs following an attack. On the airfield they found an abandoned SM.81, almost a wreck, but managed to start the engines running and get airborne just as Allied military vehicles began arriving at the airfield. With rescued army personnel, including two generals onboard, an intermediate landing for repairs was made on a makeshift dry lake bed landing strip at Sidi Kedoni near Cape Bon, before eventually reaching Castelvetrano without further incident.

In spite of the dire situation, the SAS command decided to show its bravado and make a token nuisance bombing raid over Asmara. Its target was the former Italian air base of Gura, now a major air logistics centre for USAAF bombers. For this purpose. the two long-range SM.75GA/RT were fitted with auxiliary fuel tanks, bombsights and shackles to hold 100 kg bombs, released through a ventral hatch. Leaving Rhodes at dawn on 23 May 1943, only one machine reached Gura to drop its bombs, the other was forced to unload over Port Sudan due to fuel problems. Both returned safely to Rhodes after a gruelling 24-hour mission.

SAS was often called upon to operate behind enemy lines, most recently dropping paratroops and commandos in Morocco and Algeria to sabotage enemy airfields. A similar recovery mission took Lt Col Klinger and a party of army and air force personnel to a landing in the Cyrenaica desert. Leaving Heraklion, Crete, in the early hours of 26 June 1943 in Ala Littoria SM.75, I-TETI, Klinger and his crew encountered no opposition and after 3 h 30m aloft they touched down about 70 km south of Mechili. Having spent over twelve hours on the ground, they returned safely back to base after almost 24 hours. Impending Allied landings in Sicily in July 1943 caused SAS Command to order airfields on the islands of Sicily and Sardinia rendered unusable to the enemy and all units moved to the mainland, some to Lecce, south of Brindisi, and others back to their original bases in the Rome area. These were desperate and nervous times and led to several incidences of losses due to friendly fire.

With Mussolini already under arrest and Allied forces poised to make landings on the Italian mainland, representatives loyal to King Victor Emmanuel III were flown by LATI aircraft to Lisbon for secret exploratory meetings with the Allies to extricate Italy from the war. The Lisbon service had been maintained throughout the conflict and when the Armistice was made public on 8 September 1943, LATI's Commander Fenili was flying the run on the Lisbon route in SM.75, I-MEDE. Under the terms of the Armistice the *Nuclei* fleet was declared as 78 aircraft; 18 from LATI, 43 from Ala Littoria and 17 from ALI, but most were seized by the Germans, who were in control of many Italian airfields, and incorporated into the Luftwaffe. Ten were assigned to Lufthansa, and a few were retained by Italians who elected to collaborate to operate two courier lines: Milan-Munich-Berlin with SM.75 I-AVAB, I-BALJ, I-META, I- MOND and I-TIMO, and Milan-Munich-Vienna with SM.83 I-ASSO and Fiat G.18 I-ETRA. Many of the *Nuclei* crews opted to join the *Aviazione Cobelligerante Italiana* (Italian Co-belligerent Air Force), formed in October 1943. Its transport unit, No.2 Group, 3rd Transport Wing, flying from Lecce/Galatina in southern Italy, operated a few SM and Fiat transports in support of Allied operations in the Balkans and Aegean.

As predicted by Air Marshal Balbo the war would end badly for Italy, but crews of the *Nuclei* units had acquitted themselves well and bravely, adapting quickly to wartime operations against almost overwhelming odds. But not without cost, although countless medals for valour had been awarded. Some 666 SAS personnel had lost their lives during the three-year conflict.

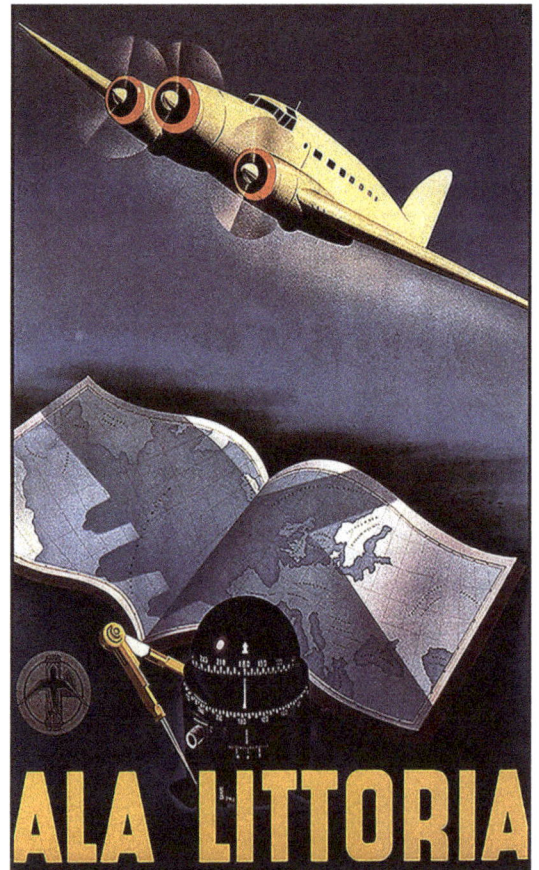

In anticipation of Italy's entry into the war on the side of Germany, which took place on 10 June 1940, aircraft, personnel and facilities of the country's three airlines - Ala Littoria, Avio Linee Aeree (ALI) and Linee Aeree Transcontinentali Italiani (LATI) - were requisitioned by the Regia Aeronautica and became an integral part of the Commando Servizi Aerei Speciali (SAS), which was divided into the communication groups (Nuclei di Comunicazione), tasked with the transport of commercial goods, and the T transport groups (Reparti Trasporto T), whose role was military communications and personnel transport. All aircraft were given military serial numbers, but many retained their civil registrations. Ala Littoria was activated on 6 June, followed on 10 June by ALI and LATI. Records of fleet allocations are incomplete and confusing, and their exact distribution among the three airlines remains unknown. Where aircraft were delivered to the airlines after Italy had entered the war, these are together with their civil and military identities.

ALA Littoria Società Anonima Fleet 1934-1943

Beech 17R Staggerwing 1937 (1)

Four-passenger touring and corporate biplane, powered by a single 313 kW (420 hp) Wright R-975-E3 engines, generating a cruising speed of 340 km/h (211 mph)

I-IBIS	71	24.04.37-	ex NC15816; to Società IOPES

Breda 39 1935-1936 (2)

Two-seat low-wing touring and liaison aircraft, powered by a single 104 kW (140 hp) Colombo S.63 engine, generating a maximum speed of 220 km/h (137 mph)

I-ABMP	3812	04.05.35-00.01.36	to Regia Aeronautica as MM55806
I-ABMQ		16.10.35-00.01.36	to Regia Aeronautica as MM58449

Breda 44 1935-1940 (4)

Six-passenger strut and wire-braced biplane, powered by either Walter Major or de Havilland Gipsy twin engines, generating a cruising speed of 175 km/h (109 mph)

I-ARIA	4301	07.01.36-06.07.40	to Regia Aeronautica as MM60424, operated by 611 Squadriglia, Tirana, Albania
I-AURA	4305	26.03.35-14.06.40	to Regia Aeronautica as MM60422, operated by 611 Squadriglia, Tirana, Albania
I-EURO	4304	10.05.38-14.06.40	to Regia Aeronautica as MM60423, operated by 611 Squadriglia, Tirana, Albania
I-ORIO	4306	14.05.35-06.07.40	to Regia Aeronautica as MM6042., operated by 611 Squadriglia, Tirana, Albania

Cant 10ter II 1934-1939 (4)

Four-passenger biplane flying-boat, powered by one 298 kW (400 hp) Lorraine-Dietrich engine, generating a cruising speed of 150 km/h (93 mph)

I-AASF	203	28.10.34-	ex SAM;
I-AASG	204	28.10.34-	ex SAM;
I-AASH	206	28.10.34-24.12.39	ex SAM; to RUNA, Ancona
I-AASI		28.10.34-	ex SAM;

Cant 22 1934-1939 (6)

Eight-passenger biplane flying-boat, powered by three Isotta-Fraschini Asso 200 in-line engines, generating a cruising speed of 140 km/h (87 mph)

I-AABN	5	28.10.34-00.02.37	ex SAM; wfu and broken up
I-AACJ	64	28.10.34-00.10.36	ex SAM; wfu and broken up
I-AACL	159	28.10.34-00.04.37	ex SAM; wfu and broken up
I-AACM	160	28.10.34-00.07.37	ex SAM; wfu and broken up
I-AAQX	162	28.10.34-00.07.37	ex SAM; wfu and broken up
I-ALFA	230	28.10.34-28.02.36	ex SAM; crashed into sea after hitting church bell-tower at Rovigno, Istria

Cant Z.506C Airone 1936-1943 (34)

15-passenger low-wing monoplane with twin floats, powered by three 560 kW (750 hp) Alfa Romeo 126 RC.34 engines, generating a maximum speed of 380 km/h (236 mph)

I-ALAL	3547	12.02.38-14.06.40	to Regia Aeronautica as MM…..
I-BUIE*	300	07.08.36-14.06.40	to Regia Aeronautica as MM60410 then Germany D-AIAO Luftwaffe AI+AO
I-DAIA/MM60638	3026	08.04.42-00.09.43	to Regia Aeronautica MM60638; seized by Germany and registered to Deutsche Lufthansa as D-ABGW
I-DAIB/MM60639	3027	17.05.42-00.11.42	destroyed by enemy action
I-DAIC/MM60640	3028	17.05.42-19.05.42	destroyed by fire at Rome/Lido di Ostia
I-DAIL/MM60641	3029	18.06.42-31.05.43	destroyed by enemy action 31.05.43
I-DAIM/MM60642	3030	21.06.42-22.11.42	destroyed by enemy action
I-DAIN	3669	02.03.40-14.06.40	to Regia Aeronautica as MM….., coded 614-6
I-DAMB	3668	05.01.40-14,06,40	to Regia Aeronautica as MM….., coded 612-1
I-DAVO/MM60670	3705	08.07.41-23.11.42	destroyed in unknown circumstances
I-DELT/MM60636	3704	02.06.41-00.09.43	seized by Germany and registered to Deutsche Lufthansa as D-ADVW
I-DENO	3549	27.06.38-07.09.38	destroyed by fire at Melilla, Spanish Morocco
I-DEVI	3552	07.10.38-10.06.40	to Regia Aeronautica as MM….., coded 614-3;
I-DICO/MM60585	3703	19.04.41-29.05.42	destroyed by fire at Rome
I-DIGO/MM60643	3031	09.07.42-24.07.43	destroyed by enemy action
I-DITO	3632	17.04.39-00.09.43	to Regia Aeronautica MM60474; seized by Germany and registered to Deutsche Lufthansa as D-ADVU
I-DIVO/MM60644	3032	05.08.42-24.07.43	destroyed by enemy action
I-DODA	3667	17.10.39-00.09.43	to Regia Aeronautica as MM60470, coded 614-5; seized by Germany and registered to Deutsche Lufthansa as D-ADVV
I-DOGA/MM60645	3033	14.08.42-00.09.43	seized by Germany and registered to Deutsche Lufthansa as D-AEGF
I-DOME/MM60648	3036	22.10.42-00.09.43	seized by Germany and registered to Deutsche Lufthansa as D- Germany D-ADVX
I-DOMI	3629	14,12,38-22.04.41	to Regia Aeronautica MM60468; destroyed by enemy action at Siracusa, Sicily
I-DOMO/MM60646	3034	24.08.42-00.09.43	seized by Germany and registered to Deutsche Lufthansa as D-AGBB
I-DOMP/MM60647	3035	03.10.42-	

I-DOMU/MM61174	3285	10.12.42-00.00.00	crashed near Taranto
I-DORA	3630	16.02.39-29.04.42	to Regia Aeronautica MM60473, coded 614-2; destroyeshot down by a Messerscjmitt Bf110
I-DOTE	3550	21.07.38-03.04.42	to Regia Aeronautica MM60466; crashed on landing Rome/Lido di Ostia
I-DUCO	3631	22.03.39-00.09.43	to Regia Aeronautica MM60469, coded 614-1; seized by Germany and registered to Deutsche Lufthansa as D-ADVT
I-DUNA	3551	06.09.38-00.09.43	to Regia Aeronautica as MM60466; seized by Germany and registered to Deutsche Lufthansa as D-ADVS
I-ELBA*	462	15.01.37-14,06.40	to Regia Aeronautica as MM.....;
I-FANO*	298	16.06.36-19.06.40	to Regia Aeronautica MM60460;
I-GORO*	302	22.10.36-4.06.40	
I-LERO*	463	20.08.37-15.12.37	reregistered I-LEVA
I-LEVA*	463	15.12.37-00.02.39	ex I-LERO; destroyed
I-POLA*	299	31.08.36-11.06.41	to Regia Aeronautica as MM....., coded 612-5; shot down off Sicily
I-RODI*	301	25.09.36-24.09.36	crashed into sea after engine explosion on approach to Benghazi, Libya

* Cant Z.506 powered by three 566 kW (760 hp) Wright Cyclone GR-1820-F52 engines

Caproni Ca 97 1934-1939 (1)

Six-passenger high-wing strut-braced monoplane, powered by three 108 kW (145 hp) Walter mars engines, generating a maximum speed of 192 km/h (119 mph)

I-ABCA	3079	28.10.34-00.11.39	ex SAM, cancelled as scrapped

Caproni Ca 101 1935-1937 (5)

Eight-passenger high-wing strut-braced monoplane, powered by three 149 kW (200 hp) Alaf Romeo Lynx engines, generating a maximum speed of 200 km/h (124 mph)

I-ABCC		01.08.35-00.08.37	ex NAA; sold to Saudia Arabia
I-ABCI	3349	01.08.35-00.08.37	ex NAA; sold to Saudi Arabia
I-ABCJ	3350	01.08.35-	ex NAA;
I-ABCK	3351	01.08.35-00.08.37	ex NAA; sold to Saudi Arabia
I-AABF			also rprtd captured N Africa, to RAF 103 MU Aboukir 5.42

Caproni Ca 111 1940- .   (1)

High-wing reconnaissance and light bomber, powered by a single 619 kW (750 hp) Isotta Fraschini Asso engine, generating a maximum speed of 290 km/h (180 mph)

I-ARSA		00.06.40-	to Regia Aeronautica as MM10644

Caproni Ca 133 1936-1940 (12)

16-passenger high-wing strut-braced monoplane, powered by three (460 hp) Piaggio Stella VII.C 16 radial engines, generating a maximum speed of 265 km/h (165 mph)

I-ADUR	01.07.37-	to Regia Aeronautica as MM60446
I-AGLE	19.02.37-	to Regia Aeronautica as MM60442
I-AXUM	29.08.36-	to Regia Aeronautica as MM60438
I-DABO	07.04.37-	to Regia Aeronautica as MM60443
I-DALI	09.06.37-	to Regia Aeronautica as MM60445
I-DAUA	20.11.36-	to Regia Aeronautica as MM60440
I-DIRE	10.10.36-13.10.39	Crashed on approach to Gabode Airfield, Djibouti, after engine failure
I-GURA	05.09.36-00.09.37	cancelled as destroyed; preserved at the Polytechnic Museum, Turin
I-NIMI	22.01.37-	
I-ROLE	22.05.37-	to Regia Aeronautica as MM60444
I-TANG	29.12.36-	to Regia Aeronautica as MM60441
I-ZULA	03.09.36-	to Regia Aeronautica as MM60439

Caproni Ca 308 Borea 1935-1938 (6)

Seven-passenger low-wing monoplane, powered by two (200 hp) Alfa Romeo 115 or de Havilland Gipsy engines, generating a maximum speed of 246 km/h (153 mph)

I-DRIA	003	09.01.36-00.03.38	wfu and broken up
I-MERA	001	11.10.35-00.03.38	wfu and broken up
I-MOLA	006	25.11.35-00.03.38	wfu and broken up
I-NTRA	004	31.10.35-	
I-SPRA	002	02.10.35-00.03.38	wfu and broken up
I-VREA	005	31.10.35-00.02.38	wfu and broken up

Caproni Ca 309 Ghibli 1937-1938 (1)

Three-seat low-wing monoplane, powered by two 291 kW (390 hp) Alfa Romeo 115 piston engines, generating a maximum speed of 250 km/h (155 mph)

I-ALAL	7	13.04.37-10.02.38	crahed on landing at Paris/Le Bourget

Caproni Ca 312

Three-seat low-wing reconnaissance and light bomber, powered by two 470 kW (630 hp) Piaggio P.XVI RC.35 radial engines, generating a maximum speed of 430 km/h (267 mph)

I-BUIA	641	00.10.41-00.11.41	to Regia Aeronautica as MM12342, operated by 611 Squadriglia, Tirana, Albania
I-BUIB	642	00.10.41-00.11.41	to Regia Aeronautica as MM12343, operated by 611 Squadriglia, Tirana, Albania
I-BUIC	643	00.10.41-00.11.41	to Regia Aeronautica as MM12344, operated by 611 Squadriglia, Tirana, Albania

I-BUID	645	00.10.41-00.11.41	to Regia Aeronautica as MM12345, operated by 611 Squadriglia, Tirana, Albania
I-BUIF	631	00.10.41-00.11.41	to Regia Aeronautica as MM12346, operated by 611 Squadriglia, Tirana, Albania
I-BUIG	632	00.10.41-00.11.41	to Regia Aeronautica as MM12347, operated by 611 Squadriglia, Tirana, Albania

De Havilland DH89 Dragon Rapide 1935-1936 (1)

Eight-passenger light biplane, powered by two 149 kW (200 hp) de Havilland Gipsy Six piston engines, generating a maximum speed of 250 km/h (155 mph)

| I-DRAG | 6260 | 29.01.35-05.08.36 | to Franco Mazotti Biancinelli, Milan and to Spanish Republicans |

Douglas DC-3 1940-1943 (1)

21-passengers low-wing, all-metal monoplane, powered by two 895 kW (1,200 hp) Pratt & Whitney R-1830-S1C3G Twin Wasp engines, generating a maximum speed of 370 km/h (230 mph)

| I-EMOS | 2093 | 26.09.40-10.06.43 | ex OO-AUH; to Regia Aeronautica as MM60520; sold to Deutsche Lufthansa as D-ATZP |

Fokker F.VIIa-3m 1935-1939 (11)

Eight-passenger high-wing monoplane, powered by three 272 kW (365 hp) Gnome-Rhône Titan Major engines, generating a maximum speed of 222 km/h (138 mph) , or 158 kW (215 hp) Alfa Romeo Lynx engines

I-AAIG	5206	06.09.35-	ex G-AATG;
I-ABBA	5212	02.10.35-00.10.38	ex ALI; wfu and broken up
I-ADUA	5238	31.10.35-00.11.39	ex HB-LAO; wfu and broken up
I-AFRO	5208	19.08.34-06.03.39	ex HB-LBQ; to RUNA Sede Provinciale, Bologna; cr Bologna 06.03.39
I-BBEC	4982	26.04.35-23.07.36	ex SAM; CofA suspended and broken up 04.37
I-BBED	5059	23.11.34-00.08.39	ex SAM; wfu
I-BBEE	5060	23.11.34-07.04.36	ex ALI; CofA suspendedand broken up 09.37
I-BBEF	5061	08.10.35-00.10.37	ex ALI; cancelled
I-UADI	5210	19.06.35-00.08.39	ex HB-LBS; wfu
I-UEBI	5195	06.09.35-00.07.37	ex HB-LAN; wfu and broken up
I-UGRI	5209	19.06.35-00.10.36	destroyed in accident

Officine Ferroviarie Meridionale-Aeroplani Romeo Ro 10 (Fokker F.VIIb-3m) 1936 (2)

Eight-passenger high-wing monoplane powered by three 158 kW (215 hp) Alfa Romeo Lynx radial engines, generating a cruising speed of
178 km/h (111 mph)

| I-AAXY | 358 | 03.05.40- | ex Compagnia Nazionale Imprese Elettriche (CONIEL); operated in East Africa |
| I-FERO | 778 | 19.02.36-08.07.36 | leased from ALI |

Junkers F 13 1934-1935 (1)

Four-passenger, cantilever wing monoplane, powered by one 136 kW (182 hp) BMW IIIa in-line engine, developing a cruising speed of 170 km/h (105 mph)

I-ABAA	2027	28.10.34-00.05.35	ex SAM; never used and traded in to Reichsluftfahrtministerium (RLM) in part payment for Junkers Ju 52/3m

Junkers G 24 gy (2)

14-passenger cantilever wing monoplane, powered by three 149 kW (200 hp) Isotta Fraschini Asso 200 engines, generating a cruising speed of 170 km/h (110 mph)

I-BAUS	924	28.10.34-14.05.35	ex SAM; traded in to RLM
I-BAZI	947	28.10.34-14.05.35	ex SAM; traded in to RLM

Junkers Ju 52/3m 1935-1943 (8)

17-passenger low-wing cantilever monoplane, powered by three 522 kW (700 hp) Piaggio P.X.R engines, generating a cruising speed of 245 km/h (152 mph)

I-ABJZ*	5942	09.11.38-00.03.39	ex D-AUJG; leased from Deutsche Lufthansa
I-BALI	6779	30.01.40-25.05.40	ex D-ARCK; leased from Deutsche Lufthansa
I-BAUS	4063	30.01.35-04.12.39	struck a hillside in bad weather near Arbersee, Bayerisch Eisenstein, Germany
I-BERO	6803	30.07.40-21.09.43	to Regia Aeronautica as MM60411; seized by Germany and registered to Deutsche Lufthansa as D-ASPE
I-BEZI	4062	03.01.35-30.03.38	damaged beyond repair on training flight when it hit the water off Venice/Lido
I-BIOS	6710	18.06.40-21.09.43	to Regia Aeronautica as MM60412; seized by Germany and registered to Deutsche Lufthansa as D-ASPI
I-BIZI	4064	08.02.35-21.09.43	to Regia Aeronautica as MM60410; seized by Germany and registered to Deutsche Lufthansa as D-AIAO
I-BOAN	6765	12.09.40-10.10.43	to Regia Aeronautica as MM60413, seized by Germany and registered to Deutsche Lufthansa as D-AIAT

* powered by BMW 132 engines

Macchi C.94 1936-1943 (12)

12-passenger high-wing monoplane flying-boat, powered by either two 574 kW (770 hp) Wright Cyclone SGR-1820-F52 or 597 kW (800 hp) Alfa Romeo 126 RC.10 engines, generating maximum speeds of 290 km/h (180 mph)

I-ANIO	94008	12,05.38-00.10.38	to Corporación Sudamaricana de Servicios Aéreos as LV-LAB
I-ARNO	94002	29.12.36-00.09.43	to Regia Aeronautica as MM60455; seized by Germany and registered to Deutsche Lufthansa as D-ADQN
I-ENZA	94007	10.05.38-00.09.43	to Regia Aeronautica as MM60459; seized by Germany and registered to Deutsche Luufthansa as D-ADQS
I-LATO	94010	21.07.38-00.02.39	to Corporación Sudamaricana de Servicios Aéreos as LV-NAB
I-LIRI	94003	31.07.36-00.09.43	to Regia Aeronautica as MM60456; seized by Germany and registered to Deutsche Lufthansa as D-ADQO

I-NARO	94006	18.12.36-00.09.43	to Regia Aeronautica as MM60453; seized by Germany and registered to Deutsche Lufthansa as D-ADQR
I-NEPI	94000	01.05.37-	
I-NETO	94009	14.06.38-00.09.43	to Regia Aeronautica as MM60458; seized by Germany and registered to Deutsche Lufthansa as D-ADQT
I-NEVA	94012	12.10.38-00.10.38	to Corporación Sudamaricana de Servicios Aéreos as LV-MAB
I-NILO	94001	26.06.40-	
I-SILE	94005	03.09.36-00.09.43	to Regia Aeronaiutca as MM60457; seized by Germany and registered to Deutsche Lufthansa as D-ADQQ
I-TOCE	94004	11.08.36-00.09.43	to Regia Aeronautica as MM60452; seized by Germany and registered to Deutsche Lufthansa as D-ADQP

Macchi MC.100 1940-1942 (3)

26-passenger high-wing monoplane flying-boat, powered by three 597 kW (800 hp) Alfa Romeo 126 RC.10 engines, generating a maximum speed of 310 km/h (193 mph)

I-PACE	4158	26.04.40-30.07.41	to Regia Aeronautica as MM60419; crashed on landinmg at Rome/Lido di Ostia after engine problems
I-PLIO	4157	22.05.39-	to Regia Aeronautica as MM60420
I-PLUS	4159	29.06.40-06.02.42	to Regia Aeronautica as MM60418; destroyed by fire at Cagliari, Sardinia

Savoia-Marchetti S.55P 1934-1936 (8)

Eight-passenger cantilever wing, twin-hull monoplane flying-boat powered by two tandem 373 Kw (500 HP) Isotta-Fraschini Asso 500 engines, generating a cruising speed of 170 km/h (106 mph)

I-BICO	10524	28.10.34-00.08.36	ex SAM; wfu and broken up
I-MERO	10515	28.10.34-00.07.36	ex SAM;
I-NACO	10516	28.10.34-	ex SAM;
I-NDRA	10513	28.10.34-	ex SAM;
I-OLAO	10526	28.10.34-00.08.36	ex SAM; wfu and broken up
I-RZIO	10522	28.10.34-00.10.35	ex SAM; wfu and broken up
I-SILI	10518	28.10.34-00.10.35	ex SAM; wfu and broken up
I-STRO	10523	28.10.34-00.10.35	ex SAM; wfu and broken up

Savoia-Marchetti S.66 1934-1940 (23)

18-22 passenger twin-hull cantilever monoplane flying-boat, powered by three 515 kW (700 hp) Fiat A.24R engines, generating a cruising speed of 222 km/h (138 mph)

I-AABF	15006	31.08.35-00.08.39	ex Aero Espresso Italiane (AEI), cancelled as wfu
I-ALGA	15016	20.07.35-01.03.37	broke adrift and destroyed in gale at Benghazi, Libya
I-ALTE	15005	28.10.34-00.10.38	ex SAM; cancelled time expired
I-BLEO	15010	28.10.34-00.02.40	ex Sam; broken up
I-CIMA	15023	20.10.37-00.02.40	broken up
I-EGEO	15011	28.10.34-00.08.39	ex SAM; wfu

I-FBAA	*Citta di Tunisi*	15008	28.10.34-00.08.39	ex SAM; crashed
I-LIDO		15019	19.02.37-14.06.40	to Regia Aeronautica as MM60450, coded 613-4
I-LAGO		15020	05.04.37-14.06.40	to Regia Aeronautica as MM60449, coded 613-3
I-MARE		15002	11.11.40-	to Regia Aeronautica, coded 608-12
I-MIRA		15021	24.04.37-14.06.40	to Regia Aeronautica as MM60448, coded 613-2
I-NAVE		15014	11.05.35-22.06.35	struck the sea at Marsaxlook Bay, Malta on landing at night
I-NEMI		15024	06.12.37-	
I-ONDA		15012	22.03.35-00.08.39	wfu
I-ONIO		15009	31.08.35-00.03.39	ex AEI; wfu time expired
I-PRUA		15018	29.01.37-14.06.40	to Regia Aeronautica as MM60451, coded 613-5
I-REDI		15004	28.10.34-07.08.35	ex SAM; crashed on landing and sank off Mahón, Menorca, Spain
I-RIVA		15017	24.12.36-00.04.37	crashed
I-SOLA		15015	11.06.35-00.08.39	wfu
I-TUTO		15003	30.05.36-00.08.39	ex AEI; wfu
I-VALE		15007	28.10.34-00.04.39	ex SAM; cancelled as destroyed
I-VELA		15022	22.05.37-14.06.40	to Regia Aeronautica as MM60447, coded 613-1
I-VOLO		15013	18.04.35-14.07.38	Lost off Terranova, Sardinia

Savoia-Marchetti S.71 1934-1939 (5)

Eight-passenger high wing cantilever monoplane, powered by three 179 kW (240 hp) Walter Castor radial engines, generating a cruising speed of 180 km/h (112 mph)

I-AAYP	7101	28.10.34-00.02.38	ex SAM; destroyed
I-AEDO	7105	09.08.35-	ex I-ROMA;
I-ALPI	7106	28.10.34-00.01.35	ex SAM; cancelled as destroyed
I-EOLO	7103	20.07.35-00.10.39	crashed
I-PALO	7104	00.00.00-28.02.38	ex I-TALO; crashed
I-ROMA	7105	28.10.34-09.08.35	ex SAM; reregistered I-AEDO
I-TALO	7104	28.10.34-	ex SAM; reregistered I-PALO

Savoia-Marchetti S.73 1935-1941 (22)

18-passenger low-wing cantilever monoplane, powered by three 596 kW (800 hp) Alfa Romeo 126 RC.10 engines, generating a cruising speed of 280 km/h (174 mph)

I-ARCO	30016	30.09.36-00.00.40	to Regia Aeronautica as MM60348
I-ASTI	30011	26.05.36-	
I-ATRI	30018	04.12.36-00.02.39	damaged beyond repair in forced-landing in desert near Cairo
I-CORI	30012	15.06.36-00.00.40	to Regia Aeronautica as MM….., coded 605-1
I-ELVO	30034	30.10.37-00.12.38	destroyed
I-ENNA	30007	18.03.36-00.00.40	reg'd to Reale Unione Nazionale Aeronautica (RUNA) by op by Ala Littoria; to Regia Aeronautica as MM….., coded 606-4
I-ESTE	30015	25.07.36-09.06.38	reregistered I-OSTE

I-GELA	30008	06.03.36-03.02.41	destroyed by British bombing at Gondar, Ethiopia
I-IESI	30036	06.12.37-16.03.40	crashed en route to Mellila, a Spanish exclave on the northern coast of Morocco
I-LODI	30039	26.03.36-00.00.40	registered to RUNA, but operated by Ala Littoria; to Regia Aeronautica as MM....., coded 606-7
I-MEDA	30020	05.02.37-30.04.38	struck a mountainside near Maranola, Formia, on flight from Tirana to Rome
I-NISA	30017	10.11.36-	
I-NOLA	30021	22.02.37-13.02.41	lost en route to Asmara, Eritrea
I-NOTO	30013	26.06.36-	
I-NOVI	30031	30.07.37-00.00.40	to Regia Aeronautica as MM60352, later coded 225-18
I-OLDA	30019	14.01.37-	
I-ORTE	30010	08.04.36-00.06.40	to Regia Aeronautica as MM603.., coded 606-3
I-OSTE	30015	09.06.38-00.06.39	ex I-ESTE; canx
I-PISA	30006	19.09.35-	
I-SUSA	30014	08.07.36-02.08.37	crashed on night landing Wadi Halfa, Egypt
I-TODI	30032	10.08.37-	
I-VADO	30033	30.09.37-	
I-VEIO	30037	11.01.38-	to Regia Aeronautica as MM....., coded 605-3

Savoia-Marchetti S.74 1935-1940 (3)

24-passenger high-wing monoplane, powered by four 522 kW (700 hp) Piaggio Stella X.RC radial engines, generating a maximum spped of 330 km/h (210 mph)

I-ALPE	21002	31.05.35-00.00.40	to Regia Aeronautica as MM60367, coded 604-11
I-ROMA*	21003	13.12.35-00.00.40	to Regia Aeronautica as MM60365, coded 604-9
I-URBE	21001	26.03.35-00.00.40	to Regia Aeronautica as MM60364, coded 604-8

* Four 630 kW (845 hp) Alfa Romeo Pegasus III engines

Savoia-Marchetti SM.75C 1938-1940 (38)

24-passenger low-wing monoplane, powered by three 560 kW (750 hp) Alfa Romeo 126 RC34 radial engines, generating a maximum speed of 370 km/h (230 mph)

I-ASSE	32033	00.00.40-16.10.41	ex I-LUEN; to LATI as I-CILE
I-LAME	32023	31.12.38-00.06.40	To Regia Aeronautica as MM60384
I-LAOS	32026	27.01.39-00.06.40	to Regia Aeronautica as MM60385, coded 601-5
I-LAST	32043	17.10.39-00.06.40	to Regia Aeronautica as MM60398
I-LAVO	32039	00.00.39-00.06.40	to Regia Aeronautica as MM60389
I-LEAL	32031	08.03.39-10.02.40	crashed in bad weather near Aiello Calabro, Cosenza, Calabria
I-LEGA	34042	28.09.39-00.06.40	to Regia Aeronautica as MM60386, coded 602-1
I-LENI	32034	30.03.39-00.06.40	to Regia Aeronautica as MM60391, coded 601-1
I-LIAN	32019	16.02.39-00.06.40	to Regia Aeronautica as MM60382, coded 223-7
I-LIGO	32035	11.04.39-00.06.40	to Regia Aeronautica as MM60392, coded 604-5

I-LINI	32028	06.02.39-00.06.40	to Regia Aeronautica as MM60387, coded 601-3
I-LISA	32036	26.04.39-00.06.40	to Regia Aeronautica as MM60393, coded 601-4
I-LIUT	32037	09.09.39-00.06.40	to Regia Aeronautica as MM60394, coded 601-6
I-LOBI	32050	00.00.39-00.12.40	registered to RUNA, but operated by Ala Littoria; to Regia Aeronautica as MM….., coded 603-1
I-LOLA	32027	03.02.39-00.06.40	to Regia Aeronautica as MM60386, coded 604-7
I-LOVE	32024	12.01.39-24.09.39	damaged beyond repair at unknown location
I-LUEN	32033		reregistered I-ASSE
I-LUME	32032	22.03.39-00.06.40	to Regia Aeronautica as MM60390, coded 602-3
I-LUNO	32048		to Regia Aeronautica as MM…….
I-LUPI	32038	12.05.39-15.05.40	crashed when controls jammed on take-off from Barcelona, Spain
I-LUSS	32041	28.09.39-00.06.40	to Regia Aeronautica as MM60395, coded 604-4
I-MAGA	32058	00.08.42-23.11.42	to Regia Aeronautica as MM60541; lost between Tripoli and Sciacca
I-TACO	32001	16.02.38-00.06.40	to Regia Aeronautica as MM60367, coded 610-1
I-TAIO	32010	05.08.38-00.06.40	to Regia Aeronautica as MM60376, coded 601-6
I-TAMO	32005	02.05.38-00.06.40	To Regia Aeronautica as MM60371, coded 602-5
I-TEBE	32014	04.10.38-00.06.40	to Regia Aeronautica as MM60378, coded 602-2
I-TEMI	32019	03.12.38-00.00.40	to Regia Aeronautica as MM60382, coded 601-8
I-TESO	32006	02.06.38-00.06.40	to Regia Aeronautica as MM60372, coded 601-3
I-TETI	32021	15.12.38-00.06.40	to Regia Aeronautica as MM60380, coded 604-6
I-TILO	32008	05.07.38-00.06.40	to Regia Aeronautica as MM60373, coded 601-5
I-TIMO	32002	07.03.38-00.06.40	to Regia Aeronautica as MM60391, coded 610-2
I-TINA	32018	14.11.38-00.06.40	to Regia Aeronautica as MM60398, coded 601-1
I-TIPO	32022	15.12.38-00.06.40	to Regia Aeronautica as MM60370, coded 604-2
I-TITO	32003	20.04.38-00.06.40	to Regia Aeronautica as MM60369
I-TOGO	32011	19.08.39-00.06.40	to Regia Aeronautica as MM60377, coded 601-7
I-TOSA	32007	21.06.38-00.06.40	to Regia Aeronautica as MM60373, coded 601-4
I-TUFO	32009	25.07.38-00.06.40	to Regia Aeronautica as MM60375, coded 604-3
I-TULE	32016	20.10.38-00.06.40	to Regia Aeronautica as MM60381, coded 604-1
I-TUON	32017	25.10.38-22.11.38	crashed in bad weather near Winklern, Austria, en route Munich-Rome

Savoia-Marchetti SM.79T 1939 (2)

Six-seat low-wing cantilever monoplane transport version of medium bomber, powered by three Alfa Romeo 128 RC.18 engines, generating a maximum speed of 460 km/h (285 mph)

I-ALAN	19052	05.01.39-	to LATI
I-ALPI			

Savoia-Marchetti SM.83 1938-1940 (13)

10-passenger low-wing monoplane, powered by three 560 kW (750 hp) Alfa Romeo 126 RC.34 radial engines, generating a maximum speed of 370 kmh (230 mph)

I-ALCE	34009	30.12.38-00.01.39	reregistered I-ATTE

I-AMER	34010	03.02.39-	transferred to LATI
I-ANDE	34011	22.03.39-	transferred to LATI
I-ARCA	34013	03.10.39-00.00.40	transferred to LATI
I-AREM	34019	04.08.39-00.00.40	transferred to LATI
I-ARIS	34021	01.04.40-00.00.40	transferred to LATI
I-ARMA	34020	28.11.39-00.00.40	transferred to LATI
I-ARPA	34017	25.07.39-24.12.39	transferred to LATI
I-ASSO	34012	08.03.39-	transferred to LATI
I-ASTA	34018	04.09.39-20.12.40	transferred to LATI
I-ATOS	34014	02.11.39-	transferred to LATI
I-ATTE	34009	00.01.39-00.08.39	destroyed in accident
I-AZUR	34015	17.10.39-00.00.40	transferred to LATI
I-LUCE	34001	13.06.39-29.08.39	reregistered I-ESTE/MM458 to Ministero dell'Aeronautica

Savoia-Marchetti SM.87

24-passenger twin-float version of the SM.75, powered by three 1,006 kW (1,350 hp) Alfa Romeo 135 RC.32 engines, generating a cruising speed of 325 km/h (202 mph)

I-IGEA/ MM450	36004	00.10.41-00.09.43	seized by Germany and registered to Deutsche Lufthansa as D-AKBE
I-IGOR/ MM447	36001	29.08.40-00.09.43	seized by Germany and registered to Deutsche Lufthansa as D-AJAB
I-ILLA/MM449	36003	11.10.41-00.09.43	seized by Germany and registered to Deutsche Lufthansa as D-AJAJ
I-INNO/ MM448	36002	05.02.41-	

LATI (Linee Aeree Transcontinentali Italiane Società Anonima) Fleet 1939-1943

Fiat G.12LGA 1942-1943 (3)

14-passenger low-wing monoplane, powered by three 560 kW (750 hp) Alfa Romeo 126 RC.34 engines, generating a maximum speed of 396 km/h (246 mph)

I-FOLG/MM60662	14	01.08.42-02.02.43	ex I-ALIH; to 48o Stormo Trasporti
I-FAUN/MM60665	17	01.08.42-02.02.43	ex I-ALIM; to 48o Stormo Trasporti
I-FELI/MM60666	18	01.09.42-09.11.42	ditched in Mediterranean Sea en route from Tobruk to Athens

Savoia-Marchetti S.73 1942 (1)

18-passenger low-wing cantilever monoplane, powered by three (700 hp) Piaggio Stella X RC engines, generating a cruising speed of 280 km/h (174 mph)

| I-DOUL/MM60448 | 30016 | 00.08.42-08.11.42 | ex I-ARCO; captured by the Allies at Maison Blanche, Algiers, Algeria |

Savoia-Marchetti SM.75C 1940-1943 (23)

24-passenger low-wing monoplane, powered by three 560 kW (750 hp) Alfa Romeo 126 RC.34 radial engines, generating a maximum speed of 370 km/h (230 mph)

I-BALI/ MM60542	32059	21.07.42-00.10.43	seized by Germany
I-BAYR	32013	12.10.40-15.01.41	ex I-TELA/MM60378; crashed into South Atlantic on flight from Natal, Brazil to Sal Island, Cape Verde
I-BELO/MM61325	32072	01.04.43-07.05.43	destroyed on ground at Carthage, Tunisia
I-BESO/MM60540	32057	13.06.42-	
I-BETA/MM60554*	001	01.02.43-14.08.43	crashed into the sea shortly after night take-off from Rhodes/Maritsa
I-BLAN/MM60933	32046	22.05.41-19.12.41	seized in Brazil
I-BONI/MM61324*	32071	01.02.43-10.04.43	crashed into the Mediterranean Sea after being shot down on flight from Italy to Libya
I-BUBA/MM60539**	32056	01.06.42-00.10.43	seized by Germany and registered to Deutsche Lufthansa as D-AJAZ
I-BUEN	32049	01.01.41-00.00.00	fate unknown, last recorded svc ROM-RIO 14.02.41 Capt Carelli
I-BUMA/MM60561*	008	01.05.43-00.11.43	seized by Germany and registered to Deutsche Lufthansa as D-AIAW
I-BUNA/MM60547	32064	01.11.42-	
I-BURA/MM421	32040	30.12.41-28.03.42	ex I-NEGH; shot down and crashed into sea off Sicily
I-BUTI/MM60550	32067	01.02.43-18.08.43	
I-MEDE/MM60534	32051	28.01.42-04.04.44	destroyed at Cagliari/Elmas
I-MELE/MM60535	32052	00.00.38-19.05.42	to Regia Aeronautica as MM60535; struck trees and crashed on take-off at Rome/Urbe
I-META/MM60536	32053	26.03.42-	
I-MONC/MM60552	32069	00.00.42-19.04.43	shot down by RAF fighter over the Mediterranean Sea
I-MONC(2)/MM60567*	014	00.00.43-	
I-MOND/MM60548	32065	00.00.42-00.00.43	seized by the Luftwaffe
I-MOND(2)/MM60569*	016	00.00.43-	
I-TALO/MM384	32004	24.07.40-	
I-TAMO/MM60543**	32060	08.06.42-	seized by Germany and registered to Deutsche Lufthansa as D-APOC
I-TELO/MM416	32047	18.12.42-15.11.42	ex I-BADO; shot down over Mediterranean Sea on route from Tunis to Castelvetrani

* Savoia-Marchetti SM.75bis with three 641 kw (860 hp) Alfa Romeo 126 RC.14 engines

** reconfigured as SM.75GA/RT (Grande Atonomia/Roma-Tokyo) with Alfa Romeo 128 engines and extra fuel tanks for Rome-Tokyo flights

Savoia-Marchetti SM.76 (1939-1940) (1)

24-passenger low-wing monoplane, powered by three 560 kW (750 hp) Alfa Romeo 126 RC.34 radial engines, generating a maximum speed of 370 km/h (230 mph)

I-CILE*	37001	16.10.41-19.12.41	ex I-ASSE; seized by Brazil

* redesignated from SM.75

Savoia-Marchetti SM.79T 1939-1940 (2)

Six-seat low-wing cantilever monoplane transport version of medium bomber, powered by three Alfa Romeo 128 RC.18 engines, generating a maximum speed of 460 km/h (285 mph)

I-ALAN	19052	00.00.39-16.07.40	ex Ala Littoria; to Regia Aeronautica as MM60399, coded 615-8; damaged beyond repair during aborted take-off at Benghazi, Libya
I-ALPI			ex Ala Littoria; to Regia Aeronautica as MM60399, coded 615-8; damaged beyond repair during aborted take-off at Benghazi, Libya

Savoia-Marchetti SM.82 Atlantico 1940-1943 (8)

10-passenger mid-wing cantilaver monoplane, powered by three 708 kW (950 hp) Alfa Romeo 128 RC.21 radial engines, generating a maximum speed of 347 km/h (216 mph)

I-BACH/MM60591*	107	00.00.41-	
I-BAIA/MM60291	23	23.05.40-21.12.40	collided with Camels on landing at Villa Cisneros, Spanish Sahara, and damaged beyond repair
I-BATO/MM60333	65	19.03.41-	
I-BELM			
I-BENI/MM60326	58	19.02.41-25.03.42	crashed after engine fire on take-off from Benghazi, Libya
I-BOLI/MM60317	49	27.12.40-19.12.41	seized by Brazil
I-BRAZ/MM60309	41	17.10.40-09.06.42	crashed due to engine malfunction after take-off from Benghazi, Libya
I-LETE/MM61247	384	00.08.43-00.12.43	seized by Germany and registered to Deutsche Lufthansa as D-ARML

NCL-37/38/39/40 and MM60780, MM60783 and MM60788 of Nucleo Communicazione LATI also reported in 1942

* later equipped with the more powerful Piaggio R.XI engine

Savoia-Marchetti SM.83 1939-1943 (15)

10-passenger low-wing monoplane, powered by three 560 kW (750 hp) Alfa Romeo 126 RC.34 radial engines, generating a maximum speed of
370 kmh (230 mph)

I-AMER	34010	15.03.39-21.09.42	ex Ala Littoria; damaged on landing at Benghazi, Libya and captured by the British
I-ANDE/MM60406	34011	22.03.39-16.08.42	ex Ala Littoria; crashed on take-off from Athens on flight to Rome
I-ANTA	34002	17.06.42-	ex YR-FAR of Prince Bibescu;
I-ARCA	34013	03.10.39-00.00.00	ex Ala Littoria, to Regia Aeronautica details unknown
I-AREM/MM60408	34019	04.08.39-10.01.41	ex Ala Littoria; disappeared without trace in the Mediterranean Sea on flight from Rome to Rio de Janeiro
I-ARGE/MM399	34016	27.01.41-18.06.42	ex I-MANU of Italo Balbo; destroyed by fire after accident at Lecce
I-ARIS	34021	14.03.40-00.11.43	ex Ala Littoria; seized by Germany and registered to Deutsche Lufthansa as D-AEAW
I-ARMA	34020	28.11.39-07.05.43	ex Ala Littoria; destroyed in air raid on ground at Tunis, Tunisia

I-ARPA	34017	25.07.39-24.12.39	ex Ala Littoria; crashed Dar el Caid Allal Bou Fenzi, near Mogador, Morocco during storm on way from Rio to Rome
I-ASSO	34012	09.03.39-	
I-ASTA	34018	10.04.39-20.12.40	ex Ala Littoria; destroyed in Allied raid on Brindisi
I-ATOS	34014	02.11.39-00.01.42	ex Ala Littoria; seized by Brazil
I-ATTO	34006	15.04.42-	ex LARES YR-SAC;
I-AZUR	34015	17.10.39-	
I-MITU	34008	17.04.42-00.11.43	ex LARES YR-SAE; seized by Germany and registered to Deutsche Lufthansa as D-ASPV

ALI (Avio Linee Italiane Società Anonima) Fleet 1928-1943

Caproni Ca 97 1929-1932 (1)

Six-passenger strut-braced high wing monoplane, powered by one 370 kW (500 hp) Alfa Romeo Jupiter VIII radial engine, generating a maximum speed of 230 km/h (140 mph)

I-AANM	2523	16.08.29-00.06.32	broken up

Douglas DC-2-115 1935-1940 (1)

14-passenger cantilever wing monoplane, powered by two 746 kW (1,000 hp) Wright GR-1820 radial engines, generating a cruising speed of 310 km/h (190 mph)

I-EROS	1319.5	25.04.35-04.06.40	later also carried military serial MM60436

Fiat G.2 1932-1936 (1)

Eight-passenger low wing cantilever monoplane, powered by three 101 kW (135 hp) Fiat A.60 in-line engines, generating a cruising speed of 209 km/h (130 mph)

I-FIAT	1	12.08.33-17.3.36	to Ministero dell'Aeronautica

Fiat APR.2 1936 (1)

12-passenger, low wing cantilever monoplane, powered by two 522 kW (700 hp) Fiat A.59 radial engines, generating a cruising speed of 349 km/h (217 mph)

I-VEGA	1	16.7.36-	to Regia Aeronautica as MM60437

Fiat G.12C 1941-1944 (17)

14-passenger low-wing cantilever monoplane, powered by three 575 kW (770 hp) Fiat A.74 RC.42 radial engines, generating a maximum speed of 390 km/h (242 mph)

These aircraft were immediately commanded by the Regia Aeronautica, with several used in the North Africa Campaign. Five were destroyed by bombing at Tunis

I-ALIA/MM60649	1	00.00.42-	

I-ALIB/MM60653	5	00.00.42-	
I-ALIC/MM60655	7	00.11.41-00.09.43	confiscated by Deutsche Lufthansa as D-ASVK and handed to the Luftwaffe 04.44 with serial AS+VK
I-ALID/MM60657	9	22.03.42-00.01.44	confiscated by Deutsche Lufthansa as D-ASVI and handed to the Luftwaffe 02.44 with serial AS+VI
I-ALIE/MM60659	11	00.00.42-	
I-ALIF/MM60660	12	00.00.42-	
I-ALIG/MM60661	13	00.04.42-00.09.43	confiscated by Deutsche Lufthansa as D-ASVJ and handed to the Luftwaffe 04.44 with serial AS+VJ
I-ALIHMM60662	14	16.04.42-00.05.42	to LATI as I-FOLG
I-ALII/MM60663*	15	00.00.42-	
I-ALIL/MM60664	16	00.00.42-	
I-ALIM/MM60665	17	00.00.42-00.07.42	to LATI as I-FAUN
I-ALIN/MM60666	18	00.00.42-00.07.42	to LATI as I-FELI
I-ALIO/MM60667*	19	00.00.42-	
I-ALIP/MM60668*	20	00.00.42-	
I-ALIQ/MM60669	21	00.00.42-	
I-ALIR/MM60694	44	10.06.43-	
I-ALIS/MM60695	47	04.07.43-	

* Fiat G.12GA with additional fuel tanks for greater range

Fiat G.18 1936-1940 (3)

18-passenger low-wing cantilever monoplane, powered by two 522 kW (700 hp) Fiat A.59R radial engines, generating a maximum speed of 340 km/h (211mph)

I-ELIO	1	05.02.36-26.11.40	later also carried military serial MM60427; destroyed by fire on landing at Milan/Linate
I-ETNA	3	06.04.36-16.11.42	later also carried military serial MM60428; destroyed beyond repair near Milan
I-ETRA	2	05.02.36-00.12.40	later also carried military serial MM60429; destroyed in ground collison with Fiat CR.42

Fiat G.18 V 1936-1944 (6)

18 passenger, low-wing cantilever monoplane, powered by two 746 kW (1,000 hp) Fiat A.80 RC.41 engines, generating a cruising speed of 340 km/h (211 mph)

I-EION	5	13.08.37-	later also carried military serial MM60431
I-ELFO	1	08.06.37-00.09.43	later also carried military serial MM60430; to D-ANYW
I-ELCE	2	08.06.37-30.04.44	later also carried military serial MM60432; damaged when being loaded with munitions at Bresso; to D-AOKW
I-ENEA	4	28.07.37-	later also carried military serial MM60434
I-ERME	3	09.07.37-	later also carried military serial MM60433; to D-AOKX
I-EURE	6	09.11.37-28.01.43	later also carried military serial MM60435; hit water and crashed on approach to Venice

Fokker F.III 1929-1932 (1)

Six-passenger cantilever wing monoplane, powered by 170 kW (230 hp) Siddeley in-line engine, generating a cruising speed of 130 km/h (84 mph)

I-AANB		10.04.31-	to Scuola Aero Turismo, Milan

Fokker F.VIIa-3m 1928-1938 (5)

Eight-passenger high-wing monoplane, powered by three 158 kW (215 hp) Alfa Romeo Lynx engines, generating a cruising speed of 178 km/h (111 mph)

I-ABBA*	5212	00.04.30-02.10.35	to Ala Littoria
I-BBEC	4982	23.05.28-12.09.33	to Società Aerea Mediterranea (SAM)
I-BBED	5059	23.05.28-03.11.33	to Società Aerea Mediterranea (SAM)
I-BBEE	5060	11.08.28-23.11.34	to Ala Littoria
I-BBEF	5061	11.08.28-08.10.35	to Ala Littoria

* Fokker F.VIIa-3m		AANB

Officine Ferroviarie Meridionale-Aeroplani Romeo Ro 10 (Fokker F.VIIb-3m) 1930-1938 (3)

Eight-passenger high-wing monoplane powered by three 158 kW (215 hp) Alfa Romeo Lynx radial engines, generating a cruising speed of 178 km/h (111 mph)

I-AAXY	358	11.08.31-14.03.38	to Cia Nazionale Imprese Eletriche (CONIEL) 14.03.38
I-AAXZ	359	11.08.31-15.04.36	crashed in fog on Monte Basso near Turin
I-FERO	778	01.05.30-12.09.33	to Società Aerea Mediterranea (SAM)

Savoia-Marchetti S.73 1937 (6)

18-passenger low-wing cantilever monoplane, powered by three 596 kW (800 hp) Alfa Romeo 126 RC.10 engines, generating a cruising speed of 280 km/h (174 mph)

I-SAMO	30022	18.02.37-	to Regia Aeronautica (605 Squadriglia coded 605-3); destroyed 02.11.41
I-SAUL	30025	05.03.37-	to Regia Aeronautica (605 Squadriglia coded 605-2; re-registered I-ADMA 08.43
I-SETI	30023	18.02.37-	to Regia Aeronautica (605 Squadriglia coded 605-4); collided with Ca 133 MM60221 11.09.41
I-SITA	30026	09.03.37-	
I-STAR	30027	06.04.37-	D-APGW
I-SUTO	30024	18.02.37-16.03.40	crashed into Monte Stromboli, Mar Tirreno

ATSA (Avio Trasporti Società Anomina) Fleet 1938-1940

Caproni Ca 148 (6)

Strut-braced, high wing monoplane freighter, powered by three 338 kW (460 hp) Piaggio Stella VII engines, generating a cruising speed of 230 km/h (143 mph)

I-ETIO	4148	11.10.38-00.03.40	ex I-EDVI; to Ala Littoria
I-GOGG	4145	01.03.39-00.03.40	ex I-POGG; to Ala Littoria
I-LANG	4147	01.03.39-00.03.40	ex I-LUIG; to Ala Littoria
I-NEGH	4151	11.10.38-00.03.40	ex I-NERI; to Ala Littoria
I-SOMA	4149	11.10.38-00.03.40	ex I-ROSA; to Ala Littoria
I-TESS	4146	11.10.38-00.03.40	ex I-TERE; to Ala Littoria

Ala Littoria Savoia-Marchetti S.66 I-ALGA

EVOLUTION OF ITALIAN AIR TRANSPORT

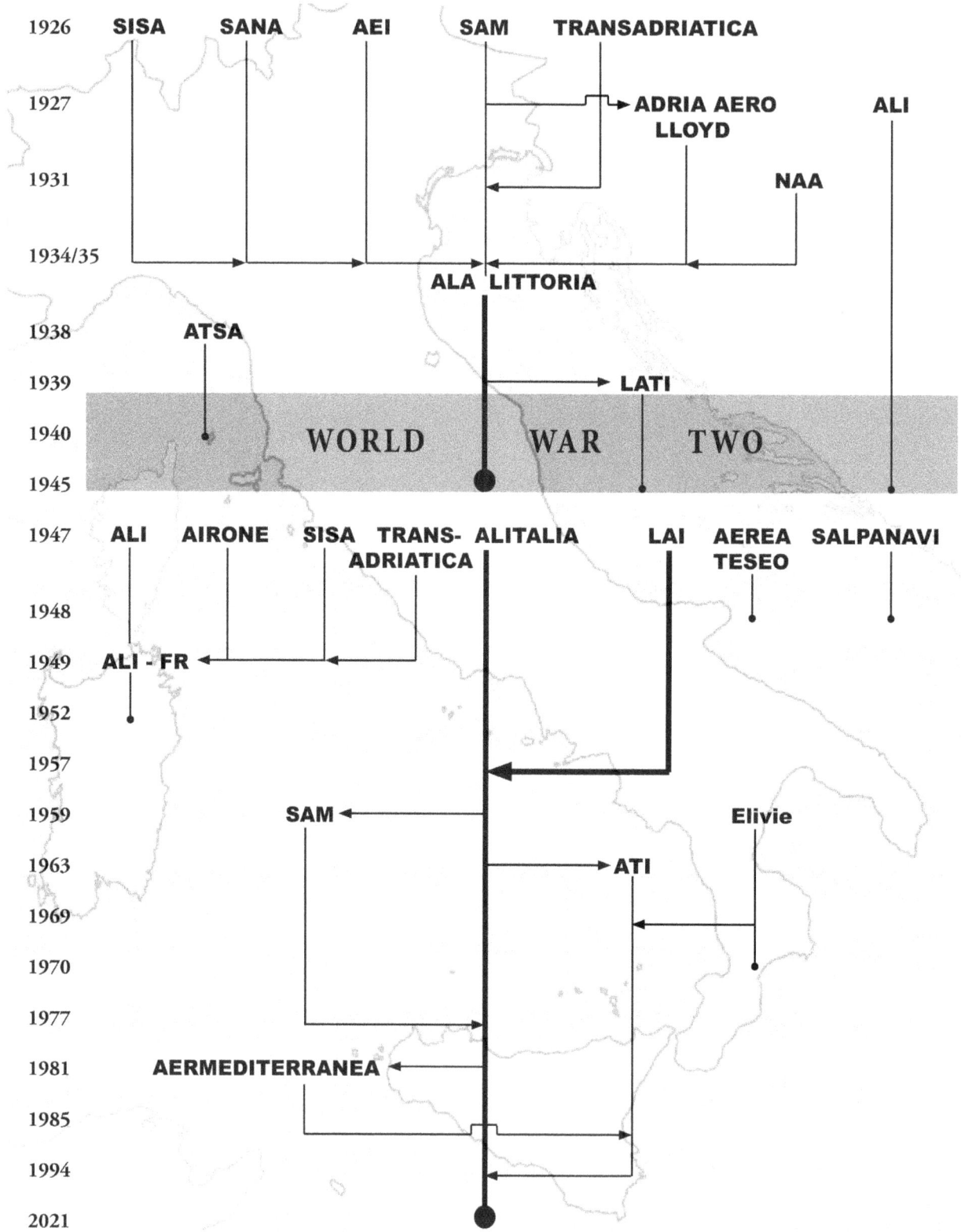

1926 SISA SANA AEI SAM TRANSADRIATICA

1927 →ADRIA AERO LLOYD ALI

1931 NAA

1934/35 ALA LITTORIA

1938 ATSA

1939 LATI

1940 WORLD WAR TWO

1945

1947 ALI AIRONE SISA TRANS-ADRIATICA ALITALIA LAI AEREA TESEO SALPANAVI

1948

1949 ALI - FR

1952

1957

1959 SAM

1963 ATI Elivie

1969

1970

1977

1981 AERMEDITERRANEA

1985

1994

2021

A new beginning

With Italy's transport infrastructure and surface communications badly devastated by the preceding years of conflict, it became a priority to regenerate the country's air services. One small concession by the Allied (Control) Commission permitted the re-establishment of limited internal services, based purely on military and administrative needs, which were begun by the *Stormo Trasporto* (Transport Wing), based at Rome's Centocelle airfield under the command of Colonel Virginio Reinero. Another, the *Stormo Notturno* (Night Wing), operated out of Guidonia airfield, commanded by Lt Colonel Ercole Savi. The Allied (Control) Commission was an integrated British-American body that had been set up in September 1943 under the Supreme Allied Commander to enforce the Italian Armistice and through which the allied powers conducted business with the Italian Government. The commission, which had arrived in Rome on 4 June 1944, took over responsibility for military government, but when a number of civil affairs were returned to the Italian Government, the word 'Control' was dropped from its title. It was abolished in March 1947, following the signing of the Peace Treaty the previous month.

With only a few war-weary Savoia Marchetti SM.75, SM.79 and SM.82 and Fiat G.12 transport machines, supplemented by a handful of hastily and crudely converted Martin Baltimore light bombers, flights were started on 1 August 1945 between Rome, now from Urbe Airport (formerly Littorio) and Italy's major cities on the mainland, including Cagliari on Sardinia and Palermo on the island of Sicily. Authorised routes were Rome-Naples-Bari-Lecce, Rome-Palermo, Rome-Cagliari, and Rome-Alghero, all

flown three times a week, with Rome-Genoa and Rome-Naples-Catania (Sicily) served twice-weekly. Only Rome-Milan-Turin and Rome-Bologna-Treviso were operated daily, except Sundays. The service was operated exclusively for the needs of the capital city, demonstrating once again that prestige and political designs were more important than economic viability.

Initially, transportation was free and allocated on a priority basis for essential government personnel, although in practice, private citizens were also carried. From 1 July 1946, fares and cargo tariffs were introduced amounting to ITL 6,990 (then USD 12.15) per seat and ITL 81 (USD 0.14) per kg of freight for longer sectors, such as Rome-Milan-Turin. Between 1 August 1945 and 30 September 1946, the *Corrieri Aerei Militari* (Military Air Couriers) as they became known, carried 49,293 passengers and 666,500 kg of mail and cargo over a total distance of 2,151,41 km during the course of 44,000 flights and 8,056 flying hours. What remained of the *Corrieri Aerei Militari* became the backbone of the 46th Stormo Trasporti of the newly-established *Aeronautica Militare*, the air force of the Italian Republic.

This operation provided a ready pool of skilled technical experts and experienced air crews with which to re-start Italy's civil airlines, a process that had begun on 16 December 1945 with the formation of the *Federazione Nazionale Imprese Trasporti Aerei Civili* (FEDAERA) (Federation of National Civil Air Transport Enterprises). FEDAERA represented the collective interests of its founder members, among whom were several emerging and revived companies, which would play a key role, albeit briefly, in the rebirth of Italy's civil air transport landscape. The founder members were the

Corrieri Aerei Militari Savoia-Marchetti SM.79 Sparviero

Douglas C-47 I-LALO was one of 16 war-surplus ex-USAAF machines allocated to LAI

Fiat-controlled concern Aviolinee Italiane (ALI), Cagliari-based Airone, and Aerea Teseo of Florence. The president was Dr Alessandro Buzio of ALI, and general secretary, Dr Attilio Morrocchi of Aerea Teseo. It should be pointed out that these companies as yet existed on paper only, with neither routes, aircraft, nor finance in place, but strong on ambition, with a long wish list drawn up of desired routes. These and their planned routes were:

- Aerea Teseo: from Florence-Bologna to Rome, Milan, Genoa, Venice, Ancona and Naples
- Airone: from Cagliari to Naples, Rome, Milan and Genoa
- Avio Linee Italiane (ALI): from Milan to Genoa, Bolzano, Venice, Trieste, Turin, Rimini, Naples and Palermo
- Transadriatica: from Treviso to Ancona, Rome, Bari, Brindisi, Milan and Genoa

By the time of the 15 November 1946 closing date for licence application to the newly constituted Directorate of Civil Aviation, some 34 submissions had been received and included several pre-war names. The elimination process on 2 December whittled these down to just 17, most with no aviation experience, finally settling on the seven deemed most likely to be able to sustain operations, although not all were expected to survive in this new competitive environment. These were: Aerea Teseo; Airone; Avio Linee Italiane (ALI), the revived Fiat-controlled airline; LATI; Salpanavi; Transadriatica, and SISA. Aeronautica Sicula, an amalgamation that included Air Sicilia and SASI, entered the fray later, as did a new Italo-Egyptian airline, Services Aériens Internationaux d'Egypte (SAIDE), founded with a capital of 250,000 Egyptian Pounds, with a 40 per cent participation by Italian industry. Before even getting off the ground, however, they were severely handicapped. Subject to high fuel costs and airport taxes and lacking any state aid, they were left with slim pickings in terms of routes.

In the meantime, the Italian Government had acquired 32 war-surplus Douglas C-47/C-53 twin-engined airliners languishing at Naples/Capodichino airport and many spares, for an inclusive price of just USD 640,000. A number of these were to be allocated proportionally to the independent airlines. The task of overhauling and converting these machines for civil use went to Fiat and its subsidiary CMASA, Piaggio and Aeroplani Caproni. Most had remained in open storage for long periods and needed repairs to the airframe and wings, and a major overhaul of the engines. In spite of civil flights requiring a special permit, on 6 September 1946, Aerea Teseo had conducted an illegal test flight between Naples and Florence's Peretola airport in C-47 I-ZOLI (actually I-VENE, falsely and conveniently marked after the company's president, Adone Zoli, commanded by chief pilot, Pietro Gaggiano. By early 1947, most of the problems facing Italy's airlines had largely been resolved, including the renewal of pilot's licences and the establishment of a joint ALI/Fiat civil aviation training school.

Arrangements had also been put in place to reinstate regional military-controlled aerodromes for civil use, which was approved by the Allied Commission on 28 February 1947. The airports under Allied control were Rome/Ciampino, Naples/Capodichino and Catania, while Milan/Linate, Florence/Peretola, Bari, and Cagliari/Elmas were under Italian military authority. Under civil control was only Venice/St Nicolò-Lido. All was now ready for the resumption of Italy's civil air routes by April.

Twin approach

Early in 1946, with the assent of the Allied Commission, the *Ministero dell'Aeronautica* (Ministry of Aviation) had begun serious preparations for the revitalisation of the

LAI's large fleet of Douglas C-47s together with DC-6B I-LYNX

country's civil aviation prospects and to seek international finance to facilitate its plans. The Ministry settled on the establishment of two national companies, one to provide international services, the other to create and maintain a comprehensive domestic network. With its commanding position in the Mediterranean, major international airlines were already staging through Italy and were quick to recognise the country's investment potential, especially for feeder traffic. The Americans were quickest off the mark and, already on 11 February 1946, the Italian Government signed an agreement with Transcontinental & Western Air Inc, which became Trans World Airlines (TWA) on 17 May 1950, for the creation of LAI (Linee Aeree Italiane Società per Azioni), giving it an equal 40 per cent stake with the *Istituto per la Ricostruzione Industriale* (IRI), the State body to oversee large industries of national interest. The remaining 20 per cent were held by private Italian interests including Fiat (7 per cent), Piaggio (6 per cent), and the Italian Southern Railway (7 per cent). Starting capital was only ITL 10 million (USD 160,000).

The British, angered by TWA's refusal to allow their participation, saw this as an open violation of the principles of the Bermuda Agreement between US and UK carriers, which discouraged monopolistic trade by its signatories. The British request for participation was bluntly rejected by the company's president, Jack Frye, citing his company's poor experience with British West Indian Airways (BWIA), an affiliate of British Overseas Airways Corporation (BOAC). Undeterred, the British put together a rival through the British European Airways (BEA) division, which took a 40 per cent stake in Aerolinee Internazionali Italiane (AII), quickly branded Alitalia. IRI also participated with 40 per cent, with the balance held by private Italian interests. The agreement was signed on 8 June and Alitalia was incorporated on 16 September 1946, on the same day as LAI. Starting capital, at ITL 900 million, was considerably higher. Italy now had two state-sponsored carriers. The creation of the

Crews and passengers on the first Alitalia flight on 5 May 1947 in Fiat G.12CA I-DALH *Alcione*

Savoia-Marchetti SM.95C I-LITA *San Cristoforo* was one of three operated by LATI across the Mid-Atlantic

two companies was decreed by Statute Law of 4 December 1946, which provided for the appropriation of ITL 1.5 billion from the IRI. The accord with LAI was for 15 years, and that for Alitalia 10 years. It also authorised the foreign shareholders to have effective control of management and administration of the airlines.

First off the ground was LAI, headed by the former Director General of Civil Aviation, Luigi Gallo, which made its debut with inaugural flights for government and military dignitaries on 12 April 1947, from Rome's Urbe airport, in the presence of Undersecretary of State for Aviation, Brusasca. Two days later, with seven of its 16 allocated Douglas C-47 - I-LAIL, I-LEDA, I-LEON, I-LIDA, I-LONA, I-LORO and I-LUCE - services were opened to the public from Milan to Turin, and on the Milan-Rome-Palermo-Catania line, flown daily. Alitalia had to wait until 5 May to get started with a fleet of four 18-passenger Fiat G.12CA on loan from the military. These were I-DALF (MM60903) *Antares*, I-DALG (MM60904)

Altair, I-DALH (MM60906) *Alcione* and I-DALI (MM60901) *Aldebaran*, all powered by the 694 kW (930 hp) Alfa Romeo 128 engines. The first service from Rome to Turin and Catania, was flown in I-DALH by Colonel Virginio Reinero, while he was still presiding over the *Corrieri Aerei Militari*, which ceased later that same month. In spring 1948, Alitalia replaced the leased aircraft with five new Bristol Pegasus-powered G.12LB - I-DALA *Castore*, I-DALB *Vega*, I-DALC *Polluce*, I-DALD *Sirio* and I-DALE *Regolo* - incorporating an underslung (Speedpak) luggage container and a 16-passenger cabin.

In a decree of 4 February 1947, the Italian Government had fused the Ministries of War, Navy and Air under the new Ministry of Defence. The Defence Minister, Cipriano Facchinetti, delegated all civil aviation affairs to Ugo di Rodino, the Undersecretary of State for his Ministry. A Civil Aviation Committee was formed to elaborate the allocation of routes, while limiting the number of airlines to be licensed. Discussions were held between the three leading

The Bristol Pegasus-powered Fiat G.12LB I-DALA *Castore*

airlines - Alitalia, LAI and ALI – with a view of creating a consortium for international services along the lines of Scandinavian Airlines System (SAS). The three reached agreement among themselves on 11 November 1947, with respect to the international routes each desired to operate, but the consortium idea was stillborn.

Alitalia:
Rome-Milan-Vienna-Prague
Rome-Madrid-Lisbon
Rome-Milan-Copenhagen-Gothenburg (with a technical stop at either Stuttgart or Hamburg
Rome-London
Rome-Milan-Brussels-Amsterdam (exclusive of traffic between Milan and Brussels
Rome-Paris
Rome-Geneva
Rome-Milan-Manchester
Rome-Tunis-Tripoli
Rome-Catania-Tripoli
Rome-Cairo and beyond to the Middle and Far East
Rome-Athens (together with LAI)-Cairo and beyond
Rome-Cairo-Khartoum-Asmara and beyond to the South
Rome-South America via Lisbon

LAI:
Rome-Marseille-Barcelona
Rome-Palermo-Tunis and beyond to Algiers and Morocco
Rome-Brindisi-Athens-Istanbul
Rome-Brindisi-Athens-(Alexandria)-Cairo-Lydda
Rome-Venice-(or Milan)-Munich-Berlin-Stockholm
Rome-Zurich

ALI:
Milan-(Marseille or Nice)-Barcelona-Lisbon
Milan-Frankfurt-Copenhagen-Oslo
Milan-Munich or other stop in German territory, which would not interfere with Alitalia
Milan-Basle-Brussels-Amsterdam
Rome-Milan-Zurich
Milan-Paris with optional extension to Ireland
Rome-Brindisi-(Thessaloniki)-Istanbul and beyond
Rome-Trieste-Budapest-Warsaw and beyond
Milan-Trieste-Belgrade-Bucharest and beyond
Rome-Moscow with intermediate stops except at Vienna and Prague
Rome-Asmara and beyond to the South (also requested by Alitalia)

Overturning the wartime decree that had merged LATI and Ala Littoria, the new government effectively reinstated LATI in September 1946, although it lacked any tangible funds or equipment. However, when overseas routes were officially determined in December 1947, LATI was not to return to its former destinations in South America. This situation came about because of LATI's controversial history in South America and an ongoing wrangle with the Brazilian Government over assets seized in 1941. The plum route to Rio de Janeiro and Buenos Aires went to Alitalia, first flown by an Avro Lancastrian on 2 June 1948. Instead, LATI was allocated a route to Santo Domingo in the Dominican Republic via Lisbon, Ilha do Sal in the Cape Verde Islands, Paramaribo in Suriname and Caracas, Venezuela. A service to Mexico City by way of Barcelona, Lisbon, the Azores, Bermuda, Miami and Havana, was also granted.

The rejuvenated carrier started flying once more on 16 May 1949, employing three 26-passenger SM.95C,

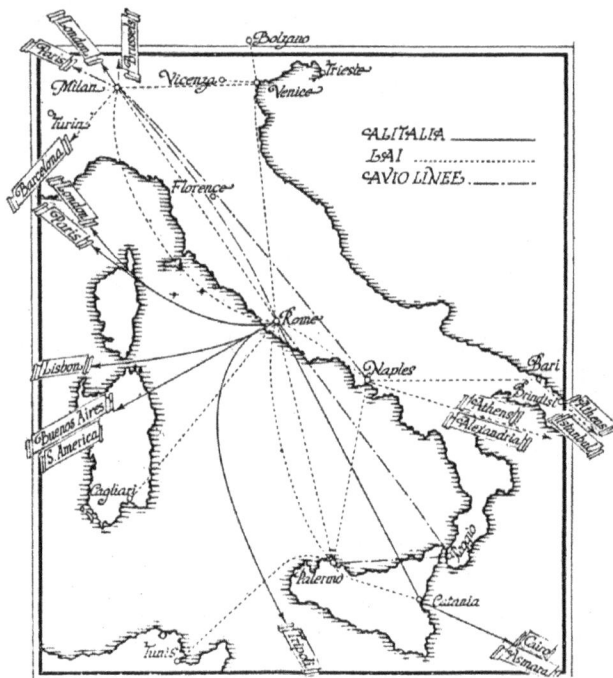

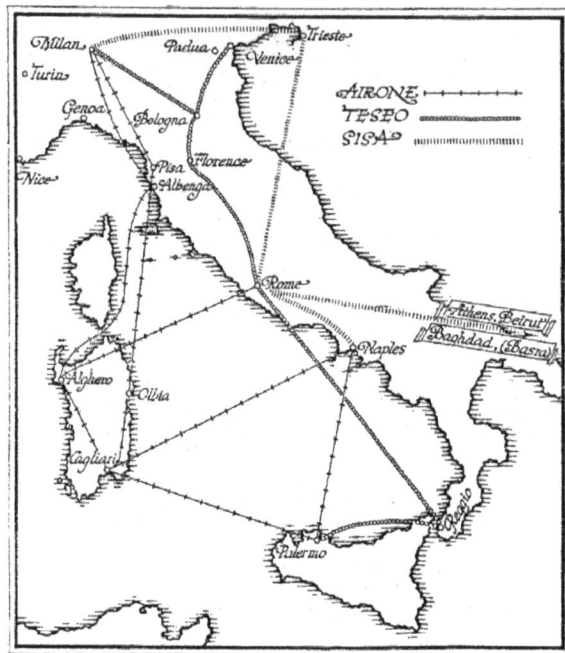

registered I-LAIT *Sant'Antonio*, I-LATI *San Francesco*, and I-LITA *San Cristoforo*. The first service was to Caracas via Seville, Ilha do Sal and Paramaribo. But instead of timetabled services, much of its activity was restricted to non-scheduled flights, especially carrying Italian workers to Caracas, where an oil boom was offering much improved prospects. By this time, however, it had to route via Dakar in Senegal rather than through Ilha do Sal, after the Portuguese Government had revoked the concession and had dismantled all facilities on the island. It was unfortunate that after only a few months, I-LATI crashed at Villa Cisneros (now Dakhla in Western Sahara) while attempting an emergency landing following engine failure on 15 November 1949. There were no casualties. LATI somehow kept going until its operations were incorporated into Alitalia in May 1950. It remained in

existence (on paper) until 1951 when reparation settlement terms were finally agreed with Brazil. Its two remaining SM.95 were not required by Alitalia and were eventually sold to Lebanese International Airlines (LIA). LATI was not legally dissolved until 1955.

Independents enter the fray

LAI had refused to concede any of its domestic route awards to the other start-ups and seeking to protect its investment, the government caved-in. This immediately put the selected candidates from the original thirty-four licence candidates at a distinct disadvantage. Avio Linee Italiane (ALI), with a capital of ITL 12 million, 94 per cent provided by the powerful Fiat concern and the remaining 6 per cent by Società Italo-Americana del Petrolo, proceeded to become

Fiat G.12T I-VIDA was leased from the military for ALI's first service between Milan and Rome

ALI's Douglas C-47 I-ELIO

a third force in the Italian aviation scene, even though its start was modest. It began operations on 16 April 1947 with an 18-seat Fiat G.12T, I-VIDA/MM60691, loaned from the *Aeronautica Militare*, initially between Milan and Rome on a daily basis. The introduction two months later of two C-47, I-ELFO and I-ETNA, and a C-53, I-ENOS, permitted the opening of services to Naples, Cagliari, Reggio Calabria and Palermo. The C-53 differed from the C-47 only in lacking the strengthened floor and large cargo door. In addition, summer flights were undertaken to the coastal resorts of Albenga and Rimini. The Fiat G.12 was a three-engined low-wing cantilever monoplane designed by Ing Giuseppe Gabrielli. It had first flown on 15 October 1940 but played a major role in the post-war revival of Italy's civil aviation, providing accommodation for 14-22 passengers. In 1947, Fiat produced three versions, differing primarily in the application of powerplants. The G.12L (*Largo*) had 575 kW (770 hp) Fiat A.74 RC.42 engines, the G.12LB (*Largo Bristol*) was powered by the 545 kW (730 hp) Bristol Pegasus 48, and the G12LP (*Pratt & Whitney*) had the much more powerful 795 kW (1,065 hp) Pratt & Whitney Twin Wasp R-1830-S13CG.

Aerea Teseo s.a.

Aerea Teseo, named after the wartime Teseo partisan group operating to the south of Florence, had been formed in the Tuscan capital in September 1945, headed by the

Douglas C-47 I-PALU was one of six operated by Aerea Teseo out of Florence

lawyer, Adone Zoli, who was determined that his city would not be deprived of air services as it had been before the war. It was formed with a capital of ITL 1 million, but became a Società Anonima (joint stock company) on 23 July 1946 with SIAI Marchetti (renamed in 1943 from Savoia-Marchetti) and Società Italiana Caproni among early major shareholders, with a capital of ITL 50 million. An inaugural ceremony took place at Florence/Peretola airport on 15 April 1947, with C-47 I-BOLO, one of six allocated to the airline, bringing dignitaries from Rome before departing for Milan via Bologna. Shortly afterwards, a second aircraft, I-TORI, left for Rome, Reggio Calabria and Palermo with the airline's first contingent of revenue passengers. Legally questionable was a Rome-Florence-Barcelona service that started in September, as no traffic rights had been granted. Aerea Teseo also made a trip to Stockholm on 27 November, carrying the Italian national tennis team. The C-47 fleet was completed with I-BARI, I-GENO, I-REGI, I-VENE, to which later came I-PALU. The eagle-eyed may realise that the registrations represented part of the name of the cities on its network.

A similar ceremony was held on the same day, 14 April, at Cagliari/Elmas airport in Sardinia, by Airone Compagnia Trasporti Aerei, which had been founded in October 1944 at Monserrato Airport to the north-east of Cagliari. With Italy devastated by war and the island of Sardinia isolated, with no regular connections to the mainland, local businessmen determined to start an airline to rectify this deficiency and 50 ITL 1,000 shares brought the initial capital ITL 50 million, increased to ITL 179 million in October 1948. The next decision to be made was the choice of aircraft. Airone (the name means Heron) sought to obtain some de Havilland DH.104 Dove twin-engine aircraft with accommodation for eight passengers, but the British company's demand for payment in cash was not acceptable, and an offer from the Italian authorities for the ex-USAAF Douglas C-47, also came to nothing, for two reasons. Although the purchase price

would have been a low ITL 500,000 each, it was estimated that the final costs after the aircraft were brought up to civil standard would be triple that figure. Furthermore, Alitalia and LAI, which were able to exert considerable political pressure, provided a serious competitive threat and persuaded Airone to spend ITL 30 million (60 per cent of its capital) on buying shares in Alitalia, leaving it financially strapped to buy the C-47s. With alternatives limited, the airline turned to Fiat.

Airone's Fiat G.12L I-AIRO *Logoduro*

Passengers ready to board Airone's Fiat G.12L I-AIRN *Barbagia* at Cagliari

ORARIO IN VIGORE DAL 1° MARZO 1949

CAGLIARI - ALGHERO - OLBIA - ROMA - NAPOLI Linea 601/604/606/608

Lunedi Mercoledi Venerdi	Martedi Giovedi	Sabato	GIORNALIERA (esclusa la domenica)			Lunedi Mercoledi Venerdi	Martedi Giovedi	Sabato
9,00 9,45 10,05	9,00	9,00	p.	CAGLIARI	a.	16,55 16,10 15,50	17,05	17,05
			a.	ALGHERO	p.			
			p.		a.			
	9,50 10,10	9,50 10,10	a.	OLBIA	p.		16,15 15,55	16,15 15,55
			p.		a.			
11,40	11,20 11,40	11,20	a.	ROMA	p.	14,15	14,45 14,20	14,45
			p.		a.			
	12,30		a.	NAPOLI	p.		13.30	

CAGLIARI - ALGHERO - TORINO - MILANO Linea 602/603

Lunedi Venerdi	Mercoledi	TRISETTIMANALE			Martedi Sabato	Giovedi
9,30 10,15 10,35	9,30 10,15 10,35	p.	CAGLIARI	a.	15.50 15,05 14,45	16,35 15,50 15,30
		a.	ALGHERO	p.		
		p.		a.		
	12,35 13,00	a.	TORINO	p.		13,30 13,05
		p.		a.		
12,50	13,35	a.	MILANO	p.	12,30	12,30

CAGLIARI - OLBIA - PISA - OLBIA - CAGLIARI - PALERMO Linea 605/607/609

Sabato				Lunedi
8,30	p.	CAGLIARI	a.	15,55
9,20 9,40	a. p.	OLBIA	p. a.	15,05 14,45
10,55 11,30	a. p.	PISA	p. a.	13,30 12,25
12,45 13,05	a. p.	OLBIA	p. a.	11,10 10,50
13,55 15,00	a. p.	CAGLIARI	p. a.	10,00 9,35
16,35	a.	PALERMO	p.	8,00

N. B. - Si avverte che l'Aeroporto di OLBIA è temporaneamente chiuso al traffico aereo e, pertanto, la linea CAGLIARI-ROMA-NAPOLI e viceversa tocca lo scalo di Alghero giornalmente (domenica esclusa).
— Il collegamento CAGLIARI-PISA e viceversa si effettua invece direttamente omettendo OLBIA.
Linea 605 CAGLIARI - PALERMO (il 1° ed il 3° sabato di ogni mese).
Linea 605 PALERMO - CAGLIARI (il lunedì successivo al 1° e 3° sabato di ogni mese.

Airone timetable of 1 March 1949

Regular services got under way on 15 April 1947 with two 20-passenger, three-engined Fiat G.12L, I-AIRN *Barbagia* and I-AIRO *Logudoro*, on the Cagliari-Alghero-Olbia-Rome, and Cagliari-Milan routes. These two aircraft were the first built by Fiat for commercial operators rather than for the Italian Air Force. A third aircraft, I-AIRE *Gallura*, was added soon after. One of these services was flown by former SISA/LATI pilot, Giuseppe Bertocco. However, it was not a good start. Even before the first service, the airline had received a communication from the Ministry of Civil Aviation stating that Airone's concession over the Cagliari-Rome service had to take in a stop at Alghero, to

The Migrant Caper – the flight of I-TROS

In the three years after the end of the war, thousands of European migrants were brought to Australia by air, principally from Rome, Athens and Singapore. One company that took advantage of this lucrative and growing business was Sydney-based New Holland Airways, which was founded in June 1947 and also offered what it grandly called luxury charter flights to all parts of the world. It operated a number of different aircraft, one of which was a Douglas DC-5. When this aircraft arrived at Rome on 10 May 1948, rather than returning with migrants to Sydney, the company decided to sell it at a profit in a deal that also included a replacement C-47, Transadriatica's I-TROS. New Holland Airways received approval from the Australian Department of Civil Aviation to transport migrants to Australia in an Italian-registered aircraft. I-TROS arrived in Sydney on 17 July 1948 with 22 migrants and six crew. I-TROS retained its Italian registration, Transadriatica name and Italian flag on the tailfin for the next four months, before receiving its Australian marks of VH-BNH on 24 November. In the intervening period, still as I-TROS, on its long-distance flights, it visited Koepang, Den Pasar, Batavia, Singapore, Mergui, Rangoon, Calcutta, Delhi, Akyab, Allahabad, Palam, Karachi, Sharjah, Basra, Baghdad, Athens, Nicosia, Penang, Medan, Palembang and Surabaya, also touching down on a Rome-Venice-Rome sector between 18 and 30 October. It was sold to Butler Air Transport on 19 May 1949.

avoid competition to the direct Cagliari-Rome service by LAI. This added considerably to its cost due to the longer flight time, fuel consumption, and additional staff needed at Alghero. This decision presaged the competitive difficulties faced by Airone and other independent airlines.

Nevertheless, on 20 April, the island was also linked with Turin. A Cagliari-Olbia-Pisa-Olbia-Cagliari-Palermo route was also soon added to the schedule. By the end of the year, Airone had carried more than 12,000 passengers. Unfortunately, Airone was hampered by the ageing and increasingly unreliable Alfa Romeo engines on its aircraft, which was not improved until delivery of a fourth machine, I-SASS, powered by Pratt & Whitney engines and thus designated G.12LP. Pratt & Whitney engines were also then retrofitted to the earlier aircraft.

Transadriatica took to the air on 23 April, with five C-47 – I-TRAS, I-TRES, I-TRIS, I-TROS and I-TRUS – operating a daily service from the airline's home base of

Venice/St Nicolò-Lido to Rome, via Padua, later extended to Pescara, with a Pescara-Ancona-Brindisi-Catania route flown three times a week. On 14 July, it opened a service between Venice and Cagliari via Padua and Novi Ligure, and in October made a special flight from Venice to Zurich/

Dübendorf, opening the first of five authorised flights to the Swiss city on 16 December 1947.

Like Airone, Transadriatica too felt the might of the political strength of LAI on its domestic routes, being forced to make intermediate stops on its Venice-Rome service at Ferrara or Ancona and Pescara, considerably lengthening the route with all the associated extra costs. Again, this was designed to avoid it competing with LAI on its direct Venice-Rome service. Transadriatica had been re-established in 1946 with a capital of ITL 4 million.

Based in the then disputed territory of Trieste in north-eastern Italy, SISA-Società Italiana Servizi Aerei was set up in 1946 and re-established services on 8 June 1947 with six C-47 aircraft – I-COSU, I-LUNA, I-NAVE, I-SOLE, I-VARO and I-VELE. Its aircraft were stationed at Gorizia/Amedep duca d'Aosta airport (an entire Italian territory, even if close to the new 'hot' borderline with Yugoslavia). Its initial network provided direct services from Trieste to Milan/Linate, Rome and Bari/Palese, with Rome also linked to Bari/Palese via Naples/Capodichino. The Trieste-Milan and Trieste-Rome services were operated daily, except Sundays, while the other connections provided two flights a week.

Transadriatica Douglas C-47 I-TRES at Venice/Nicelli Airport

Douglas C-47 I-TRIS pictured at Zurich/Dübendorf on one of several flights to Switzerland

SISA Doulgas C-47 I-LUNA, one of six operated

The smallest of the six independents was SNA-Società, generally known as Salpanavi, because it was backed by the Salpanavi shipping company of Milan with ITL 100 million, which almost immediately ran into difficulties. On the strength of its route allocation – Milan to Rome, Alghero and Bari – it had ordered three new 33-seat Savoia-Marchetti SM.95, the company's biggest transport aircraft. On 19 July 1947, with I-SALP poised to depart on the inaugural service, Salpanavi was faced with an official directive prohibiting the use of a four-engined aircraft on this run, forcing it to arrange the urgent loan of a C-47 from SISA. It was further specified that when Alitalia commenced its Milan-Bari-Catania service, Salpanavi would have to terminate its route at Ancona/Falconara airport, half-way towards the intended final destination and, furthermore, make a compulsory stop at Grosseto *en route* to Rome. Stymied before it really got going, Salpanavi saw two of its SM.95 re-allocated to rival

Alitalia, while the third went to the Italian-backed SAIDE in Egypt. Penalised by such limitations, the company halted operations in April 1948.

Another name revived from the pre-war period, Aero Espresso Italiana (AEI), was formed in February 1947 with a capital of ITL 100 million and was headed as chairman by Count Carlo Felice Trossi, and Dr Vittorio Bonetti as managing director. The registered corporate name was AIAX-Aero Espressi Italiani. AEI began flying on 15 June 1947. Although its services were of a non-scheduled variety, such as air-taxi, charter, newspaper delivery, aerial advertising. tourist flights and pilot training, by 30 November 1947 it had flown 264,186 km, carried 1,856 passengers and 26,000 kg of freight and newspapers. A not inconsiderable achievement, bearing in mind the limitations of its equipment, a hotch-potch fleet of six Lombardi (Avia) F1.3, five two-seat Macchi MB.308, two modern

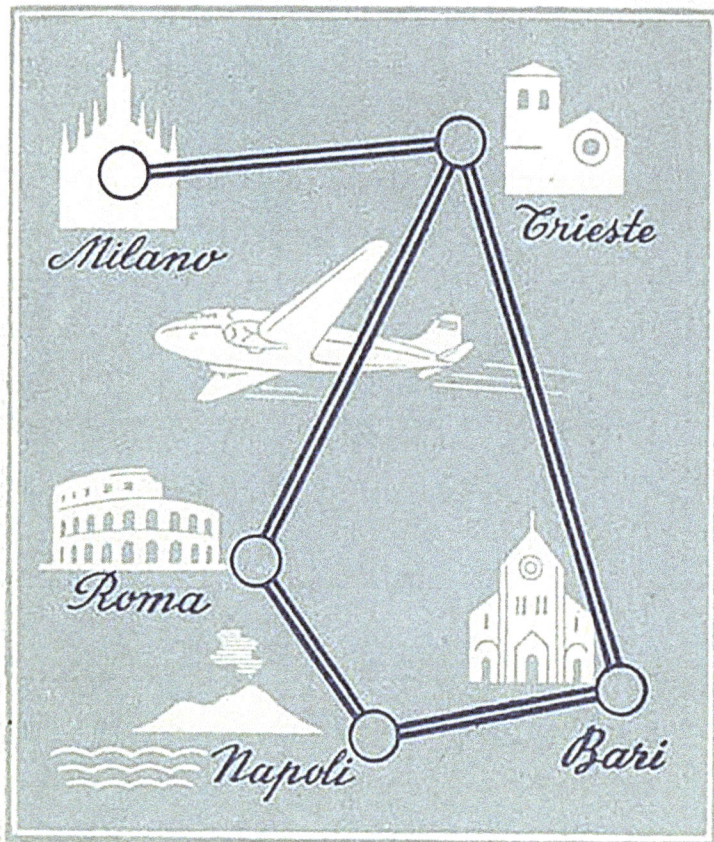

SISA route map December 1947

four-seat single-engine North American Aviation Navion, two Republic Seabee amphibians, a single Norduyn Norseman and seven war-surplus UC-61K (Fairchild 24R). The most useful was the Norseman, which was able to transport nine passengers in addition to the pilot. Bases were maintained at Milan/Linate, Rome/Urbe, and Varese (both Venegono and Vergiate airfields).

A total of eight scheduled carriers were in regular operation by mid-July, but not long afterwards all were temporarily grounded by a strike over wage demands. Nevertheless, by the end of 1947, despite a lack of up-to-date facilities and airports, a rudimentary network of domestic air services connecting most major centres had, nevertheless, been established. LAI's performance was indisputably superior, and by the end of the year, it had transported 54,253 passengers, 62,243 kg of baggage, 46,343 kg of airmail and 338,590 kg of cargo at 98 per cent regularity. Alitalia recorded 9,415 passengers on its scheduled services. It is worth noting that this had in part been made possible by an agreement signed with the US on 4 June 1947, covering the transfer of navigation, communication and weather facilities at Rome, Naples, Pisa, Milan, Palermo and Tropani and providing the training of Italian communications personnel at Rome's Ciampino airport.

Four SISA Douglas C-47 at its Trieste base

Savoia-Marchetti SM.95C I-DALL *Marco Polo* in flight

Savoia-Marchetti SM.95C I-DALJ and Fiat G.12LB I-DALB, both powered by Bristol Pegasus engines

International resumption

On 10 February 1947, the Treaty of Peace with Italy (one of the Paris Peace treaties) was signed, formally ending hostilities. It came into general effect on 15 September. As a result, Italy was once again free to restart flying beyond its own shores. Alitalia immediately took advantage of the new-found freedom and dispatched one of its larger aircraft, the SM.95 I-DALM *Marco Polo*, which had been delivered on 13 May 1947. This was also on loan from the *Aeronautica Militare* (Italian Air Force) and, in its military guise serialled MM61635, had carried the last King of the Savoia dynasty, Umberto II, to exile in Portugal on 13 June 1946. I-DALM, piloted by Commander Pivetti, departed Rome for Oslo on 6 July 1947 with 38 Norwegian passengers aboard, with an intermediate stop at Frankfurt. A second flight was

made two days later in a G.12 commanded by Olivieri. Meanwhile other SM.95 joined the fleet, I-DALJ *Cristoforo Columbo,* I-DALK *Amerigo Vespucci,* I-DALL also named *Marco Polo*, because I-DALM had been returned to the military as MM61635, I-DALN *Sebastiano Caboto* and I-DALO *Ugolino Vivaldi*. The first two were powered by four 641 kW (860 hp) Alfa Romeo 128 RC18 engines, but the next batch had 552 kW (740 hp) Bristol Pegasus 48 engines, which also replaced the Alfa Romeo engines on the first two. Normal accommodation was for six crew and 26 passengers. As the aircraft was unpressurised, passengers had to wear oxygen masks when crossing the Alps. A big advantage was that the aircraft was able to operate from short grass strips, such as Rome/Urbe, a capability also accredited to the Fiat G.12.

Five Avro Lancastrian civilianised bombers were acquired by Alitalia at the instigation of shareholder BEA including I-DALR *Borea*

In Rome, Italy's airlines were confined to Urbe airport until 25 July 1947, when Ciampino, occupied on 1 June 1944 by Anglo-American forces, was handed over to the Italian authorities. Combining the buildings and facilities of the two sides (Ciampino East and Ciampino West), it was one of the best airports in the Mediterranean area, with a long runway created from pierced steel planking, two terminal buildings, several hangars and offices. Situated some 12 km to the south-east of the centre of Rome, it was opened in 1916 and is one of the oldest airports still in operation today. After being captured by Allied Forces, it immediately became a USAAF military base. A new 2,250 m long by 60 m wide concrete runway with modern lighting was put into operation on 27 November 1948. Nevertheless, Alitalia kept a small number of G.12s aircraft at Urbe for its Rome-Turin and Rome-Catania services. Although there had been a gradual improvement of the major aerodromes – on 21 November 1948, Milan/Malpensa was opened to traffic with a 2,000 x 60 m runway and two taxiways – navigation aids remained woefully inadequate for some time to come, with instrument let-downs at best accomplished by a combination of antiquated ground-based radio direction finding (RDF) or radio compass and stopwatch!

Anticipating the awards of significant international routes, Alitalia had also begun taking delivery of five Avro 691 Lancastrian Mk III, purchased on its behalf by BEA, together with a sole Lancaster as a spares source. A single Avro 652 Anson I, I-AHBN, was also transferred for instrument training and the development of night flying capability, but was not used and languished in a corner of the airport until scrapped. The Lancastrian was a close derivative of the Lancaster heavy bomber, with its armour and armament removed and its gun turrets replaced with metal fairings. A new lengthened, streamlined nose section and tail cone were also fitted. It was powered by four 1,210 kW (1,620 hp) Rolls-Royce Merlin 24/2 piston engines and provided accommodation for 13

passengers. With two extra 1,818-litre fuel tanks in the former bomb bay fitted as standard, it achieved a range of 5,750 km, at a fast cruising speed of 425 km/h (264 mph). The five Lancastrian Mk III in the fleet were I-AHBX *Maestrale*, I-AHBY *Libeccio*, I-AHCB *Grecale*, I-AHCD *Scirocco* and I-DALR *Borea*. The first aircraft, I-AHCB, was delivered on 21 July 1947. On 16 November 1947, I-AHBY, flown by Pivetti and Orlandini, made a non-stop flight from Rome to Asmara in 10 hours 15 minutes, although a regular service was not initiated until the following April. I-AHBX *Maestrale*, commanded by Ulivi and Martinelli, made an exploratory flight to South America in April 1948, with the Alitalia management on board, staging via Dakar, Natal, Rio de Janeiro, São Paulo, Montevideo to Buenos Aires. A few weeks later, on 2 June, a regular weekly, if gruelling, 28-hour service on this route was inaugurated, increased to twice-weekly from the summer of 1949. Unfortunately, I-AHBX was destroyed having suffered an engine fire on landing at Dakar, Senegal on 23 December 1949. There were no casualties among the 13 people on board.

In the meantime, Alitalia had added a Rome-Catania-Malta-Tripoli service on a weekly frequency with the G.12 in August 1947 and, in September, extended the Rome-Brindisi-Athens-Cairo route to Khartoum and Lagos, also flown weekly. In addition, Alitalia also operated a number of special flights to Nigeria, Kenya and Rhodesia, although their exact purpose has not been recorded. It also started to make inroads into Europe, first inaugurating a Rome-Nice-Paris service on 11 January 1948, followed by Rome-Milan-London/Northholt, first flown by SM.95, I-DALN, on 3 April and extended to Manchester four days later. Rome-Nice-Geneva was added on 22 July and the airline also operated a French Riviera service, which linked Rome and Cannes via Nice and Juan-les-Pins. An interesting experiment was conducted in 1949, when Alitalia installed an onboard post office. During the flight, passengers were

ALI's Pratt & Whitney-powered Fiat G.212CP I-ENEA

able to post their private correspondence in special collection boxes. Towards the end of the flight, a crew member would empty the boxes and sort the mail, which was carefully franked for onward transportation. When international routes were finally allocated on 16 April 1948, contractual agreements meant that Alitalia obtained the lion's share of routes, although LAI was not far behind.

Operating largely with outdated equipment of British and Italian manufacture, and being under pressure to support local manufacturers, Alitalia expressed an interest in several new designs, most of which never left the drawing board, such as the Fiat G.218, the SIAI-Marchetti S.95S, the latter an all-metal variant of the type already in service, and the imaginative 26-seat Santangelo Orsa. Showing more promise was the Breda-Zappata B.Z.308, which made its first flight on 27 August 1948 under the control of Mario Stoppani, with Alitalia placing an order for four aircraft. The B.Z.308 was a low-wing cantilever monoplane with twin fins powered by four 1,865 kW (2,500 hp) Bristol Centaurus 568 radial engines. It provided accommodation for 55 passengers in two cabins and had a range of 7,700 km. However, serial production never got started due to financial problems of the Breda aviation branch, and the only aircraft was handed over to the *Regia Aeronautica*, which used it in Africa until 1954 with the serial MM 61802.

The third company with some profitable routes out of Milan was ALI, which banked on its close relationship with the Fiat empire. On 19 April 1948, it opened a twice-daily Milan-Paris service with the Fiat G.212, and also operated a Milan-Brussels route in collaboration with the Belgian carrier, Sabena with the Douglas C-47, and a Milan-Zürich service with the Fiat G.212. All international flights were operated three times a week.

End of the road

With the two largest carriers carving up the market, Italy's post-war independent airlines were left with unprofitable routes and never really stood a chance commercially, and it was not long before the first casualties were suffered.

The ill-fated Fiat G.212CP I-ELCE which crashed into the Superga Basilica Hill in Turin

ALI-Flotte Reunite Fiat G.212CP I-Este

Throughout its brief existence, Aerea Teseo had struggled financially, and continued boardroom battles over shareholding and capitalisation failed to resolve its problems. The first shut-down occurred from 18 to 26 December 1947 when personnel failed to obtain an assurance about the future of the company. It was but a short reprieve as, in February 1948, when the administrative control passed to the Nocentini Group, operations were suspended again and the entire management resigned. Plans to increase the capital to ITL 100 million had also not been implemented.

The airline appeared to have overcome the obstacles in its way through the intervention of the Lord Mayor of Florence and new financing from Florentine credit institutions, when, soon after resuming operations, the airline suffered a serious accident on 20 February 1948, when its C-47, I-REGI, crashed into the side of a hill close to Collesalvetti village to the south of Pisa and east of Livorno. The crew of Captain Pellizzari, co-pilot Guazzetti and radio operator Cammareri, had been authorised to take-off from Florence for Rome during severe weather

including snowfall, but had to make an unscheduled stop at nearby Pisa to pick up some passengers who were stranded there due to a mechanical defect of their aircraft. The pilot chose to fly the short Florence-Pisa leg below the cloud base. Presumably, the weather suddenly deteriorated further, and the aircraft entered the clouds at a very low level and drifted from the route, causing it to impact the hill. The crew, an employee of Aerea Teseo and three passengers died in the crash, while three passengers survived. The accident and attendant negative publicity helped seal Aerea Teseo's fate. Although it once again resumed flying on 25 May under new management, it was declared insolvent in June 1948 with a deficit of ITL 1.3 million and stopped operations. Its aircraft were sold to Egypt. In April, Salpanavi had already closed down after a long and unsuccessful fight for concessions. It supplied DC-3 and crew for the formation of Yemenite Airways, the forerunner of Yemen Airways/Yemenia.

Of the remainder, only the Fiat-backed ALI, with several significant European routes, appeared to be holding its

Passengers disembarking from the ALI-Flotte Reunite Douglas C-47 I-TRAS

own, even though its progress was marked by several tragic accidents. On 1 July 1948, Fiat G.212, I-ELSA, inbound to Brussels, caught fire in-flight and crashed near Keerbergen, north of the Belgian capital, with the loss of four crew and four passengers, including the pilot Riva Romanò. A second mishap on 6 December that same year, saw C-47, I-ETNA, departing for Brussels, apparently fall victim to the winter fog of Padana Valley, fatally crashing shortly after take-off from Milan/Linate. All five crew – Commander Piero Bondin, co-pilot Luigi Lisardi, wireless operator Pasquale Del Sorbo, engineer Alassandro Valisi, and stewardess Janette Paroli - and the single passenger lost their lives. The airline survived these setbacks and, on 1 February 1949, officially announced that it had begun absorbing the operations of the remaining carriers – Airone, SISA and Transadriatica – under the title of ALI-Flotte Reunite. The fleets of the three companies were registered to ALI-Flotte Reunite on 12 September that year. The combined fleet of four Fiat G.12, five G.212CP and 12 C-47 now served a network encompassing Amsterdam, Athens, Barcelona, Beirut, Brussels, Nice, Paris, Prague and Vienna, served regularly from Italy's main cities.

At the announcement, General Luigi Biondi had outlined the objectives and hopes for the new organisation. His words painted an optimistic picture when he said: "….the new society has all the existing rights, whether in Italy or abroad and this powerful Italian organisation has the possibility of carrying the nation's flag wherever necessary….

It has a conspicuous inheritance, a nominal capital greater than 1 million lira, a diffuse radius of action in many parts and regions of the country, so that it will never fall prey to fluctuations of a capitalistic or monopolistic nature". It was an ambitious assessment but one that soon proved a step too far. The four carriers' operational integration was fully completed on 1 March 1949, but ALI-FR was not legally established until the following summer.

The newly-formed ALI-FR got off to a bad start on 4 May 1949, with the crash of the Fiat G.212, I-ELCE, which struck the Superga Basilica hill on approach to Turin airport at an altitude of 670 m in a lowering cloud-base. The whole of the active Turin football team, the *Grande Torino*, (almost all of the Italian national side) and coaching staff perished in the accident, as well as the crew and three well-known Italian sports commentators. The aircraft was carrying the football team home from Lisbon, where they had played a friendly match against Benfica. Having made a stop at Barcelona, the G.212, under the command of Lieutenant Colonel Pierluigi Meroni and Cesare Biancardi, set off for Turin heading over Cap de Creus, Toulon, Nice, Albenga and Savona, where the aircraft turned north towards the Piemontese capital, lining up with the runway. The weather in Turin was poor, with clouds almost touching the ground, rain showers, strong wind gusts, and very limited horizontal visibility of just 40 m. Having prepared for landing, the aircraft crashed into the back of the retaining wall of the Basilica. One theory advanced for the deviation was that the

LAI forged ahead by acquiring modern Douglas DC-6 aircraft including I-LADY and I-LOVE

strong crosswinds forced the aircraft to starboard and lined the aircraft up with the Hill of Superga.

The airline never recovered from this disaster. It continued to ply the inherited routes, but soon discontinued its services to Paris, Brussels and Rome, finally succumbing to financial difficulties and ceased flying on 15 December 1951. Almost all of its assets and concessions, except for the Alghero-Cagliari route, together with nine serviceable C-47 aircraft, were acquired by LAI for ITL 400 million in January the following year. ALI-FR's four surviving G.212CP returned to Alitalia from whom they had been purchased and three briefly carried French registrations while on temporary lease to Compagnie Air Transport (CAT). One G.212CP had a particularly interesting history after returning from France. Following its re-entry on the Italian aircraft register as I-ENEA, it was for a short while in the employ of Società Italiana per il Trasporto Aereo (SIPTA), an obscure outfit created by a Mr Brenner, who ran an import-export business in Milan. On 7 June 1952, it left Milan for Hong Kong loaded with medical supplies. On the return flight it carried Italian expatriates who had been detained by the Chinese. At least one more return flight was made to Hong Kong before I-ENEA was sold to Arabian Desert Airlines as G-ANOE.

In September 1951, another new airline, TAC-Trieste Airways, had been founded to continue SISA's international routes. It had planned to use a fleet of Martin 2-0-2 and Douglas DC-3 and DC-4 aircraft for scheduled routes, but conflicts of interest and concern over foreign funding doomed the venture before it got started.

Last two standing

And now there were only two left to battle it out over the international long-haul market. A scramble ensued for traffic, which was forecast to increase by some 20 million of Italians expected to descend on Rome for the 1950 celebration of the Roman Catholic's Holy Year announced by Pope Pious XII in his papal bull *Jubilaeum Maximum*. A priority in the shopping list to attract new passengers for both airlines was the replacement of the ageing fleets, to meet the competition from foreign carriers, which had upgraded with the latest US-built aircraft. LAI stole a march on its rival by purchasing three brand-new Douglas DC-6 airliners, obtained through a substantial USD 4.3 million loan under the USA's European Recovery Program (Marshall Plan), most likely facilitated through the political clout of its part-owner TWA. The DC-6 was the latest product from the Douglas Aircraft works at Long Beach, California. Powered by four 1,800 kW (2,400 hp) Pratt & Whitney R-2800-CA15 Double Wasp piston engines with reverse thrust, it cruised at 500 km/h and had a transcontinental range of 7,350 km. Accommodation was provided for 64 mixed first/tourist passengers in a pressurised cabin, offering superior comfort over the earlier Italian aircraft. One aircraft was equipped for luxury service with 46 couchettes and eight berths. The first DC-6, I-LUCK, was delivered on 1 September 1950, followed by I-LOVE on 5 October, and I-LADY on 17 December 1950. On 13 July, LAI had already opened a prestige service from Rome to New York with a leased standard DC-6 version. I-LUCK was damaged

A LAI Douglas C-47 being met by a vehicle of the Hevra Kadisha to take on the ashes of Holocaust victims for burial in Jerusalem (National Photo Collection of Israel)

beyond repair when it overran the runway on landing at Milan/Malpensa on 23 December 1951. There were no casualties among the four crew and 24 passengers.

This left Alitalia at a distinct disadvantage, rendering its make-shift Lancastrians all but obsolete. Unable to match its competitor's superior political connections and secure funding through the European Recovery Programme, Alitalia was forced to secure second-hand equipment, which it achieved quickly with four Douglas DC-4 from Pan American. Although not the most modern of types and without cabin pressurisation, the DC-4, nevertheless, had the advantage of being able to carry 44 passengers in a comfortable cabin, as compared to the 13 in the Lancastrian. The first aircraft, I-DALT *Città di Milano*, arrived at Ciampino on 25 April 1950, flown by Orlandini, Balletti and Ulivi, and entered service on 5 May on the prestigious South American service, which was now flown via Lisbon and the Cape Verde Islands. At the same time, Alitalia introduced its first female flight attendants. The next two aircraft, I-DALV *Città di Napoli* and I-DALZ *Città di Roma,* arrived later on 28 and 26 April respectively, with the final DC-4, I-DALU *Città di Palermo*, joining the fleet on 18 August. The five G.12LB were impressed in the Aeronautica Militare on 23 June 1950, followed by the four remaining SM.95 on 31 October 1952, where they continued to fly for many more years.

The end of the SM.95B was precipitated by a tragic accident of I-DALO *Ugolino Vivaldi* on 27 January 1951. On the London-Rome service, the aircraft crashed in flames between Tarquinia and Cittavecchio, along the Tyrrhenian Sea coastline. Only the steward and three passengers were saved, while among the victims were the two pilots, Renato Torelli and Cesare Balli. Lightning had struck the wing, setting a fuel tank on fire and forced the pilot into an attempted emergency landing at an abandoned pre-WWII airfield, which ended in disaster. On 17 May 1949, the same aircraft, flying the same route, commanded by Cesare Balli, had suffered a similar occurrence north of Lyon, with two metres of the right wing ripped off. That time, the pilot brought the aircraft down safely at Lyon. An investigation found that the anti-lightning application was ineffective, but Alitalia failed to make the necessary modifications for cost reasons, thus bearing some culpability for the later accident. The withdrawal of the SM.95B forced the suspension of the London service until August 1951, when it was reinstated by the DC-4 withdrawn from the Malta-Tripoli sector.

The four remaining Lancastrians were also taken out of service and cancelled on 5 November 1952, leaving only the four DC-4 in the fleet.

This left Alitalia woefully short of aircraft to maintain its network, causing it to fall further behind its competitor, which had started to replace its Douglas C-47 fleet with four ex-Braniff Airways Convair 240-2 twins, representing considerable enhancements in speed, range and passenger capacity. The first aircraft, I-LAKE, was delivered in April 1953, with the remaining three aircraft, I-LARK, I-LIFE and I-LIFT, arriving later that year. The new aircraft enabled LAI to improve and develop its European network,

Alitalia Douglas DC-4 I-DALZ

LAI's Convair 240 twin provided considerable enhancements in speed, range and passenger capacity

Convair 340 I-DOGU of Alitalia

Only two Convair 440 Metropolitans were operated by Alitalia including I-DOVE

which then served Frankfurt, Munich, Zürich, Barcelona, Athens and Istanbul, as well as Tunis, Alexandria and Cairo in North Africa. Alitalia quickly followed suit, taking advantage of a cancelled Northeast Airlines order and taking delivery of the first of three brand-new Convair 340 aircraft, I-DOGI, on 5 May that same year. I-DOGI was almost immediately placed on the Rome-Nice-Geneva route. The subsequent delivery of the remaining aircraft permitted the full reinstatement of the London service on 8 July 1953, now flown via Paris, releasing the DC-4 back to the Malta-Tripoli route. The short/medium-range Convair 240 was the first pressurised airliner and provided accommodation for 40 passengers. It was powered by two Pratt & Whitney R-2800 Double Wasp air-cooled radial engines, which generated a cruising speed of 450 km/h. Range was 1,900 km. The Convair 340 was lengthened to provide 44 seats and had better performance at higher altitudes.

Late in 1953, Alitalia at last stole a march on its competitor by acquiring four new improved Douglas DC-6B at a cost of USD 1 million each, the first being I-DIMA, which flew into Rome on 17 November. The new aircraft was quickly placed on the South American run and, with deliveries completed by March 1954, the still pristine DC-4 fleet was sold. On the basis of having offset previous losses and recorded a healthy profit, two further DC-6B were ordered for 1956 delivery. LAI countered with its own

DC-6B, I-LAND, delivered on 24 July 1954, and I-LYNX, delivered on 12 May 1954.

Six accidents, four with heavy loss of life, took the shine off LAI's growing reputation and ultimately led to its incorporation into Alitalia. The spate of accidents began on 26 January 1953, when the Douglas C-47, I-LAIL, crashed in mountainous terrain near Sinnai (Sardinia), following failure of the left wing on a service from Cagliari to Rome, with the loss of all 19 people on board. Another C-47, I-LENT, came to grief at Rome/Ciampino, when it was destroyed by fire after force-landing following an engine failure on take-off on 10 April 1954. It was a training flight and there were no casualties. On 18 December that same year, Douglas DC-6B, I-LINE, crashed in flames and sank into Jamaica Bay after its fourth attempt to land at New York's Idlewild airport, killing 26 of the people on board the aircraft. After a two-year lull, LAI suffered three further accidents in quick succession. On 24 November 1956, DC-6B, I-LEAD, lost altitude seconds after take-off from Paris/Orly and crashed into a house past the runway end. All 10 crew and 24 of the 25 passengers died. Twenty-one people perished on 22 December, when C-47, I-LINC, crashed into snow-capped Monte Giner in the Italian Alps, having inexplicably greatly deviated from its Rome-Milan course. Contributing to this accident was apparent confusion on the ground as to which ATC sector had

Alitalia's first Douglas DC-6B I-DIMA was delivered in November 1953 and was quickly put onto the South American run

LAI also operated the DC-6B

responsibility for its safe passage, reinforcing concerns, especially by foreign carriers, about worrying deficiencies in the country's radar and radio-navigation services. On 2 January 1957, another C-47, I-LEDA struck a wall after landing at Reggio Calabria airport on a flight from Rome to Catania. The seven occupants were unhurt.

Nevertheless, LAI, having increased its capital to ITL 5.5 million, pressed on with a bold re-equipment programme. In 1956, with the help of a USD 6.2 million bank loan, LAI placed an order for four Lockheed L.1649A Starliner, an elegant four-engined aircraft, for the prestigious Rome-New York route, specifying a configuration for 45 tourist-class passengers forward, and

for 26 first-class passengers aft, the latter accommodated in two cabins with eight couchettes and one of 10 at the rear. A special galley for the preparation of hot food was also to be incorporated. Although all four aircraft had already been built and painted in LAI colours at the Lockheed factory at Burbank, and had received their official registrations and names – I-LAMA *Romano*, I-LETR *Ambrosiano*, I-LIRA *Vesuviano*, and I-LODO *Siciliano* - LAI never took delivery, and the order was cancelled by Alitalia after it had succeeded LAI. However, it did take delivery of its order for six Vickers V.785D Viscount turboprop airliners, the first of which, I-LIFE, was delivered to Rome on 27 March 1957, followed by

LAI took delivery of six Vickers Viscount turboprop aircraft before being integrated into the new Alitalia

five more over the following five months. Unfortunately, its service life with the airline was short and ended with the merger of LAI into Alitalia on 31 October that same year. All six were transferred to Alitalia. In contrast, Alitalia had opted for two Convair 440 with improved soundproofing and weather radar, and four Douglas DC-7C, having declined the extra expense of switching to turboprop aircraft.

However, there was no way back for LAI. For some time, there had been periodic calls for the amalgamation of the two airlines, motivated both by a political desire for Italian civil aviation to divest itself of foreign influence, and the commercially dubious situation of having two competing majority state-owned carriers, which were clearly unable to compete with the larger European airlines on the major international routes, both in terms of operational efficiencies and greater cost levels. These voices resurfaced with renewed vigour early in 1957 following the latest LAI fatal crashes. The forced resignation of LAI's general manager, General Luigi Gallo, and a management reshuffle, including the replacement of the president, Prince Marcantonio Pacelli, by General Aldo Urbani, in the wake of these tragedies, did nothing to allay fears over the airline's future, hastening its ultimate demise. Furthermore, Alitalia's financial position

was far stronger than that of LAI, this and the fact that Alitalia had the firm support of IRI and thus the Italian Government, probably influenced TWA's decision to extricate itself from the airline, although this was not without cost to the US airline. IRI did rather well out of the deal, having to pay only a quarter of the ITL 1,688 million due to TWA, according to the 1946 agreement, to liquidate its interest in LAI. The remainder was offset against the four Starliners, which were handed to TWA.

The merger between LAI and Alitalia was announced on 10 August 1957, exactly in the middle of Italy's traditional summer holiday season. Following negotiations with foreign investors, LAI was legally merged into Alitalia on 1 September, its assets being taken over on 6 October. LAI entered voluntary liquidation on 31 October 1957, and the next day, its operations were integrated into the re-named Alitalia-Linee Aeree Italiane, which now assumed the position of sole Italian flag-carrier. Capital was increased from ITL 4.5 million to ITL 10 million, with the issue of new shares valued at ITL10,000, with the majority 71.5 per cent retained by IRI, and 15 per cent in the hands of private Italian interests, mostly Fiat. BEA's holding was reduced to 13.5 per cent and relinquished completely in April 1961.

Four Lockheed L.1649A Starliner aircraft were ordered by LAI but never delivered

Aerea Teseo Società Anonima Fleet 1946-1948

Douglas C-47/C-47B 1947-1948 (7)

21-passengers low-wing, all-metal monoplane, powered by two 895 kW (1,200 hp) Pratt & Whitney R-1830-S1C3G Twin Wasp engines, generating a speed of 370 km/h

I-BOLO	15603/27048	30.01.47-01.12.48	ex USAAF 43-49787; to Royal Egyptian Air Force
I-GENO	15475/26920	14.05.47-01.12.48	ex USAAF 43-49659; to Royal Egyptian Air Force
I-PALU	4233	03.07.47-01.12.48	ex USAAF 41-7746; to Royal Egyptian Air Force
I-REGI	4312	30.01.47-28.02.48	ex USAAF 41-7813; crashed at Collesalvetti on approach to Pisa
I-TORI	14310/25755	09.12.46-01.12.48	ex USAAF 43-48494; to Royal Egyptian Air Force
I-VENE	15474/26919	09.12.46-01.12.48	ex USAAF 43-49658; to Royal Egyptian Air Force

Airone Compagnia Trasporti Aerei Fleet 1947-1949

Fiat G.12L 1947-1949 (4)

18-passenger low-wing cantilever monoplane, powered by three 575 kW (770 hp) Fiat A74 RC.42 engines, generating a cruising speed of 310 km/h

I-AIRE	*Barbaggia*	94	00.00.47-01.02.49	to ALI-FR
I-AIRN	*Gallura*	93	00.00.47-01.02.49	to ALI-FR
I-AIRO	Logudoro	92	00.00.47-01.02.49	to ALI-FR
I-SASS*		100		to Aeronautica Militare

* Fiat G.12LP with three 795 kW (1,065 hp) Pratt & Whitney R-1830-S1C3-G Twin Wasp radial engines

ALI (Avio Linee Italiane Società Anonima)/ALI-Flotte Reunite 1947-1952

Douglas C-47/C-47B/C-53 11947-1952 (11)

21-passengers low-wing, all-metal monoplane, powered by two 895 kW (1,200 hp) Pratt & Whitney R-1830-S1C3G Twin Wasp engines, generating a speed of 370 km/h

I-COSU	4291	00.00.49-14.03.52	ex SISA; to LAI as I-LULA
I-EBRO	7325	11.01.48-14.03.52	ex USAAF 42-15530; to LAI
I-ELFO	4260	10.05.47-13.07.51	ex USAAF 41-7773; to Aeronautica Civil as MM61800
I-ENOS	7397	10.10.47-14.03.52	ex USAAF 42-15880; to LAI
I-ETNA	4396	06.06.47-06.12.48	ex USAAF 41-18358; crashed on take-off at Milan/Linate
I-SOLE	4506	12.09.49-03.02.52	ex SISA; to LAI
I-TRAS	15355/26800	15.11.49-14.03.52	ex Transadriatica; to LAI
I-TRES	14128/25573	12.09.49-30.04.52	ex Transadriatica; to LAI as I-LILI
I-TRIS	15262/26707	05.11.49-21.06.51	ex Transadriatica; to Aeronautica Militare as MM61799
I-TRUS	15201/26646	18.11.49-14.03.52	ex Transadriatica; to LAI
I-VARO	6011	14.12.49-18.03.52	ex SISA; to LAI as I-LICE

Fiat G.12LP (3)

22-passenger low-wing metal monoplane, powered by three 795 kW (1,065 hp) Pratt & Whitney R-1830-SIC3G radial engines, generating a cruising speed of 295 km/h

I-AIRE	94	01.02.49-00.00.51	ex Airone; to Aeronautica Militare as MM
I-AIRN	93	01.02.49-00.00.51	ex Airone; to Aeronautica Militare as MM
I-AIRO	92	01.02.49-00.00.51	ex Airone; to Aeronautica Militare as MM

Fiat G.12T (3)

14-troop or cargo transport, powered by three 575 kW (770 hp) Fiat A74 RC.42 radial engines, generating a maximum speed of 390 km/h (240 mph)

I-VIDA	40	ex MM60691; lsd from Aeronautica Militare
I-VIDI	72	exMM60718; lsd from Aeronautica Militare
I-VIDO	71	ex MM60717; lsd from Aeronautica Militare

Fiat G.212CP (6)

34-passenger low-wing metal monoplane, powered by three 795 kW (1,065 hp) Pratt & Whitney R-1830-SIC3G radial engines, generating a cruising speed of 300 km/h

I-ELCE	5	01.06.48-04.05.49	crashed on Superga Hill on approach to Turin/Aeritalia
I-ELSA	4	01.06.48-01.07.48	crashed near Keerbergen, Belgium
I-ENEA	10	01.10.48-	to SIPTA
I-ERBE	2	01.04.48-	
I-ERME	7	01.08.48-	leased to SAIDE as SU-AFX 11.48-06.49
I-ESTE	3	01.03.48-	leased to SAIDE as SU-AFY 11.48-06.49

LAI (Linee Aeree Italiane Società per Azioni) Fleet 1947-1957

Douglas C-47/C-47B/C-53 1947-1957 (27)

21-passengers low-wing, all-metal monoplane, powered by two 895 kW (1,200 hp) Pratt & Whitney R-1830-S1C3G Twin Wasp engines, generating a speed of 370 km/h

I-EBRO	7325	14.03.52-18.11.52	ex ALI-FR; to Aeronautica Militare as MM61817
I-ENOS	7397	14.03.52-18.11.52	ex ALI-FR; to Aeronautica Militare as MM61818
I-LAIL	4308	02.05.47-26.01.53	ex USAAF; crashed near Sinnai, NE of Cagliari/Elmas
I-LALO	19484	07.07.48-31.10.57	ex USAAF 42-101021; to Alitalia
I-LAMA	4389	12.03.48-14.04.55	ex USAAF 41-18351; to Aeronautica Militare as MM61823
I-LEDA	4411	12.04.47-02.01.57	ex USAAF 41-18373; struck wall while landing at Reggio Calabria
I-LENE	4325	04.09.47-31.10.57	ex USAAF 41-7826; to Alitalia
I-LENT	4548	31.03.52-10.04.54	ex ALI-FR I-VELE; damaged beyond repair on take-off from Rome/Ciampino
I-LEON	4316	12.04.47-31.10.57	ex USAAF 41-7817; to Alitalia

I-LETR	4686	15.01.48-28.11.51	ex USAAF 41-18561;damaged beyond repair on take-off at Milan/Malpensa
I-LICE	6011	18.03.51-31.10.57	ex ALI-FR I-VARO; to Alitalia
I-LIDA	4261	12.04.47-31.10.57	ex USAAF 41-7774; to Alitalia
I-LILI	14128/25573	30.04.52-10.08.56	ex ALI-FR I-TRES; to Transair as G-AOUD
I-LINA	4236	10.06.47-31.10.57	ex USAAF 41-7749; to Alitalia
I-LINC	9101	30.11.47-22.12.56	ex USAAF 42-32875; crashed into Monte Giner en route Rome-Milan
I-LIRA	4380	20.09.47-14.04.55	ex USAAF 41-18342; to Aeronautica Militare as MM61826
I-LODO	4221	13.10.47-03.04.55	ex USAAF 41-7742; to Aeronautica Militare as MM61825
I-LONA	4500	12.11.47-31.10.57	ex USAAF 41-18438; to Alitalia
I-LORD	4496	21.06.47-31.10.57	ex USAAF 41-18434; to Alitalia
I-LORO	4297	12.04.47-31.10.57	ex USAAF 41-7805; to Alitalia
I-LOTT	4506	31.03.52-31.03.55	ex I-SOLE; to Aeronautica Militare as MM61624
I-LUCE	4387	17.04.47-31.10.57	ex USAAF 41-18349; to Alitalia
I-LULA	4291	14.03.52-31.10.57	ex ALI-FR I-COSU; to Alitalia
I-LUNA	4346	25.02.52-31.10.57	ex USAAF 41-7847; to Alitalia
I-SOLE	4506	03.02.52-31.03.52	ex ALI-FR; reregistered I-LOTT
I-TRAS	15355/26800	14.03.52-09.10.52	ex ALI-FR; to Aeronautica Militare as MM61815
I-TRUS	15201/26646	14.03.52-09.10.52	ex ALI-FR; to Aeronautica Militare as MM61816

Douglas DC-6 1950-1957 (6)

64-passenger low-wing, all-metal monoplane powered by four 1,790 kW (2,400hp) Pratt & Whitney R-2800-CA15 Double Wasp engines, generating a speed of 500km/h

I-LADY	43034/136	15.03.50.08.09.50	ex LV-ADV; lsd from Aerolineas Argentinas
I-LADY(2)	43216/165	17.09.50-31.10.57	to Alitalia
I-LIKE	43152/161	28.05.53-31.10.57	to Alitalia
I-LOVE	43030/124	31.03.50-22.09.50	ex LV-ADR; leased from Aerolineas Argentinas
I-LOVE(2)	43217/166	17.09.50-31.10.57	to Alitalia
I-LUCK	43215/164	01.09.50-23.12.51	crashed on landing at Milan/Malpensa

Douglas DC-6B 1953-1957 (4)

68-passenger, low-wing monoplane, powered by four 1,865 kW (2,500 hp) Pratt & Whitney R-2800-CB17 Double Wasp engines, generating a speed of 510km/h

I-LAND	44419/491	24.07.54-31.10.57	to Alitalia
I-LEAD	45075/731	29.10.56-24.11.56	crashed on initial climb out of Paris/Orly
I-LINE	44418/487	28.05.54-18.12.54	crashed into Jamaica Bay on approach to New York/Idlewild
I-LYNX	44417/473	12.05.54-31.10.57	to Alitalia

Convair 240 1952-1956 (4)

40-passenger short-range airliner, powered by two 1,800 kW (2,400 hp) Pratt & Whitney R-2800-CA3 Double Wasp radial engines, generating a cruising speed of 465 km/h

I-LAKE	71	31.12.52-00.00.56	ex Braniff International Airways N90667; to Air Jordan as JY-ACA
I-LARK	84	09.04.53-00.00.56	ex Braniff International Airways N90669; to Iran Air as EP-ADX
I-LIFE	9	07.03.53-00.00.56	ex Braniff International Airways N90655; to Iran Air as EP-ADY
I-LIFT	55	20.05.53-00.00.56	ex Braniff Interantional Airways N90663; to Air Jordan as JY-ACB

Vickers V.785D Viscount 1957 (6)

48-passenger short/medium-range aircraft, powered by four 1,175 kW (1.575 hp) Rolls-Royce Dart RDa3 Mk.510 turboprop engines, generating a speed of 550 km/h

I-LARK	329	30.06.57-31.10.57	to Alitalia
I-LIFE	325	27.03.57-31.10.57	to Alitalia
I-LIFT	326	17.04.57-31.10.57	to Alitalia
I-LILI	327	26.05.57-31.10.57	to Alitalia
I-LOTT	330	28.07.57-31.10.57	to Alitalia

Lockheed L.1649A-98 Starliner (4)

102-passenger triple-finned airliner, powered by four 2,525 kW (3,400 hp) Wright R-3350-EA-2 Turbo Compound engines, generating a maximum speed of 605 km/h

(I-LAMA)	*Romano*	1026	N8081H; never delivered, taken over the TWA
(I-LETR)	*Ambrosiano*	1037	N8082H; never delivered, taken over the TWA
(I-LIRA)	*Vesuviano*	1038	N8083H; never delivered, taken over the TWA
(I-LODO)	Siciliano	1039	N8084H; never delivered, taken over the TWA

LATI (Linee Aeree Transcontinentali Italiane) Fleet 1949-1950

Savoia-Marchetti SM.95C 1949-1950 (3)

20-passenger cantilever monoplane of mixed construction, powered by three 552 kW (740 hp) Bristol Pegasus 48 radial engines, generating a speed of 295 km/h

I-LAIT	*Sant'Antonio*	19	00.00.49-01.04.50	to Alitalia
I-LATI	*San Francesco*	17	00.00.49-15.11.49	crashed on landing at Villa Cisneros, Western Sahara
I-LITA	*San Cristoforo*	18	08.06.49-01.04.50	to Alitalia

Salpanavi (Salpanavi Società per Azioni) Fleet 1947-1948

Douglas C-47 1948-1949 (2)

21-passengers low-wing, all-metal monoplane, powered by two 895 kW (1,200 hp) Pratt & Whitney R-1830-S1C3G Twin Wasp engines, generating a speed of 370 km/h

I-NAVE	4345	25.08.48-09.10.48	lsd from SISA; to Yemenite Airlines as YE-AAB Shiban
I-PADO	4329	05.10.48-02.03.49	lsd from Transadriatica; to Royal Egyptian Air Force

Savoia-Marchetti SM.95 1947 (1)

20-passenger cantilever monoplane of mixed construction, powered by three 552 kW (740 hp) Bristol Pegasus 48 radial engines, generating a speed of 295 km/h

I-SALP	6
(I-TANC)	

SISA (Società Italiana Servizi Aerei) Fleet 1946-1949

Douglas C-47 1947-1949 (6)

21-passengers low-wing, all-metal monoplane, powered by two 895 kW (1,200 hp) Pratt & Whitney R-1830-S1C3G Twin Wasp engines, generating a speed of 370 km/h

I-COSU	4291	11.03.47-	ex USAAF 41-7799; to ALI-Flotte Reunite
I-LUNA	4346	30.09.46-12.09.49	ex USAAF 41-7847; to ALI-Flotte Reunite
I-NAVE	4345	29.03.47-25.08.48	ex USAAF 41-7846; lsd to Salpanavi
I-SOLE	4506	10.05.47-12.09.49	ex USAAF 41-18444; to ALI-Flotte Reunite
I-VARO	6011	30.01.48-14.12.49	ex USAAF 41-18650; to ALI-Flotte Reunite
I-VELE	4548	22.05.47-12.09.49	ex USAAF 41-38599; to ALI-Flotte Reunite

Transadriatica (Società Anonima di Navigazione Aerea Transadriatica) Fleet 1946-1949

Douglas C-47/C-47B 1947-1949 (6)

21-passengers low-wing, all-metal monoplane, powered by two 895 kW (1,200 hp) Pratt & Whitney R-1830-S1C3G Twin Wasp engines, generating a speed of 370 km/h

I-PADO		4329	21.08.48-05.10.48	ex USAAF 41-7830; lsd to Salpanavi
I-TRAS		15355/26800	05.12.46-15.11.49	ex USAAF 43-49539; to ALI-Flotte Reunite
I-TRES	*Guido Bottoli*	14128/25573	14.02.47-12.09.49	ex USAAF 43-48312' to ALI-Flotte Reunite
I-TRIS	*Oreste Bossi*	15262/26707	05.12.46-05.11.49	ex USAAF 43-49446; to ALI-Flotte Reunite
I-TROS		15230/26675	05.12.46-24.11.48	ex USAAF 43-49414; to New Holland Airways as VH-BNH
I-TRUS		15201/26646	05.12.46-18.11.49	ex USAAF 43-49385; to ALI-Flotte Reunite

*A*litalia

Having been embroiled in a bruising competitive battle with LAI over the past ten years, Alitalia now had the international market to itself. With a workforce of approximately 3,100, including 300 pilots and, together with three DC-6, two DC-6B, six Viscount and 12 C-47 taken over from LAI, and its own six DC-6B, six DC-7C, four CV-340 and two CV-440, the Alitalia fleet now totalled 41 aircraft of seven different types, including maintained deliveries of the new Viscounts. The four-engined turboprops gradually took over from the Convair twins on higher density routes and, from 1 January 1958, were put on the four times weekly London-Milan route, continuing on to Naples and Catania.

Since 1950, Italy had enjoyed unprecedented growth that transformed a largely backward economy into one of the world's most dynamic industrial nations with an average GDP of 5.9%. Further boosted by Italy's status of one of the founder members of the EEC in 1957, Alitalia too had grown and by the end of the decade in terms of passenger/kilometres flown, ranked sixth overall among Europe's leading airlines.

At a time when the airline was still directing its energies towards the process of integration with LAI, most of its counterparts were well advanced along the path of re-equipping with the new generation of jet airliners. Indeed, LAI had already looked ahead, by placing options on the Boeing 707-420 for delivery in November 1959. Although this order was now void, Alitalia was forced to reappraise its position. Remaining loyal to Douglas, four Rolls-Royce-powered DC-8 with two options were ordered on 16 July 1959 for delivery through 1960. One of the reasons being that Douglas also offered better delivery times in comparison with Boeing. A similar study led to the choice of the Sud-Aviation SE-210 Caravelle III for medium-haul European routes, where Air France's introduction of the type between Paris and Rome had led to a 23 per cent drop in traffic on Alitalia's parallel Viscount service. The order for four Caravelle III was signed on 15 October 1959. To finance the new acquisitions Alitalia's capital was increased to ITL 20 billion (USD 32.2 million) and, perhaps not unsurprisingly, a loss was recorded for 1958/59, although turned around for 1959/60. Globally, Alitalia was now ranked number 12 and, in keeping with its status as a major international carrier, felt moved to open a second transatlantic service, from Naples to New York with the DC-7C on 2 April 1960, as well as new routes to India and Pakistan.

The arrival of the jets posed fresh problems; a vast increase in available seating capacity and increased aircraft noise. The latter causing a temporary ban at Ciampino, which in reality had as much to do with the lack of suitable handling facilities and runway surface deficiences. After many delays, Rome's new purpose-built airport at Fiumicino (now Leonardo da Vinci) was finally opened on 15 January 1961, though it was a cause for much political scandal that it had not been finished in time for the city's hosting of the 1960 Summer Olympic Games a year earlier - more so in view of the fact that Alitalia was designated official carrier for the XII Olympiad. However, it had been in partial use since 20 August 1960, to relieve the heavily congested Ciampino. To ensure sufficient aircrew would be available for the new jets, in 1962 Alitalia opened a flying training school based at

Vickers V.700D I-LINS was operated for seven years before being sold to Uruguay as CX-BHB

The Douglas DC-7C was an interim long-haul aircraft pending the acquisition of jet aircraft

Brindisi employing Aermacchi MB326B twin-jet trainers, adapted from the military version.

The delivery of Alitalia's first Douglas DC-8-40, I-DIWA *Amerigo Vespucci,* on 28 April 1960, was quickly followed by the Sud-Aviation Caravelle III, I-DAXE *Aldebaran,* on 19 May 1960, and both aircraft were officially presented at Ciampino four days later, after which the Caravelle immediately left on its maiden flight to London. Alitalia's first DC-8 flight took place between Rome and New York on 1 June. The Caravelle also inaugurated a Rome-Athens- Cairo service on 12 July. With its new generation of airliners, Alitalia extended its horizons by opening Rome-Vienna-Prague on 5 April 1960, the first post-war service between Italy and Eastern Europe. By the year's end, eight jets were in service and for the first time Alitalia carried

in excess of 1 million passengers over a 64-city network spanning 110,533 km.

Alitalia's DC-8-40 was powered by four 77.8 kN (17,500 lb) Rolls-Royce Conway 508-12 turbofan engines and was configured for 12 first-class and 130 economy-class passengers. Full payload range was 7,800 km. The 80-passenger, rear-engined Caravelle III twinjet was powered by two 50.7 kN (11,400 lb) Rolls-Royce Avon RA.29 Mk.527 turbojets and had a range up to 2,500 km. Alitalia later also acquired the improved Caravelle VI-N with more powerful 54.28 kN (12,200 lb) RA.29 Mk.531B turbojets, and the earlier Caravelle III models were upgraded to VI-N standard. It is worth mentioning that on 2 November 1963 the airline also placed a USD 300,000 deposit to reserve a slot for six of Boeing's projected supersonic airliners, the

The Douglas DC-8-43 was Alitalia's first long-haul jet aircraft (Jon Proctor)

2707, but that project never saw the light of day. It was not a popular move in political circles, who would have preferred support for the Anglo-French Concorde.

But two serious accidents spoiled Alitalia's hitherto excellent recent safety record. Viscount I-LIZT was lost at Ciampino on December 21, 1959 during a training flight, crashing out of control while conducting an impromptu two-engined asymmetric 'touch and go'. Both crews lost their lives. More serious was the fatal accident to DC-7C, I-DUVO, which inexplicably lost height during climb-out from Shannon on February 26,1960 and crashed into the nearby Clonloghan Church with the loss of 11 crew members and 23 passengers. One steward and 17 passengers survived the accident. No definite reasons for this accident were revealed by the investigation.

Charter diversion

The advent of the new jets and the measured move towards an all-jet fleet, finally accomplished in 1968, marked the slow demise of Alitalia's piston-engined airliners, which had served the airline well. Although the Convair fleet was disposed of *en masse* in 1961/62, a number of its Douglas aircraft received a new lease of life. It had become apparent that there was new scope to serve the growing tourist charter market with high-capacity aircraft and, not wanting to be left out, Alitalia revived the pre-war name of Società Aerea Mediterranea SpA (SAM), as its non-IATA charter subsidiary, formed on 1 December 1959, with the state airline holding 70 per cent of the capital. It was based at Rome/Ciampino. The first of three Douglas DC-6B, I-DIMA, was transferred to SAM on 1 April 1961, and began flying between Rome and Copenhagen, Madrid and London/Gatwick on 19 April, configured for 82 passengers. I-DIMD and I-DIME, joined the fleet in May and enabled

SAM's Douglas C-47 at Trieste Airport

an extension of flights, also including frequent services to London/Gatwick from Milan and Turin. With the expansion of flights to the Middle East and North Africa on behalf of major tour operators such as Club Méditerranée, Alitalia added another DC-6B, I-DIMU, to the SAM fleet. The DC-6B fleet, eventually numbering eight, was reconfigured for 86 passengers and provided with weather radar, which gave rise to the designation Super DC-6B. Unfortunately, one aircraft was lost on 8 May 1962, when I-DIMO crashed into Monte Velino, while returning to Rome/Ciampino on a cargo flight from Khartoum. The crew had started the approach at night and impacted the mountain at an altitude of 2,350 m (7,710 ft). All five crew members were killed. It is believed that the accident was caused by a premature descent. I-DIMO was immediately replaced by I-DIMI. I-DIMB was shared with the Aeronautica Militare Reserve between 1963 and 1968, where it carried the serial MM61900 on military flights.

Charter work continued to grow both in terms of numbers and variety. Summer services brought UK and German holidaymakers to the seaside resort of Rimini on the Adriatic, and the Côte d'Azur also became increasingly popular, especially Nice and the casinos of Monte Carlo, as did other resort areas in Southern Europe. There were also frequent flights from Italy to such destinations as Prague, Stockholm, Madrid, Moscow, Tenerife and Las Palmas de Gran Canaria. Intercontinental charters were also flown to Hong Kong, Johannesburg and Perth, carrying inclusive-tour passengers, religious groups, immigrants, ships' crews and government officials. Prior to the 18 March 1962 peace agreement that ended the seven-year Algerian War of Independence, refugees were flown from Algiers and Oran to Bordeaux, Lyon, Toulouse and Ajaccio. In the winter periods, from October to April each year, the DC-6Bs were busy in transporting Italian flowers from Albenga to Malmö and Stockholm in Sweden making three flights a week.

SAM bought two Curtiss C-46A Commando twin-engined aircraft from US-based Boreas Corporation for freight charter operations, the first of which, I-SILV, was delivered on 6 December 1961, with the second, I-SILA,

Douglas DC-6 I-DIMB at Rome Fiumicino (Bob Proctor)

The two Curtiss C-46A Commando I-SILA and I-SILV used on cargo charter flights

Sud-Aviation Caravelle VI-N I-DABL at Turin (Tom Singfield)

147

following on 6 January 1962. Powered by two 1.420 kW (2,000 hp) Pratt & Whitney R-2800 radial piston engines, the C-46A was equipped with a large cargo door on the port side of the fuselage, a strengthened cargo floor and a hydraulic winch and had a cargo capacity of 6.8 tonnes. Freight flights were conducted with flowers from Albenga to Malmö and Stockholm, and another important source of income came from transporting car parts on behalf of Fiat and Maserati. On 31 October 1962, both were taken over on lease by Alitalia for its own freight business, which included the Rome-Milan-Frankfurt and Rome-Tripoli routes, both being flown three times a week. These services connected with Douglas DC-7CF Freighters from Rome and Milan to New York.

In December 1961, SAM had also been tasked with taking over Alitalia's secondary services, using some of Alitalia's Douglas DC-3 fleet, starting at the end of 1961 with I-LALO and I-LORD, initially connecting Trieste with Venice, before adding the Venice-Florence-Rome service on 16 April 1962, by which time two more DC-3s, I-LENE and I-LORO, had been added. From 1 November 1962, the DC-3 fleet was also deployed on a daily service linking Rome with Reggio Calabria, Palermo and Trapani in Sicily and the island of Pantelleria in the Strait of Sicily to the south-west. In addition, three flights a week were operated between Milan and Tarbes (Lourdes airport) in south-western France. These services were transferred to a new domestic airline, Aero Trasporti Italiani (ATI), which was established by Alitalia on 16 December 1963 to take over and expand the domestic network. All four DC-3s were then sold to different operators in Africa.

Having been relieved from operating scheduled domestic services, SAM now concentrated entirely on passenger and cargo charters. A new departure was its involvement from 1967 in the emerging cruise market in the Mediterranean, launching flights for the Greece-based Chandris Line operating out of Venice, soon supplemented with flights for the Lauro Line and Lloyd Triestino, both cruising from Genoa. Although the emphasis remained on European charters, SAM also operated many long-haul charters, with Canada and Australia new destinations. When Alitalia started replacing its Caravelles with the new Douglas DC-9, three Caravelle VI-N were transferred to SAM and re-equipped for the transport of 99 passengers. The first to enter service on 1 May 1968 was I-DABT, followed by I-DAXA on 10 June and I-DABV on 1 November that same year. Although I-DAXA remained with SAM for only a few months before being returned to Alitalia, SAM acquired more Caravelles, eventually operating ten different aircraft. Their arrival marked the end of the DC-6B fleet, several of which passed to the Aeronautica Militare, where, assigned to 302° and 306° Gruppo Volo, they operated long-haul flights for the *Reparto Volo Stato Maggiore* (General Staff Flying Unit) out of Rome/Ciampino.

However, two aircraft, I-DIMU and I-DIMB, were converted to DC-6A freighter configuration by Officine Aeronavali at Venice in December 1968 and May 1965 respectively. Among their most lucrative work was the transport of race horses around Europe, but they also operated scheduled services for Alitalia.

In April 1972, SAM made plans for a serious move into the transatlantic charter market with an Alitalia Douglas DC-8-43. Although landing rights were granted, these plans were not implemented. The 1973 oil crisis and the first moves towards airline deregulation in the US made the prospect less attractive. Having a non-IATA subsidiary now was less and less important and from 1972, SAM started the process of becoming merely a paper airline, utilising Alitalia aircraft for charter work as and when required. By 1974, it was just an Alitalia business unit and it was finally dissolved in 1977.

Caravelle VI-N I-DABG was one of several of the type operated by SAM

Domestic dilemma

Domestic operations had at best been only marginal for both Alitalia and LAI, and had often been a distraction from the main thrust of serving the financially more rewarding markets. But for some time, Alitalia had been considering a further development of domestic multi-stop services, especially on secondary routes in the poorer south of the country, with an emphasis on using smaller aircraft and a separate organisation with a lower cost base.

Having instructed SAM to serve its secondary routes for a time with outdated aircraft, Alitalia, with the support of the government, now established a new company, ATI-Aero Trasporti Italiani SpA on 16 December 1963, with the initial capital of ITL 10 million divided between Alitalia (90 per cent) and IRI (10 per cent). The capital was substantially increased to ITL 450 million on 3 July 1964, and again on 3 March 1966, this time to ITL 600 million. Led as president by General Giovanni Buonamico, and as director-general by Marcello Mainetti and based at Naples/Capodichino, the establishment of ATI was in part due to a growing influence of the private airline, Aerolinee Itavia, but its main purpose was to improve and increase the links between the north and the poorer southern parts of Italy, using smaller aircraft at reduced prices. Alitalia had long been criticised for neglecting local services in favour of international routes, but providing cabin service equal in standard to international routes, while also using unsuitable aircraft, made no economic sense, especially at the fares charged.

The aircraft chosen was the twin-engined, Rolls-Royce Dart-powered Fokker F.27-200 Friendship turboprop aircraft, with accommodation for 44 passengers, bought new from the Dutch manufacturer. The first, I-ATIP, was delivered on 25 May 1964, enabling the start of operations on 2 June. With two further aircraft, I-ATIM and I-ATIS, arriving at Naples in June and July respectively, the network quickly expanded to four multi-stop routes: Milan-Grosseto-Rome, Trieste-Venice-Florence-Rome, Rome-Naples-Palermo-Trapani-Pantelleria Island, and Rome-Naples-Reggio Calabria-Catania-Palermo, linking 12 destinations

ATI began operations with a fleet of Fokker F.27-200 turboprop aircraft (Piergiuliano Chesi)

Douglas DC-8-43 I-DIWT in the new Alitalia branding (Paul J Morton)

with 26 daily flights. ATI also operated the Rome-Naples-Rome service on behalf of the parent company.

In March 1966, ATI won the international tender for the management and operation of the domestic network of Kingdom of Libya Airlines (KLA), which the local airline wanted to improve and expand. Two F.27s, PH-FSD leased from Fokker and its own I-ATIS, together with flight and cabin crews, technical, administrative and operational personnel were dispatched to Tripoli, and ATI was also made responsible the provision of spares, and for line maintenance in Tripoli, although major overhauls were undertaken at Naples. Operations began on 15 June that year. Services operated on each day of the week, except Friday, which is the weekend in the Muslim world, linking Tripoli with Ghadames, Ghat, Sebha, Marsa Brega and Benghazi, where extensions were operated

to Beida, Tobruk and Kufrah, although not all destinations were served on each day. The F.27s were also serving Malta four times a week from Tripoli, as well as Djerba and Tunis in Tunisia twice a week, and later, Alexandria from Benghazi on Sundays only.

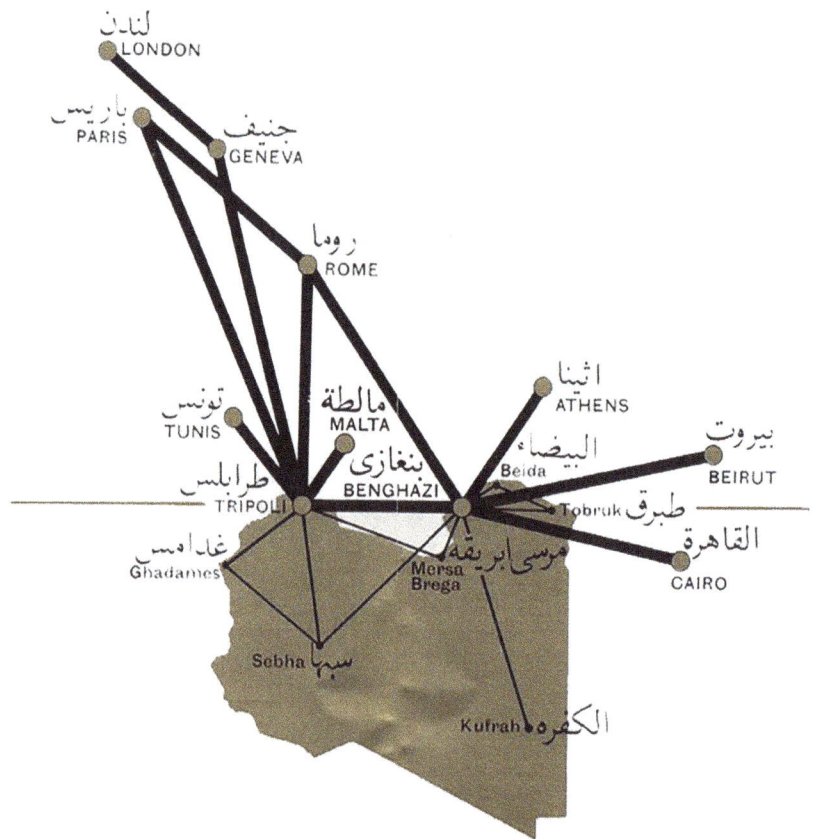

Kingdom of Libya Airlines (KLA) route network

ATI Fokker F.27-200 Friendship I-ATIM operated on behalf of Kingdom of Libya Airlines (David Parker Brown)

PH-FSD was returned to Fokker in May 1967 and replaced by I-ATIM. A third aircraft, I-ATIB, joined the KLA fleet in November 1968. US carrier Trans World Airlines (TWA) was contracted by KLA to provide an analysis of future equipment needs and its final report of 1968 recommended that the airline end the ATI F.27 leases, stating that ticket receipts from the domestic operation, where fares were kept low to enable more people to fly, were insufficient to recoup the cost of the lease deal. Nevertheless, ATI continued its services in Libya while KLA finalised arrangements for a new fleet, but the *coup d'etat* on 1 September 1969 that brought Muammar Quaddafi to power, ended the Italian airline's Libyan adventure.

ATI expansion

In the meantime, ATI had added a route down the Aegean from Venice to Ancona, Bari and Brindisi/Lecce, and from Bari to Tirana, Albania, and in August 1967, had taken over operational, technical and commercial management of helicopter operator Società Italiana Esercizio Elicotteri (Elivie), which had been established by Alitalia (62.5 per cent) and IRI (10.0 per cent) as ELI-Linee Italiane SpA as early as 23 November 1956 but did not start seasonal operations until 20 July 1959. Other participants in the initial capital of ITL 250 million were Fiat-Società per Azioni (14.5 per cent), Dr Lamberto Micangeli (12.0 per cent) and Alisud Compagnia Aerea Meridionale SpA (1.0 per cent). In 1967, the capital was fully written-off and the company recapitalised at ITL 400 million, now held by Alitalia (90 per cent) and IRI (10 per cent).

Operations had started with four Agusta-manufactured Bell 47J helicopters – I-EDUE, I-EQAT, I-ETRE and I-EUNO – linking Naples across the Gulf of Naples with the islands of Capri and Ischia twice a day. Services were flown from both, the Naples/Capodichino airport and from the downtown Marittima heliport on Piazza Municipio. Flights from the airport to the downtown heliport were co-ordinated to connect with all incoming and outgoing national and international flights. Passenger demand was light during the winter months between November and April, and spare capacity was leased out to charter and aerial work operators. A seasonal service was also flown in 1961 and 1962 with the newly-delivered Agusta A 102 between Turin downtown heliport and Milan/Malpensa, although this proved unsuccessful and was quickly discontinued. The fleet was later bolstered by five Agusta-Bell 204B and two Agusta-Bell 206A JetRanger helicopters.

A major improvement in equipment was implemented in 1968 with the acquisition of two Sikorsky S-61N, I-EVMA and I-EVME, configured for 26 passengers. Also that year, a seasonal service was added to Sorrento/Positano, picturesque towns along the rocky Amalfi Coast. A redistribution of

Agusta-Bell AB 47J Ranger I-EQAT in original Elivie paint scheme (Angelo Gialanella/Archive Ottogalli)

Agusta-Bell AB 102 I-ECIN pictured at the Vigna di Valle Museum (Angelo Gialanella/Archive Ottogalli)

Agusta-Bell AB 204B I-ENOV in new Elivie colours (Angelo Gialanella/Archive Ottogalli)

Agusta-Bell AB 206A JetRanger I-EVBA at Naples/Capodichino (Angelo Gialanella/Archive Ottogalli)

Alitalia and IRI shares resulted in full control of Elivie taken by ATI in 1969. ATI promptly added new services from Venice to Cortina d'Ampezzo, a winter sports resort in the Veneto region of the Dolomites, and from Naples to Catania on the Island of Sicily. On 14 January 1970, Elivie lost its AB 204B helicopter, I-EVCA, which crashed during an emergency landing on an oil platform in the Adriatic Sea during fog after leaving Ancona. All nine occupants lost their lives. Another AB 204B, I-EVCO, had already been damaged beyond repair at Pesaro on 1 December 1969, as was the AB 47J, I-ETRE, on landing at Naples on September 1969. These events probably hastened the company's demise, although continuing unprofitability was cited as the most valid reason, when Elivie was closed down on 30 June 1970. Aerial work on behalf of oil companies continued for another two years.

By 1971, the Fokker fleet had increased to 13 units, and ATI's first jet aircraft, the Douglas DC-9-32, was added in July 1969 and now numbered three units, I-ATIA, I-ATIK and I-ATIX. The initial cabin layout provided accommodation for 105 passengers, but ATI later increased capacity to 120 seats. The dense network criss-crossed Italy and now also included the towns and cities of Turin, Verona, Pisa; Catania and Comiso/Ragusa on the island of Sicily; Alghero-Sassari and Cagliari on the island of Sardinia, and the island of Lampedusa, bringing the total number of destinations to 25 radiating from all the major cities, and including the international service to Albania. Many of the multi-stop services, especially in the south, were promoted as *aèrobus*. A total of 1.8 million passengers were carried that year.

Sikorsky S-61N I-EVMA approaching Ischia Heliport (Angelo Gialanella/Archive Ottogalli)

Douglas DC-9-32 I-RIKT photographed at Düsseldorf (Konstantin von Wedelstaedt)

Three fatal accidents, together with the global fuel crisis dented ATI's progress. On 16 April 1972, the F.27-200, I-ATIP, lost altitude in poor weather with local thunderstorms and crashed into the ground near Ardinello di Amaseno on a service from Rome to Foggia. All 18 persons on board, three crew and 15 passengers, died. Later that year, on 30 October, another F.27-200, I-ATIR, struck a hillside near Poggiorsini on approach at night and limited visibility on descent into Bari, killing all three crew and 24 passengers. I-ATIT, with five crew and 31 passengers, had already been lost on 25 May 1969, when it struck a concrete embankment on the Agata River on approach to Reggio Calabria. One passenger was killed, and nine others were seriously injured. These setbacks were further compounded when F.27-200 - I-ATIS was hijacked between Trieste and Bari on 6 October 1972, although this incident was brought to a safe conclusion with the hijacker shot by the police.

These accidents highlighted deficiencies in the management of Italy's fast-growing aviation sector and, in 1973, ATI was entrusted by the *Amministrazione della Difesa* (Administration of Defence) for the NavAid Flight Inspection Service, the *Servizi di Radiomisure*, on behalf of the Aeronautica Militare. The service had been created within the air force in 1952, and became the *Centro Radiomisure* in the early 1960s, before another re-organisation created the *Reparto Radiomisure*. At the end of 1976, this became the 14th *Stormo* (Squadron). The Fokker F.27s, which were being phased out as more DC-9s were delivered, were considered ideal for this service on behalf of the military. Three F.27 aircraft, the F.27-200 I-ATIC, and I-ATIC and I-ATIN, both F.27-600 models, were deployed and modified with a ventral antenna under the fuselage, and a manual flight inspection system installed in the cabin, now devoid of all passenger seating. This equipment enabled control to be maintained

Fokker F.27-600 employed on navaids flight inspection (John Visanich)

154

RETE ATI
ATI NETWORK

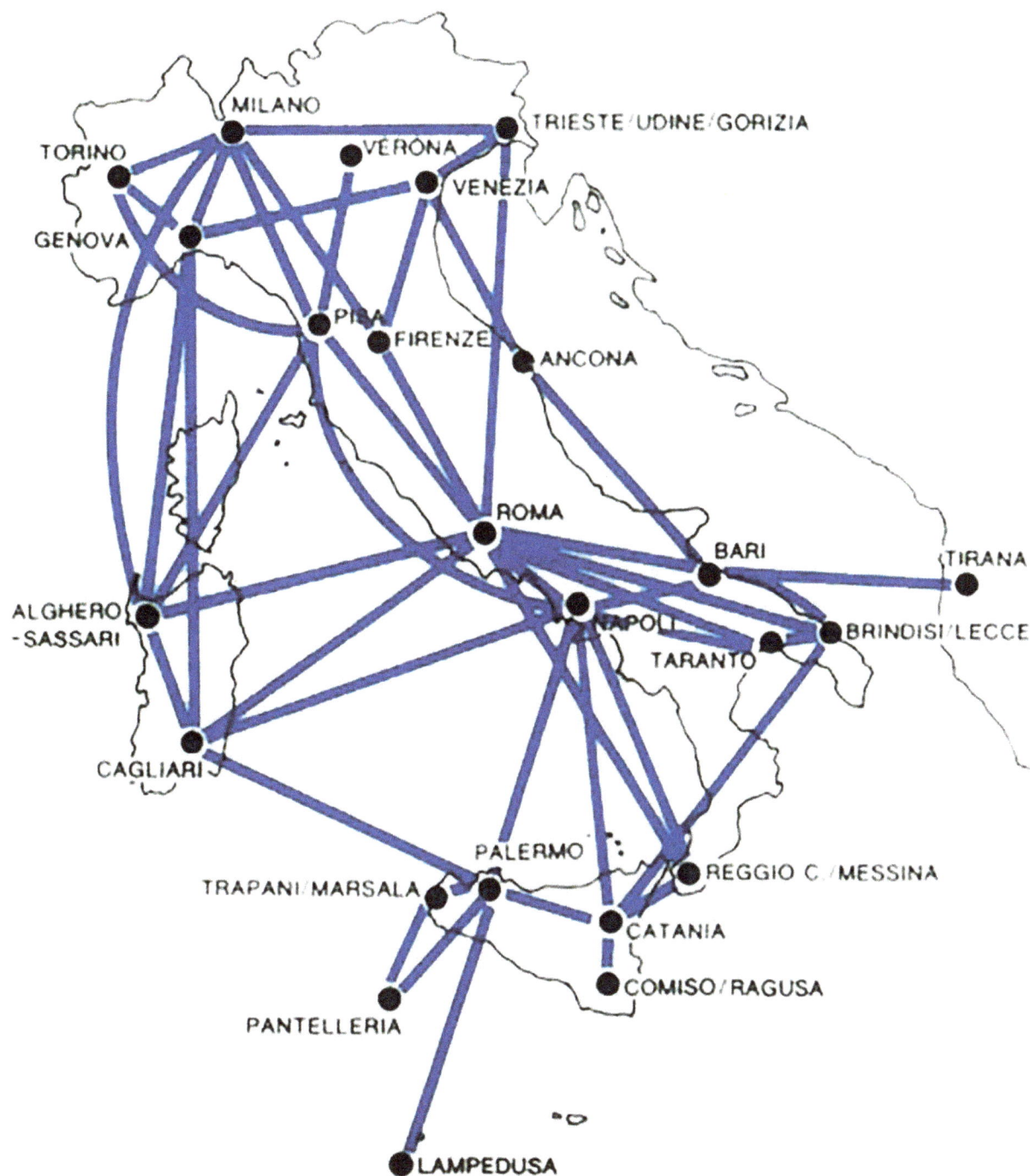

A map of Italy showing the ATI network with the following destinations connected by routes: MILANO, TORINO, GENOVA, VERONA, VENEZIA, TRIESTE/UDINE/GORIZIA, PISA, FIRENZE, ANCONA, ROMA, BARI, TIRANA, ALGHERO-SASSARI, NAPOLI, BRINDISI/LECCE, TARANTO, CAGLIARI, PALERMO, REGGIO C./MESSINA, TRAPANI/MARSALA, CATANIA, COMISO/RAGUSA, PANTELLERIA, LAMPEDUSA

McDonnell Douglas MD-82 I-DANG in hybrid Alitalia/ATI colourscheme (Aldo Bidini)

of the ground stations and provide radio assistance for flight and navigation. ATI provided this service for 10 years, but in 1985, the Italian Government divided the responsibility between the military (*14th Stormo*) and the civil air traffic control agency, founded by presidential decree on 24 March 1981, then known as *Azienda Autonoma di Assistenza al Volo e al Traffico Generale* (Company for Flight Assistance and General Traffic/AAAVTAG), which later became ENAV.

Having concentrated entirely on its scheduled domestic services, the expansion of the fleet with more DC-9-32s arriving every year, provided the extra capacity for ATI to embark on charter flights in 1974. While these principally served the German and United Kingdom markets and holiday destinations along the Mediterranean at first, this aspect of the airline's operation soon expanded into longer flights to Africa. However, the loss of DC-9-32, I-ATJC, brought more unwelcome publicity. On 14 September 1979, I-ATJC took of from Alghero, Sardinia bound for Rome/Fiumicino, with a planned stop at Cagliari on the southern part of the island. As a result of wrong or misinterpreted instructions from air traffic control, the aircraft hit the rocky mountainside of Conca d'Oru near Sarroch at an altitude of 610 m (2,000 ft) with the lower part of the fuselage, causing the aircraft to break up and cause a fire. The impact was 18 km (11 miles) south-west of Cagliari Airport. All four crew and 27 passengers perished in this tragedy.

Convoluted consolidation

Meanwhile, the privately-supported Itavia, had started operations on 15 July 1959 over a small domestic network with a single de Havilland D.H.104 Dove, soon supported by six de Havilland D.H.114 Heron. The British-built aircraft were replaced in 1962 by four Douglas DC-3, and the airline became an established scheduled and charter

operator with a substantial Douglas DC-9 and Fokker F.28 Fellowship fleet. However, its fortunes ebbed and flowed throughout its history and, following a number of controversial accidents, including the crash of Douglas DC-9-15, I-TIGI, on 27 June 1980, in the Tyrrhenian Sea while flying from Bologna to Palermo, with the loss of all 81 people on board, probably due to a bomb on board or a missile strike, forced the airline to cease operations on 10 December 1980. Rather than absorbing Itavia's assets into ATI, Alitalia (55 per cent) and ATI (45 per cent) formed a new company, Aermediterranea-Linee Aeree Mediterranee SpA, on 20 March 1981, at the instigation of the then Minister of Transport, Rino Formica.

AERMEDITERRANEA

After the revocation of Itavia's air operator's certificate, all flight crew were transferred to Aermediterranea and services were begun on 1 July that year, with two Douglas DC-9-32 twinjets, I-DIBO *Conca d'Oro*, and I-DIZF *Dolomiti*, from Rome and Milan. Aermediterranea quickly re-established the former Itavia network of 22 domestic cities with a DC-9-32 fleet that soon increased to eight aircraft. International passenger and cargo charters were introduced within Europe and to North Africa and the Near East on 1 April 1982, but the airline's ambitions went much further. In 1983, an application was made to the US authorities for authorisation to commence charter services across Atlantic, stating that it would carry 20,000 passengers on its proposed 1984 Italy-US operation, on which it intended to use Boeing 747 and Douglas DC-10 aircraft maintained by Alitalia in Rome. Having been found financially and operationally fit,

Aermediterranea Douglas DC-9-32 I-DIZF, one of eight operated in its short history

the Civil Aeronautics Board (CAB) granted an air operator's certificate to Aermediterranea on 5 January 1984, subject to reciprocal arrangements for US charter traffic to Italy. The AOC was to be effective from 14 February and was valid for five years. This was never implemented, and the inefficient duplication on short-medium-haul charter operations resulted in a mutual agreement to merge Aermediterranea back into ATI. The full integration was completed on 1 April 1985.

ATI was now faced with a significantly increased network and a burgeoning charter market and persuaded its majority owner that it would need additional DC-9-32 aircraft, as well as a brand-new fleet of the higher-capacity McDonnell Douglas MD-82, configured for 172 passengers in single-class, which, by 1992, had grown to 40 in total. The first MD-82, I-DAWJ, entered service on 8 April 1985. Ten 48-seat ATR 42-300 turboprop aircraft were also acquired for less dense routes and those destinations with limiting runway capacity, with the first, I-ATRB *Ravello*, entering

service on 10 July 1986. On a flight from Milan/Linate to Cologne in Germany, the ATR 42-300, I-ATRH *Verona*, crashed nose down into the 700 m (2,300 ft) high Conca di Crezzo after an uncontrolled descent on 15 October 1987, killing all three crew and 34 passengers. Icing conditions existed.

ATI's 30-year history came to an end when it was absorbed into the Alitalia operation on 30 October 1994. A shareholders' meeting on the previous 25 July, had unanimously agreed to this move, convinced that elimination of duplication and overlaps between the two companies would generate savings of several billions of lire a year. The reintegration, while it proceeded, did not go down well with the various unions, with the pilots particularly fearing redundancies and their chances of advancement. Talks were held between the airline and the Minister of Transport, Publio Fiori, to clarify the situation, but these did not change the outcome.

The ATR 42-300 twin-turboprop aircraft was operated on less dense routes (Michel Gilliand)

Twin-engined Piaggio P.166DL-3 at Malta (Peter Tonna)

SIAI-Marchetti SF260C light training aircraft

Piper PA-420-720 Cheyenne IIIA (Peter Bakema)

Fast forward

For 10 years after its establishment, Alitalia had been able to use the training facilities of British European Airways (BEA) and British Overseas Airways Corporation (BOAC) to ensure a sufficient supply of pilots as its operation was growing. With the imminent arrival of new jet aircraft and a significant increase in traffic, Alitalia decided that it would be more cost-efficient to establish its own flying school and placed an order for four Aermacchi MB.326 two-seat jet trainers that had entered service with the Aeronautica Militare's flying school at Lecce. The MB.326D was a dedicated civilianized version for Alitalia, equipped with navigation and communications systems tailored, including a Collins VHF omni-directional radio range localizer, instrument landing system and automatic direction-finding, Bendix radio magnetic indicator, Sperry pictorial deviation indicator, and a dual Collins VHF radio kit.

The Centro di Addestramento di Brindisi (Training Centre at Brindisi) became operational on 1 July 1963 and training commenced of 105 cadets, who had been assessed at the Centro Addestramento Alitalia at Rome/Fiumicino. The first MB.328D, I-ADIA, arrived in Brindisi on 27 May 1963, followed by I-ADIE on 3 June, I-ADIO on 8 July, with deliveries completed by I-ADIU on 16 July. The average duration of the training procedure was some 18 months, and included 80 one-hour missions, of which 68 were with an instructor and 12 solo, both undertaken during day and night. Upon completion, the successful graduates had to do their military service, which had been deferred, to gain experience as air force pilots, before being able to join the airline initially as navigators on the Douglas DC-8, third pilots on the Caravelle, or co-pilots on the Viscount turboprop.

The MB.326D provided excellent performance and good reliability. Apart from an isolated wheels-up landing, only one was involved in a serious accident, which cost the life of a student and caused the destruction of the aircraft. On 12 December 1966, during a solo night training sortie, I-ATIA flew into the ground near Cellino San Marco. In 1967, economic realities forced Alitalia to close down its flying school. During 10 courses at Brindisi, with more than 20,000 hours flown, 200 pilots were qualified. The remaining three aircraft were handed over to the Aeronautica Militare Italiane, which had a large training operation and spare capacity and agreed to train 30 Alitalia pilots each year. The MB.326Ds were assigned military serials MM54266, MM54267 and MM54268.

A shortage of pilots to meet increasing demand forced Alitalia to re-establish a flying school in 1980. Based at Alghero on the island of Sardinia, the school was equipped with four three-seat, single-engined SIAI-Marchetti SF.260C light trainers and two twin-engined Piaggio P.166DL-3 utility aircraft. The fleet was boosted in 1987 by three twin-engined Piper PA-42-720 Cheyenne IIIA and more SF-260s. However, air traffic slumped following the September 2001 terrorist attacks and took many years to recover, leaving Alitalia no choice but to slowly wind down its training programme, and the school was finally closed in 2007.

Douglas DC-9-32 I-DIBN *Isola di Palmaria* at Rome Fiumicino (Jon Proctor)

All-jet fleet

Having successfully integrated the Douglas DC-8 into its long-haul network, Alitalia decided to remain with the US manufacturer to replace its Viscount turboprops and Caravelle jets on its short/medium-haul routes, and placed a large order for the DC-9-32. It had faced a strong lobbying by the British to buy the similar BAC 11-500 twinjet, but the Douglas counter-offer, which included an agreement for the Naples-based airframer, Aerfer, to build fuselage panels for all DC-9 throughout the production cycle, swung the decision towards the Long Beach, California company. The first DC-9 aircraft, I-DIKA *Isola di Capri*, was delivered on 8 August 1967. By the time, the Vickers Viscount operated the last flight in December 1968, leaving Alitalia an all-jet operator, the airline had already taken delivery of over 20 of the new Douglas twinjets, including three DC-9-32F freighters. The DC-9-32 was a single-aisle airliner powered by two rear-mounted 54.5 kN (12,250 lb) Pratt & Whitney JT8D-9A turbofan engines and offered a range of up to 2,800 km. In Alitalia service, the aircraft was configured in either a 102-seat two-class layout, or for 123 passengers in economy.

Alitalia also boosted its long-haul fleet by signing an order in 1966 for four stretched McDonnel Douglas DC-8-62 airliners, capable of carrying a full payload of 289 passengers over a distance of 9,650 km. The first two,

I-DIWN *Giuseppe Verdi*, and I-DIWJ *Antonio Vivaldi*, were delivered on 28 October 1967 and 26 July 1968 respectively. Also part of the initial order were two DC-8-62CF-H convertible freighters. The DC-8-62 incorporated various improvements over earlier models, including increased wingspan and modifications to the engine pylons and nacelles for reduced drag, and increased fuel capacity. Alitalia's fleet, which totalled 10 aircraft, comprised the basic -62 with four 80 kN (18,000 lb) Pratt & Whitney JT3D-3B turbofans, and the -62H and -62CF-H with increased take-off weight of 136.080 kg and more powerful 84.5 kN (19,000 b) JT3D-7 engines.

The DC-8-62 fleet, configured for 20 first-class and 138 economy-class passengers, was mostly deployed on the extensive South American network, which included services from Milan/Malpensa to Buenos Aires, Montevideo, Rio de Janeiro, São Paulo and Santiago de Chile, and from Rome and Milan/Malpensa to Caracas and Lima. They also saw service on the routes to Chicago, Philadelphia, Johannesburg and Tehran, and operated the first trans-polar flight in April 1970 from Italy to Tokyo via Anchorage.

Other notable events were the order for four Boeing 747-100 wide-body jets, including one freighter, in April 1966, and Alitalia's participation with its acclaimed engineering facility in the ATLAS purchasing and maintenance consortium, to co-ordinate activities across

Douglas DC-9-32 I-RIZR *Marche* (Aldo Bidini)

Alitalia's first McDonnell Douglas DC-8-62 I-DIWN *Guiseppe Verdi* delivered in October 1967

The same DC-8-62 I-DIWN in the new colours adopted in 1969 (Guido Allieri)

Boeing 747-100 I-DEMA *Neil Armstrong* was put onto the Rome-New York service in June 1970 (Alain Durand)

Boeing 747-200B I-DEMB *Carlo del Prete* differed from the other early Pratt & Whitney-powered aircraft by having eight upper deck windows instead of three (Aldo Bidini)

Boeing 747-200B Combi I-DEMF *Portofino* celebrating the 90th anniversary of Italy's famous chocolate confectionary company Perugina (Perry Hoppe)

members' wide-body fleet. The ATLAS consortium also included Air France, Lufthansa and Sabena. At the same time, Alitalia was the first airline to introduce an automatic passenger reservation system with video terminals, which it named ARCO. Based on three IBM 360/65 processing units, ARCO administered the total passenger seat capacity offered by Alitalia on its worldwide network, which in 1968, already exceeded 11 billion passenger/km. The first Alitalia reservations office to come on line was Naples, which started processing passenger reservations through ARCO on 12 March 1968. The ARCO network was soon expanded to cover Rome, Milan, Venice, Turin, Genoa, Catania and Palermo in Italy, and international destinations in Europe and North America. In February 1972, the system was expanded to include cargo reservations, again making Alitalia the first airline to offer this facility. When becoming an all-jet airline on 1 January 1969, Landor Associates created a new corporate identity by replacing its traditional winged arrow with a highly visible stylised 'A', with the colours of the national flag, and shaped to fit perfectly on the aircraft tail. Capital letters were replaced with lower case, and green was made the dominant colour.

The first four-engined Boeing 747-100A, I-DEMA *Neil Armstrong,* was delivered on 13 May 1970 and entered

service between Rome and New York on 5 June, closely followed into service by the second aircraft, I-DEME *Arturo Ferrarin,* on 16 July. A first batch of five was completed with deliveries of three 747-200B over the next two years. All five were powered by the Pratt & Whitney JT9D-7 turbofan engines and provided accommodation in Alitalia service for 382 passengers, with 18 in first class and 364 in economy. Visually, the two types were almost identical, having three upper deck windows on each side to allow for upstairs lounge areas. Only I-DEMB *Carlo del Prete* differed with having eight upper deck windows. The 747-200B also had more powerful engines and increased fuel capacity for greater range. Alitalia operated with these early aircraft for nearly a decade, until the first batch of eight General Electric CF6-50E2-powered 747-200B, including three 747-200B Combi aircraft, were taken into service in 1980 and 1981. The first was I-DEMC *Taormina,* delivered on 26 November 1980. After that a number of small top-up orders, all with General Electric engines, brought the total numbers to nineteen. On 16 March 2000, Alitalia placed an order for five of the substantially improved 747-400, but this was never fulfilled, although the airline leased a 747-400F Freighter, N409C, from Atlas Air between1 July 2000 and 1 January 2002.

African adventure

In the mid-1960s, Alitalia embarked on two adventures in Africa in two different nations, both of which had recently proclaimed independence.

Zambia Airways was officially incorporated on 1 September 1967 as the flag carrier, taking over a company of that same name that had been a subsidiary of the dissolved CAA-Central African Airways. The network was domestic-only and used Douglas DC 3 and de Havilland Canada DHC-2 Beaver light aircraft. Alitalia was chosen to provide assistance from both managerial and technical point of view, and the first general manager, Francesco

Casale, was an employee of Alitalia. The first flights to Kenya, Malawi, Tanzania and Zaire began on 1 January 1968 with BAC 111-400 twinjets originally ordered by CAA and never delivered because of Southern Rhodesia's UDI. In November, a fully-staffed Alitalia DC 8-40 began operations along the weekly Lusaka-Nairobi-Rome-London route, and a second shorter intercontinental weekly route - Lusaka-Rome-London - was added in February 1970 after an Alitalia DC 8-40 was fully leased by Zambia Airways and re-registered 9J-ABR (ex I-DIWE). In the years following, the collaborative relationship with Alitalia weakened until it had ceased altogether by the beginning of 1976.

Somaliland had been an Italian colony until it was occupied by British armed forces in February 1941 during the Second World War. Given the previous long relationship, on 21 November 1949, the United Nations Organization entrusted Italy with the territory trusteeship to prepare it for full independence, which took place on July 1, 1960. The Somali Republic was formed by the union of the territory administered by Italy with British Somaliland. Somali Airlines was formed on 9 March 1964 as a 50 per cent partnership between the government and Alitalia, the

latter also providing operational and technical assistance, initially contracted for five years. The first scheduled flight took place on 7 July between the capital Mogadishu and Hargeisa, the capital of the former British Somaliland, with one of the four DC 3 aircraft previously presented by the US government. In September, a modest network of internal connections was already in operation, while in March the following year, the first international connection was opened to Aden, in pool with Aden Airways. In August 1968 and June 1969, Alitalia sold two VickersViscount 700 turboprops, 60S-AAJ (ex I-LIRP) and 60S-AAK (ex I-LIFE), to improve both domestic and international networks. Unfortunately, 60S-AAJ, was lost on 6 May 1970 when, after an on-board fire, the four-engined aircraft made a hard landing at Mogadishu airport and crashed. It was replaced by another former Alitalia Viscount, 60S-SAN (ex I-LIRC), the following December.

The different political situation in the country after Siad Barre took power in October 1969, the progressive approach to the Soviet Union, and the first armed skirmishes with Ethiopia, put an end to Alitalia's involvement in the airline and in 1977, the government bought all the Alitalia shares.

Alitalia's Douglas DC-8-43 I-DIWE was leased to Zambia Airways and reregistered 9J-ABR

Somali Airlines Vickers Viscount 60S-AAK, ex I-LIFE (Clinton Groves)

Alitalia Cargo

Cargo had become an increasingly important aspect of Alitalia's operations, especially on the North Atlantic, which had almost doubled between 1959 and 1961. To maximise advantage in this most profitable sector, two DC-7C, I-DUVA and I-DUVE, were converted to freighters by Lockheed in 1961 at a cost of USD 250,000 each, with two large freight doors on the port side and a payload capacity of 13.6 tonnes. Both were disposed of to Airlift International on 25 March 1966. On 31 October 1962, Alitalia took over the two Curtiss C-46A Commando, I-SILA and I-SILV, from SAM, which began three weekly flights from Rome to Milan and Frankfurt, and from Rome to Tripoli on 1 November. Flights were timed to

meet the Douglas DC-7C services from Rome and Milan to New York. The two C-46A were sold to American Air Export and Import Company (AAXICO) on 17 July 1968, being the last piston-engined airliners in the Alitalia fleet.

Cargo capacity was quickly replaced in 1968 with the introduction of three Douglas DC-9-32F and two DC-8-62CF. The first DC-8-62CF-H, I-DIWC *Titano*, arrived in Rome on 10 April 1968, followed by I-DIWQ *Ciclope* on 30 June that same year. In all-freighter configuration, the DC-8-62CF-H offered a total capacity of 38,000 kg, with 153.44 m³ usable space in the main cabin for 13 standard pallets, and 45.4 m³ usable space in the four underfloor cargo compartments. The first DC-9-32F, I-DIKF *Atlante*, was delivered on 3 May 1968, followed

Curtiss C-46A Commando I-SILA was taken over from SAM

Alitalia Cargo Douglas DC-9-32F I-DIBK *Ercole* at Turin (Tom Singfield)

Alitalia Cargo System McDonnell Douglas DC-8-62H I-DIWQ *Ciclope* (Guido Allieri)

Boeing 747-200B I-DEMC *Taormina* (Paul Spijkers)

Alitalia Cargo System DC-8-62CF-H I-DIWQ

by I-DIKG *Anteo*, which joined the fleet six days later, and I-DIBK *Ercole*, delivered on 12 February 1969. The DC-9-32F, for which Alitalia was the first customer, was equipped with a large 3.45 x 2.06 m forward cargo door and strengthened floor, and provided a 70.4 m³ cargo space in the main cabin, which, together with the 25.3 m³ underfloor hold, enabled it to carry eight full cargo pallets and two half-pallets, for a total payload capacity of 15,000 kg. All windows were removed.

Its new jet fleet enabled Alitalia to operate extensive all-cargo services, with the DC-8 scheduled on the Rome-Milan-Boston-New York, and Milan-Rome-Tripoli-Mogadishu-Nairobi-Lusaka routes. DC-9-32F routes included Rome-Milan, Milan-Turin, Rome-Milan-Frankfurt, Rome-Milan-London, Rome-Milan-Paris and Milan-Brussels-Amsterdam. The Rome-Milan service was for a time shared by SAM's DC-6A, I-DIMB and I-DIMU, which also flew from Rome to Tripoli and Benghazi, and from Milan to Copenhagen. The DC-8-62CF-H and DC9-32F were withdrawn from service in 1981and replaced with the Boeing 747.

Alitalia took delivery of its only new Boeing 747-200F(SCD), I-DEMR *Stresa/Titano*, on 18 December 1981. It was the longest-serving 747 in the fleet, making its last flight on 15 February 2004. Boeing 747-200B, I-DEMC *Taormina*, served as a passenger aircraft from 26 November 1980 until converted into a freighter in February 1994. It was used by Alitalia Cargo System for 10 years, before being sold to AirBridgeCargo on 20 September 2004 after storage. I-DEMW *Spoleto*, was also active with Alitalia Cargo for 10 years before it was given to Atlas Air for conversion to a freighter. It was then leased again by Alitalia as N518MC as a cargo aircraft between April 2002 and 11 December 2003. Other leases from Atlas Air were 747-200F, N536MC, from 15 March 2003 to 10 April 2006, and 747-400F, N409MC, from July 2000 to January 2002. Boeing 747-200F, I-DEMX *Ciclope*, was leased from Lufthansa, ex D-ABYZ, between 21 May 1992 and 29 February 1994. The 747-200F has a volumetric loading capacity of 759m³ and a maximum payload of 111,583kg. The raised cockpit allows front loading of cargo. Range with maximum payload was 5,680km.

The Atlas Air Boeing 747-400F N409MC was leased by Alitalia for eighteen months from July 2000 (Konstantin von Wedelstaedt)

McDonnell Douglas MD-11F EI-UPI at Mumbai's Chhatrapati Shivaji International Airport (Sean D Silva)

In March 2005, Alitalia took into service the first of five McDonnell Douglas MD-11F freighters, converted at Venice by Aeronavali, by then already an Alenia subsidiary, from the airline's MD-11C Combis. The five aircraft were I-DUPA *Teatro all Scala/Giaocchino Rossi*, I-DUPE *Arena di Verona/Giuseppe Verdi*, I-DUPI *Fontana di Trevi/Giacomo Puccini*, I-DUPO *Canal Grande/Nicoló Paganini,* and I-DUPU *Ponte Vecchio/Antonio Vivaldi.* However, the financial crisis of 2008 made them uneconomical to operate and all were taken out of service in January 2009 and disposed of. The MD-11F retained the unusual 3.6 x 2.6m rear cargo door of the Combi version, but had all windows removed. The main deck provided a cargo volume of 440 m^3 and could accommodate 26 standard pallets or containers. Together with another 10 pallets or containers in the lower cargo hold, this added up to a maximum payload of 90,000 kg.

After the sale of the MD-11F fleet, Alitalia transported all cargo in the belly-hold of its passenger fleet and, later, also through Air France and KLM Royal Dutch Airlines. Although the privately-owned, Milan/Malpensa-based Cargoitalia tried to plug the gap from July 2009 and had plans to order five A330-200F freighters, it ceased operations on 21 December 2011, leaving much of the Italian cargo market, Europe's third-largest, in the hands of Cargolux Italia and Lufthansa. The potential of the market was recognised by Etihad Airways, when it acquired a 49 per cent stake in 2014 and made the revitalisation of Alitalia cargo a priority, especially based at Milan/Malpensa, but the word cargo was strikingly absent when it announced its strategic plan on 21 January 2015. Alitalia continued using the belly-hold of its passenger aircraft.

Amidst the Corona Virus pandemic, when passenger traffic declined, Alitalia converted two of its Boeing 777-200(ER) passenger aircraft, EI-ISD and EI-WLA, to freighters. EI-ISD operated its first cargo flight on 3 July 2020 between Rome and New York/JFK, having made its last passenger flight on 13 June from Palermo to Rome. EI-WLA operated its first cargo service between Rome and Mumbai on 20 June 2020 and from New York/JFK to Milan/Malpensa on 10 October. On 9 October, EI-ISD uplifted a record 57, 616 kg of cargo on a single flight from Delhi to Rome, the highest ever tonnage to be carried on the 777-200(ER). Alitalia began operating the weekly cargo only flights from India on 20 June 2020 from Mumbai and Delhi. Typical load comprised heavy automotive and engineering equipment, together with garments and spare parts, as well as pharmaceuticals, having received the CEIV Pharma (Centre of Excellence for Independent Validators in Pharmaceutical Logistics) certification from the International Air Transport Association (IATA) in November 2019.

The famous Norge airship taking off from Ciampino

The Rome Airports
Urbe (Littorio), Ciampino and Fiumicino

The first truly civilian airport was Urbe, in the northern outskirts of the city, then known as Aeroporto del Littorio, which was inaugurated in the presence of Benito Mussolini and Italo Balbo in 1928. All flights to and from Rome used Littorio, which served as the main base of Ala Littoria from 1934 well into the Second World War. However, the airport suffered heavy bombardment in 1943, but, after hasty reconstruction at the end of the war, it was renamed and re-activated as the main civil airport until all commercial flights were transferred to Ciampino in 1950. Since then, Urbe has hosted mainly flying club activities, and private, air taxi and helicopter flights, which continue to this day. Also based at the airport is the Corpo Forestale del Stato (CFS, Italian Forestry Service), an armed corps, which manages a fleet of aircraft for firefighting and early spotting of wildfires. Urbe has a single 1,084 m runway.

Ciampino G B Pastine International is Rome's oldest airport, whose history goes back to 1916, when it began its long life as a military airbase and home to regular airship flights. It was on 10 April 1926, that Umberto Nobile took off from the airport on the airship Norge, the first aircraft to reach the North Pole and the first to fly across the polar ice cap from Europe to North America. Ciampino was captured by the Allied forces in June 1944 and became a base for the United States Army Air Force (USAAF), primarily as a transport

base by the Douglas C-47 Skytrain aircraft of the 64th Troop Carrier Group. North American A-36 Apache combat aircraft were also flown from the airport, but when this ceased, it was used by the Air Transport Command as a major transhipment hub for cargo, transiting of aircraft and personnel for the remainder of the war. In July 1947, it became Rome's main airport after taking over all commercial flights from Urbe but this ended with the official inauguration of Fiumicino Leonardo da Vinci International on 15 January 1961. Today, Ciampino remains an important hub for low-cost carriers, domestic and charter flights and general aviation traffic, recording an annual passenger throughput of nearly 6 million on its single 2,208 m runway. The airport also serves the military and is the headquarters of 31° Stormo and 2nd Reparto Genio of the Italian Air Force. It also hosts a fleet of Bombardier 415 aerial firefighting aircraft managed by SOREM. The airport is named after Giovan Battista Pastine, an Italian airship pilot who served in World War I.

Rome Fiumicino International Leonardo da Vinci is the major international airport, one of the busiest in Europe with 43.5 million passengers annually, and was the main hub of Alitalia. The new airport was a merger between two designs and the final project was approved in August 1958. Although not officially opened until 15 January 1961, with the landing of a Trans World Airlines (TWA) Lockheed Super Constellation from New York, it had already come into use on 20 August 1960, to help relieve the increased traffic experienced

Rome Fiumicino Leonardo da Vinci International

during the Summer Olympics. When it opened, it had two runways of 3,800 m and 3,900 m in length, but a third, 3.900 m long was added in 1973, as were hangars and maintenance centres under a heavy investment programme by Alitalia. The airport eventually had three terminals and, in 2004, inaugurated its Cargo City. A dedicated fast railway line connecting it with the Rome city centre was opened to the public on 27 May 1990. The airport suffered two tragic events, both through terrorist attacks. In the first, on 17 December 1973, Palestinian gunmen stormed the terminal, took hostages and firebombed a Pan American Boeing 707-320B, killing 30 persons on the aircraft and two in the terminal. On 27 December 1985, seven Arab terrorists walked up to the ticket counter shared by Israel's El Al Airlines and TWA, and fired assault rifles and threw grenades, killing 16 and wounding 99 people. The airport authority, Aeroporti di Roma, has several plans for the long-term development of the airport, the major one being the Masterplan Fiumicino Nord, which envisages a new terminal, two new runways, additional aircraft aprons and a new system of taxiways to allow a smooth flow of aircraft, to bring the annual passenger capacity to 100 million. Also planned is a 50-hectare environmental park.

Ciampino G B Pastine International is Rome's oldest airport

Testing Times

Since its inception, Alitalia had been competently guided by pilot, engineer and businessman Bruno Velani (CEO from 1964), but his departure in 1973 heralded a change of fortune. The 1970s would prove challenging for Alitalia and indeed, many other carriers. The excitement of the big new Boeings was tempered by the doubling of capacity they afforded, especially on premium routes such as the North Atlantic; overall traffic growth was halved over the previous decade. Alitalia responded by rejecting the new round of increased IATA fares and promoting lower fare packages between Rome and New York, but the results were disappointing.

Then came the 1973 fuel crisis leading to severe financial losses. A new CEO initiated a drastic plan to retire a significant proportion of the DC-8 and Caravelle fleets and a subsequent recapitalisation wrote off all debts and made the state the majority shareholder. At the same time the country's economy was in trouble and the civil aviation sector was not immune from numerous strikes inspired by strong leftist unions. Remedies included a radical shake-up of the airline's top-heavy management and redirecting long-haul capacity towards the Middle East, Asia, Australia and South America.

Alitalia's approach to its problems was fleet modernisation and product overhaul, particularly addressing poor punctuality. Having had a satisfactory operating experience with its DC-8 and DC-9 fleets, it came as no surprise when Alitalia ordered the McDonnell Douglas DC-10-30 to supplement the larger 747 on the thinner long-haul routes. The airline signed a contract in June 1970 for four aircraft plus six options, only four of which were taken up. In the meantime, McDonnell Douglas had entrusted Aeritalia (born out of the merger of Aerfer and the Fiat Aviation Division) with the task of manufacturing the trijet's fuselage panels. The eight aircraft were delivered between 6 February 1973 and 5 May 1975, with the first, I-DYNA *Galileo Galilei*, entering service between Rome and South America on 1 April 1973. The type also quickly replaced the DC-8-62 on the services to Tokyo and Johannesburg, but had a relatively short life with the airline, as Alitalia decided to standardise on the new wave of the Boeing 747 and all DC-10 aircraft were progressively withdrawn from 1985. The last aircraft, I-DYNE *Dante Alighieri*, left for Eastern Air lines in the US on 15 January 1986. The DC-10 was designed to replace the DC-8 for long-range flights. Powered by three 226.85 kN (51,000 lb) General Electric CF6-50C2 turbofan engines, with two on underwing pylons and the third at the base of the vertical stabiliser, it had a maximum speed of 940 km/h (Mach 0.88) and a typical range of 9,600 km. In Alitalia service it was configured for 242 passengers, with 38 in business-class and 204 in economy.

In spite of a poor reputation of the type for early crashes, the DC-10 was safely operated by Alitalia throughout its service life, although one incident is worth recalling. After leaving Johannesburg to Rome via Nairobi on 5 October 1973, the DC-10-30 I-DYNA, flown by Captain Carlo Frappi and First Officer Fulvio Chianese, encountered a storm about halfway to Nairobi, when the flight crew noticed fluctuations in the No.3 engine followed by substantial vibrations. When the cabin crew noticed flames coming out of the engine, Frappi shut it down. After an amber warning light that had indicated a partial fire at No.2 engine proved false, the flight proceeded normally, only to be replaced by high temperatures in two hydraulic pumps, followed by total loss of fluid in the No.2 system. No.3

The McDonnell Douglas DC-10-30 I-DYNA *Galilieo Galilei* entered service on 1 April 1973 (Alain Durand)

Eighteen Boeing 727-200 joined the Alitalia fleet but were operated only for a few years (Alain Durand)

engine was shut down to prevent damage to the turbine and now, only one hydraulic system was operating. Although the aircraft had difficulty in banking as flight controls were locked and not responding, Frappi managed to land it safely at Nairobi's Embakasi International at 2 am on 6 October.

Engineers were due to be sent to Nairobi from Rome, and a spare CF6 engine was expected to be delivered by a French Bristol Freighter cargo aircraft, but this got caught up in the Yom Kippur War that started that same day as Tunisia, Libya and Egypt closed their airspace and it never arrived. A spare engine, together with 25 engineers, arrived from

Rome in a Douglas DC-8 on 12 October, and the engineers proceeded to replace No.3 engine and repair the hydraulic system, giving the all-clear two days later. After climbing out of Nairobi on 14 October, the No.1 engine EGT was higher than the other two, and was shut down after two hours. Having negotiated the Sahara and Mediterranean and passed Caraffa di Catanzaro village inbound to Ponza, the crew noticed a drop of the RPM in No.3 engine, which went all the way to zero. All attempts to restart No.1 engine failed, but the aircraft was brought down safely at Rome/Fiumicino on only one engine. A satisfactory conclusion to

McDonnell Douglas MD-82 taking off from Perugia

a difficult flight, negotiated with skill by the flight crew and the two onboard engineers, Miglione and D'Ettore.

There was also a need to find a new medium-range jet to fill the gap between the DC-9 and DC-8-40. The DC-8 also needed replacing, as did the smaller Caravelle twinjet. Alitalia evaluated and deliberated between the new Airbus A300 wide-body, the DC-9-50, and the Boeing 727-200 Advanced. Given the foreseeable Italian aerospace's involvement in Boeing's projected 7X7, later to become the Boeing 767, the Airbus was not a high priority at the time and, to the surprise of many, Alitalia opted for the Boeing jet. Boeing's willingness to take seven DC-8-40 in part exchange and commonality of the JT8D engine with its DC-9-30 fleet, may have swung the decision in Boeing's favour. Alitalia placed an order for seven aircraft, with all seven delivered in 1976, the first, I-DIRA *Città di Gubbio,* arriving on 7 October 1976. Powered by three rear-mounted 77 kN (17,400 lb) Pratt & Whitney low-bypass turbofan engines, the 727-200 Advanced had a good short-field performance and a range of 4,720 km. Other distinguishing features were an integral rear airstair and an auxiliary power unit (APU), which provided independence from ground facilities. In Alitalia service it carried 155 passengers in a two-class arrangement, or 181 in all-economy. A further 11 727-200 aircraft were acquired in 1978/79. In a startling move, in early 1982, Alitalia accepted an offer in 1982 from McDonnell Douglas to replace the 727 with the MD-82. An option for 30 MD-82 was signed on 3 November 1982, some of them to be operated by ATI subsidiary. Again, a sub-contract for the manufacture of fuselage panels by Aeritalia at Naples, had a persuasive effect. The trijets were removed from service, even though they were only a few years old, the last one, I-DIRS *Città di Sulmona,* leaving the fleet on 2 May 1985.

By that time, the first 16 MD-82 had already been delivered, starting with I-DAWA *Roma* on 9 December 1983. By 31 March 1995, the fleet had grown to a substantial 90 aircraft, including aircraft acquired through the absorption of Aero Trasporti Italiani (ATI) in October the previous year. The single-aisle, rear-engined twinjet was powered by two 89 kN (20,000 lb) Pratt & Whitney JT8D-217A/C turbofan engines and had a full payload range of 3,800 km. It also had a good hot-and-high performance. In Alitalia service it was configured either in two classes with 22 passengers in business and 119 in economy, or in an all-economy layout for 141 passengers. Some later deliveries were fitted out in a single-class arrangement for 164 passengers. Alitalia successfully operated the McDonnell Douglas twin for almost 27 years, with the last aircraft, I-DAVV, leaving the fleet for Bulgarian Air Charter on 3 May 2010. Apart from an incident on 20 April 1994, when I-DAWR *Venezia* hit a truck on the taxiway after landing at Trieste, ripping off the outer part of the wing and rupturing a fuel tank, Alitalia had a perfect safety record with the type.

Alitalia had been targeted by Airbus from the very beginning as a likely customer, but it was not until 28 November 1978 a firm contract was signed (announced on 31 October) for eight A300B4-200, plus three options. These options were never taken up, but the airline acquired six Eastern Air Lines aircraft, including two A300B2-200 and four A300B4-100 variants, bringing the fleet to fourteen. The first aircraft, I-BUSB *Tiziano,* entered service on 28 April 1980, with deliveries of the eight new aircraft completed on 23 February 1982. The ex-Eastern models were delivered between 1 September 1988 and 12 July 1989. All were powered by the General Electric CF6-50C turbofan. The Airbuses entered service on Alitalia's routes from Rome to London, Paris, Cairo, Jeddah, Khartoum and Tel Aviv, and were also scheduled on the high-density Rome-Milan sector. The Airbus was configured for 18 first-class and 251 economy-class passengers.

Airbis A300B4-200 I-BUSH coming in to land at Athens Ellinikon International (Alan Lebeda)

Shepherd One

Flying the Pope around the world has always been the task of Alitalia, the pontiff typically travelling with the Italian airline on the outbound leg, and returning to Italy on the national carrier of the country visited, but only if deemed safe. Aircraft used depended on availability, but the Vatican has reserved a specific flight number, AZ4000, for each volo papale (papal flight). After each flight, aircraft used returned to normal passenger service. In more recent times, the Pope and his entourage numbering about 30 people, were guaranteed space in business class, with the Pope sitting by himself in the first row, while the 70 or so journalists had to make do with economy. The entourage, known in Italian as the seguito, literally the 'following', is typically

composed of the Cardinal Secretary of State; one or two other cardinals and bishops; 10 priests, most of them officials of the Secretariat of State; and laity, employees of the Vatican Press Office, as well as plainclothes agents of the Vatican security service and the Swiss Guard. In the distant past, however, papal travel was much more luxurious. Especially on long journeys, two rows of seats in business class were removed to install a double bed for the Pope. One such bed, complete with seat belt, used by John Paul II in 1979 when returning to Italy by TWA, can still be seen in a museum at the old airport site at Kansas City. Pope Paul VI was the first to travel by aircraft, when he made the first papal pilgrimage to the Holy Land on 4 January 1964 in the Alitalia Douglas DC-8-40, I-DIWS Leone Pancaldo, and the first to venture outside Italy since Pius VII in 1809. For this special flight, the Vatican's yellow and white flag replaced the Italian flag on the aircraft's tail. But it was Pope John Paul II who was the most well-travelled, clocking up 1,160,000 km, the equivalent of 29 times around the world, more than all his predecessors before him, visiting 129 of the world's nations. The present Holy Father, Francis, has also logged an impressive number of flights but introduced a less rigid programme, for example replacing the inflight question and answer sessions with the press by individual discussions with the journalists, and generally being more informal. When flying longer distances, Alitalia assigned its wide-body Airbus A330 and Boeing 777. Upon landing, the pilots open the cockpit windows and display the flag of the country being visited, alongside the Vatican's yellow and white flag with the papal tiara and keys. On shorter journeys, the Pope flew on the Airbus A320 family aircraft, while on short trips within Italy, he travelled mostly in an AW139 helicopter.

Pope Francis with the Papal coat of arms beside the passenger door; Airbus A320 EI-DSY *Aldo Palazzeschi* with the Irish and Vatican flags; and Douglas DC-8-43 I-DIWS *Leone Pancaldo* in Papal colours in the Holy Land

A difficult decade

On 26 May 1989, Alitalia (45 per cent), Olivetti (45 per cent) and San Paolo Finance (10 per cent) founded Eurofly SpA at Turin to provide charter flights, which were begun on 21 February 1990 with a Milan/Malpensa-Girona-Rome-Milan on behalf of Ford Italy, using Alitalia's Douglas DC-9-32 aircraft. In summer 1991, Eurofly became the first Italian airline to operate to the Red Sea area, with services to Sharm-el-Sheikh in Egypt. While charter flights were largely limited to Europe, major expansion took place in 1998/1999 with an entry into the long-haul market, with flights to the Caribbean, Mexico, Maldives, Sri Lanka, Cape Verde, Kenya and Tanzania, all operated by three Boeing 767-300. Medium-haul operations were performed with types such as DC-9-32, DC-9-51 and MD.82, mostly leased from the parent company. In December 2000, Eurofly, now fully owned, was designated as Alitalia's official charter company, leading to the acquisition of five Airbus A320-200 in May 2001, and of two Airbus A330-200 the following summer, to facilitate a major upgrade of its medium- and long-range network respectively. However, on 15 September 2003, the airline was sold to Spinneker Luxembourg and continued operations with A320 and A330 aircraft. On 28 February 2010, it was merged with the private airline Meridiana under the new MeridianaFly brand.

Having disposed of its DC-10 trijets, Alitalia was now short of long-haul aircraft for its thinner routes and, in 1986, placed an order for the McDonnell Douglas MD-11 successor, acquiring three passenger aircraft and five MD-11C Combis. Once more, the Aeritalia involvement in the manufacture of several structural components (winglets, tails, rudders, and upper fuselage panels) had its weight inside the intricacies of Italian state-owned companies. The first aircraft, I-DUPE *Arena di Verona/Giuseppe Verdi,* was delivered on 27 November 1991 and entered service on 17 December between Rome and Buenos Aires. Configured for either 210 passengers in three classes (12 first, 24 business and 174 economy), or for 204, with 30 in business and 174 in economy, a total of eight General Electric CF6-80C2S1F- powered aircraft served with Alitalia in passenger configuration until 2005, when five remaining aircraft, I-DUPA *Teatro all Scala/Giaocchino Rossi,* I-DUPE *Arena di Verona/Giuseppe Verdi,* I-DUPI *Fontana di Trevi/ Giacomo Puccini,* I-DUPO *Canal Grande/Nicoló Paganini,* and I-DUPU *Ponte Vecchio/Antonio Vivaldi,* were converted to cargo by Aeronavali at Venice and continued operating until 2009. I-DUPO had sustained considerable damage in a hard landing at Chicago/O'Hare International on 19 August 1994, although there were no injuries to the 14 crew and 253 passengers. The nose tyres failed during the

McDonnell Douglas MD-82 I-DANG *Benevento* operated by eurofly (Marco Dotti)

McDonnell Douglas MD-11 I-DUPC *Vincenzo Bellini* at Hong Kong Kai Tak International (Robbie Shaw)

landing, there was damage to the nose landing gear support structure, and foreign object damage to No.1 and No.3 engines. The aircraft was repaired at Phoenix, Arizona, and re-entered service on 11 February 1995.

In the late '80s, Alitalia was already planning a brand new 'over 100 seats' fleet and, because of the nation's deepening involvement with Europe aerospace manufacturers, it signed a contract for 40 Airbus A320 family aircraft on 27 July 1989. The contract anticipated a further confirmation of specific types to be selected between the basic A.320, the shortened A.319, and the longer A.321. The innovative A320 twin-engined narrowbody airliner family pioneered the use of digital fly-by-wire and side-stick flight controls and underwent a continuous programme of enhancements and efficiency improvement with large winglets, aerodynamic refinements, weight savings and reduced fuel consumption through engine developments. The pan-European type went on to become the highest-selling jet airliner, surpassing the Boeing 737, which had entered service 20 years earlier.

Alitalia first introduced the stretched, minimum change A321-200, becoming an early operator when introducing I-BIXA *Piazza del Duomo-Milano* in March 1994. The first basic A320-200, I-BIKA *Johann Sebastian Bach*, joined the fleet in March 1994, with the shorter A319-100, I-BIMA *Isola d'Elba*, delivered on 19 June 2002. All were powered by the CFM International CFM56 high-bypass turbofan engine, a joint venture between GE Aviation of the United States and Snecma (now Safran Aircraft Engines) of France. Thrust ratings for the Alitalia aircraft ranged from 100 kN (23,500 lb) to 140 kN (31,000 lb). Alitalia eventually operated a total of 99 different A320 family aircraft, including 22 A319, 54 A320 and 23 A321. Typical two-class accommodation was 138 in the A319, 165 in the A320, and 200 in the A321.

In 1995, Alitalia leased three Boeing 767-300ER twinjets from Ansett Worldwide Aviation Services (AWAS), followed later that year and early in 1996 by three more from Singapore Aircraft Leasing (SALE). All six were first operated with British registrations, before being put onto the Italian register. The first aircraft, operated as VH-ITA and G-OITA, before becoming I-DEIB *Pier Paolo Racchetti*, was delivered on 21 January 1995, together with VH-ITB/G-OITA, later I-DEIC *Alberto Nassetti*. From 1999, the 767-300ER fleet was boosted by three new aircraft, delivered direct from Boeing, three transferred from Eurofly, and two ex-Air Canada aircraft, which brought the fleet to 14 aircraft in total. All were powered by two General Electric CF6-80C2B6F turbofan engines and, in Alitalia service, provided accommodation for 25 business-class and 189 economy-class passengers. The extra fuel capacity and higher gross weight compared to the standard model, gave the 767-300ER as range of over 11,000 km. It was used on Alitalia's services to North and South America, and to Africa and the Middle East. The last commercial 767 flight was completed by EI-DDW *Sebastiano Caboto* on 24 October 2012 on the Los Angeles-Accra-Rome service.

In 15 December 1992, Alitalia purchased a 30 per cent stake in Malév Hungarian Airlines to gain access to the Budapest hub, but this was bought back by the Hungarian State in December 1997, when Alitalia was in the midst of a restructuring programme. But a major step forward was made in 1995 with the signing of a partnership with KLM Royal Dutch Airlines that was intended to develop Milan/Malpensa as a hub, along with Amsterdam/Schiphol and Rome/Fiumicino. To avoid a monopolistic situation, some slots had to made available to existing competitors and new entrants at all three airports. The ambitious alliance was to cover

Boeing 767-300ER I-DEIG *Francesco Agello* (Enrico Pierobon)

Airbus A320-200 EI-DTE *Francesco Petrarca* in the snow

Airbus A321 I-BIXD soon after take-off from London Heathrow with the undercarriage doors still closing (Adrian Pingstone)

the core businesses of both airlines, including KLM and KLM Cityhopper, and Alitalia mainline, Alitalia TEAM and Alitalia Express, effectively amounting to virtually all the groups' revenues. Profits were to be shared on an equal basis, and another important element of the agreement was an integrated fleet policy. Furthermore, the fleets of both airlines were to be made available to the joint venture at no charge, and proceeds from aircraft disposal were to be split equally. KLM was also to make a contribution to Alitalia towards the investment in the new Malpensa hub. It was

an ambitious deal, but one that never really lived up to expectations as Alitalia priorities soon turned to a desperate fight for survival. The venture was also eventually to lead to a full merger, but this never took place.

Regional experiments

The decade was also one of forging formal and informal alliances with local reginal airlines, to ensure that Alitalia maintained its extensive control over the domestic market, the biggest in Europe after France and Germany. But the

Airbus A319-100 I-BIMD *Isola di Capri* landing at London Heathrow (Adrian Pingstone)

first experiments dated back to 22 December 1986 and the foundation of Naples-based Aliblu SpA, in which Alitalia participated with a 10 per cent holding. Aliblu began domestic flights in August 1987 with British Aerospace Jetstream 31 twins, but traffic and economic results were below expectations, and operations ceased in 1989 and the company was liquidated the following year.

The role of Avianova SpA would become much more important. The company was set up as a subsidiary of Alisarda on 18 December 1986, to carry out regional flights, especially to and from Sardinia, with smaller aircraft more suited to this type of traffic. Operations began in August 1987 with a pair of ATR 42 turboprop aircraft, but expectations remained unfulfilled, as passenger flow turned out to be essentially as seasonal one. This forced Avianova to seek a partner and on 12 June 1989, ATI officially acquired 50 per cent of the Avianova shareholding. Over the following years, the ATR 42 fleet grew to 11, nine of which were transferred from ATI, and four brand-new of the larger ATR 72. Expansion was swift, with flights carried out on

British Aerospace Jetstream 31 I-BLUU of the short-lived Aliblu domestic airline in which Alitalia held a small stake (Aldo Bidini)

Avianova ATR 72-212 EI-CLB at Stuttgart Echterdingen (Jetpix)

behalf of ATI and Alitalia, until the entire shareholding was acquired by ATI in 1993. After the integration of ATI into the parent Alitalia was completed in July 1995, 55 per cent of Avianova's shares were acquired by Alitalia. Between 1 November 1996 and 1 October 1997, Avianova flew with the Alitalia TEAM brand.

Alitalia became the sole shareholder and, on 1 October 1997, the Avianova fleet, network and personnel was transformed into the operational activity of Alitalia Express, which had been formally established on 23 July 1996 as a subsidiary for regional flights. On that date, the fleet consisted of nine ATR 42, four ATR 72, and six Fokker 70 twinjets. The first of 14 Embraer ERJ145, a 50-seat jet powered by two rear-mounted Rolls-Royce AE 3007-A1E turbofan engines, and a range of 3,700 km, was delivered on 1 June 2000, and these were followed by the larger 78-seat E170, with more powerful engines and a range of 4,000 km.

Minerva Airlines SpA started scheduled operations on 1 September 1996 and operated with a fleet of 30-seat Dornier 328-100 twin turboprop aircraft, with Alitalia code-share flights accounting for some 70 per cent if its business. In March 1998, it became a full Alitalia franchisee. It ceased its loss-making activities on 25 October 2003, but reports that it would resume regional services on behalf of Alitalia with ATR 42 turboprops, or that Alitalia would take over the carrier, proved unfounded. Another short-lived airline was Azzurra Air SpA, established in December 1995 by Italian investment group Air International Services with 51 per cent, and Air Malta with the remaining 49 per cent. From April 1998 until March 2002, two of its four-engined BAe 146 jet aircraft were based at Milan/Linate, operating for Alitalia Express to such destinations as London City, Valencia, Munich, Frankfurt and Geneva. Suggestions that it might be fully integrated into the Alitalia Group in 1998 did not come to pass and Azzurra Air stopped flying

in March 2004 and was eventually declared bankrupt the following July after non-payment of leasing fees.

It is difficult to understand why Alitalia risked its reputation by linking up with Alpi Eagles, which had a turbulent history since starting flying scheduled services in December 1996. Its operation was plagued by management upheavals and delayed flights due to the unreliability of its Fokker 100 twinjets. After competing head-on with Alitalia on the Venice-Rome service with a ticket-less, low-fare, full-service, two-class operation, it started code-sharing with Alitalia in 1997, before reverting to independent flying. Palermo-based Air Sicilia was poised to provide code-share flights for Alitalia between Sicily and some of the smaller islands, but talks collapsed the day before service was due to begin. Of more substance was the code-sharing deal with Meridiana on its nonstop north-south routes. In April 2004, Alitalia had taken over the network of the short-lived and bankrupt regional carrier Gandalf Airlines, which had been operating a fleet of Dornier 328 aircraft in both jet and turboprop versions from its base at Milan/Orio al Serio to domestic destinations and some European points since March 1998. Alitalia's move was to gain valuable slots at some European airports.

Questionable solutions
But these were only side issues that detracted from the dire financial state Alitalia found itself in through a combination of undercapitalisation, difficulties resulting from the First Gulf War, the recession of the airline industry, and the increasing competition from liberalisation of the air transport market. Although it made progress in reducing costs and improving productivity, and managed to harmonise union relations and lowering labour costs, a considerable achievement given the previous confrontational environment, it failed to return the airline to profitability. Debts spiralled out

Alitalia Express Embraer 170LR EI-DFH *Via Aurelia* (Aldo Bidini)

of control and rose from ITL 653 billion in 1990, to ITL 3,420 billion by the end of 1995.

As a result, Alitalia instigated a restructuring plan for 1996-2000, which was to be accompanied by a large capital increase from IRI. The agreement reached between the company and the trade union representatives on 19 June 1996 was to save costs, during the five-year period from 1996 to 2000, of more than ITL 1 000 billion. In return for that reduction in wage costs, the staff were to receive Alitalia shares to a value of ITL 310 billion (representing for the company a cost of ITL 520 billion with tax and social charges), corresponding to the annual saving achieved in labour costs.

The plan also provided for the formation of a self-contained company, wholly controlled by Alitalia, which would engage new cabin personnel on less expensive terms. This new division, Alitalia TEAM, was formally established on 23 July 1996, as a low-cost branch. A quarter of the mainline 6,000 plus flight and cabin crew were transferred to Alitalia TEAM and a large number of aircraft (6 Boeing 767-300, 17 Airbus A321, 20 McDonnell Douglas MD-82, 9 ATR 42 and 4 ATR 72) began operating under the TEAM logo. Following a shareholder meeting in July 1999, the ATR fleet and associated personnel was transferred from Alitalia TEAM to Alitalia Express.

The financial component of the plan notified to the European Commission on 15 July 1996 provided for

Minerva Airlines Dornier 328-110 twin-turboprop aircraft D-CPRU operating for Alitalia (Konstantin von Wedelstaedt)

Airbus A320-200 I-BIKE with Alitalia TEAM markings (Konstantin von Wedelstaedt)

capital injections totalling ITL 3 310 billion: ITL 1 500 billion to be provided by IRI by the end of 1996, 1 500 billion to be the subject of a second instalment to be paid in 1997 and ITL 310 billion for staff. Of the ITL 1 500 billion corresponding to the first instalment, ITL 1 000 billion had already been advanced by IRI in June 1996. The development phase (1998-2000) was chiefly based on bringing the Malpensa hub into service as from 1998. Milan, centre of the wealth-generating industrial north, was one area where Alitalia's traffic suffered particularly, much having been lost to Zürich and Munich. The city's Linate airport, though much closer to the city, was hardly adequate to handle heavy traffic and long-haul flights and was notorious for winter fogs, causing expensive and disruptive delays. For years, the better alternative, Malpensa 50 km to the north, had remained underutilised due to lack of fast surface transport links, resulting in concentration of resources on Rome. According to the plan, the creation of the Malpensa hub was to be accompanied by restructuring of the terminal at Rome-Fiumicino Airport. During the development phase, Alitalia also planned to introduce shuttle services on the main domestic Italian routes, to reorganise its international network and to develop a series of alliances with foreign partners. Fleet rationalisation was also high on the agenda, with 14 DC-9-32 and 14 A300B4 sold, and orders for five MD-82 and 15 A320-200 cancelled. As part of a restructuring plan agreed with the European Commission, IRI began a part-privatisation process on 18 May 1998, by placing a 14 per cent rights issue with institutional investors, and allocating 20 per cent to staff. This effectively reduced the state holding to 51 per cent, the minimum that was then allowed under Italian law.

Alitalia TEAM Boeing 767-300ER I-DEIC (Ken Fielding)

State-managed failure

Throughout its history, Alitalia led a charmed life, with low productivity, a bloated workforce with high labour costs, hostile unions and much government and political interference, contributing to a poor and loss-making existence. If its first profit in 1998 provided some relief and hopes for a better future, it was but a false dawn, as the airline racked up accumulated losses of some EUR 3.7 billion over the next ten years. This in spite of state aid of EUR 1.5 billion in 1998 from the government of Romano Prodi, a capital increase of EUR 1.4 billion in 2002 under the government of Silvio Berlusconi, and another increase of EUR 1.6 million in 2005. In September 2004, the Berlusconi government also provided a bridging loan of EUR 400 million, when Alitalia once again found itself in financial difficulties, following an agreement with the unions for pay cuts and layoffs to keep the airline out of bankruptcy. It all added up to an investment by the Italian Government and other organisations of EUR 4.7 billion.

Notwithstanding its own perilous position, Alitalia wanted to buy the smaller airline Volare for EUR 38 million, as part of its strategy to regain domestic market share lost to low-cost airlines, but this was blocked on 23 May 2006 by the *Consiglio di Stato* (State Council), Italy's highest appellate court for administrative affairs, which ruled in favour of its chief rival, Air One, which had been the next highest bidder. Alitalia was particularly after Volare's prized slots at Milan/Linate and the airline estimated that it would lose EUR 125 million in revenues by 2008 if Volare went to Air One. Volare, later volareweb.com, which had begun operations in 1997, collapsed in November 2004 under heavy losses and

debts and filed for bankruptcy. On 25 March 2006, the EU gave the green light to the Italian Government for a EUR 25 million rescue aid to enable it to keep operating. Alitalia was eventually declared the winner in the battle against Air One and formed Volare SpA as a subsidiary on 14 April 2006, with all former Volare employees transferred on 15 May. In the following year, Volare served as Alitalia's low-cost subsidiary but was dissolved and its operations integrated into Alitalia mainline on 11 February 2015.

As to Alitalia itself, the expected return to profit did not materialise and, as the government was forbidden by the European Union to inject new capital into the failing airline, it reluctantly agreed to reduce its 49.9 per cent holding in the airline. It invited bids for a 30.1 per cent stake on 29 January 2007, but specified that the successful bidder was to guarantee the airline's 18,000 jobs, its domestic routes, and retain the Alitalia brand. There were initially 11 bidders, but all gradually dropped out, forcing the government to scrap the auction. While there was serious consideration of liquidating the airline, the government opted to engage in direct negotiations with companies that had previously expressed an interest, to buy at least 39.9 per cent, although the government was also willing to divest itself of its entire stake. Heading this list were Air One, the country's second-largest airline, a local investment group and Air France-KLM partnership. All three presented proposals to purchase Alitalia on 6 December 2007.

Air France-KLM was always considered a natural candidate, because it already enjoyed a partnership with Alitalia in the SkyTeam airline alliance. Although it had not participated in the earlier failed auction and

Airbus A320-200 I-PEKF of Volare

Airbus A320-200 (Konstantin von Wedelstaedt)

Alitalia shareholdings in other airlines

Airline	Maximum holding	Duration
Air One, Rome*	100.0 per cent	2009-2014
Aliblu, Naples	100.0 per cent	1986-1989
Avianova, Cagliari*	100.0 per cent	1997
Eurofly, Rome	45.0 per cent	1989-2003
Malév Hungarian Airlines	30.0 per cent	1992-1997
Somali Airlines	50.0 per cent	1964-1977
Volare, Milan*	100.0 per cent	2006-2015

*Fully integrated into mainline operation

subsequently declared that it did not envisage going after Alitalia, it was announced the winner in March 2008. Air France-KLM offered a share swap of EUR 0.10 per share, for a total of EUR 184 million, pay EUR 608 million for the convertible bonds issued by Alitalia, and invest EUR 1 billion in new shares. But it was the terms of the agreement that fell foul of the powerful unions, especially the proposed dismissal of 1,620 employees of Alitalia, a substantial reduction of the workforce of its maintenance subsidiary, Alitalia Servizi, the intention to base the bulk of the flight network at Rome/Fiumicino, with all international flights from Milan/Malpensa to be stopped, and the complete discontinuation of Alitalia's freight service. The talks with the unions collapsed, leading to the resignation of Alitalia's chairman, Maurizio Prodi, and an announcement by Air France-KLM on 21 April 2008 that it had withdrawn its offer.

New ownership, same brand

After returning to office as prime minister, Berlusconi launched a third attempt to secure Alitalia's future, having given an emergency loan of EUR 300 million on 22 April in an attempt to stave off the airline's imminent collapse on the threat by the *Ente Nazionale per l'Aviazone Civile* (ENAC). Italy's civil aviation authority, to revoke its licence. However, he made it clear that Italy must continue to have its own flag-carrier and a complete take-over by a foreign airline would be inconceivable. In May, he asked the bank Intesa Sanpaolo to draw up a

Embraer E175STD EI-RDF *Parco Nazionale Dolomiti Friulano* at Perugia

plan that would ensure Alitalia's survival. The central part of the plan was for Alitalia to file for bankruptcy as protection from its creditors, which was implemented on 29 August, along with splitting the company into two parts, and to sell a stake to a foreign carrier. One part of Alitalia was to contain the debts and less viable parts, which was to be liquidated, while the profitable short-haul routes, landing rights and part of the aircraft fleet would be separated into a new business, controlled by a consortium of Italian investors and including the competitor Air One.

Hastily-assembled CAI-Compagnia Aerea Italiana, a consortium of Italian investors, which submitted a proposal to take over Alitalia, subject to several conditions, including productivity-linked contracts and a wage reduction of at least 25 per cent, which were rejected by half of the airline's unions on 8 September, and on 12 September, CAI broke off all negotiations. However, pressured by the Italian government, negotiations resumed, but on 22 September, CAI withdrew its buyout offer. But Berlusconi was determined to secure a positive outcome and forced a new meeting on 25 September and, on 29 September, following the withdrawal of ENAC's threat to suspend the licence and some concessions by CAI, the last union agreed to the buyout plan. On 30 October 2008, CAI presented a binding offer of EUR 1.052 billion to the bankruptcy administrator, Augusto Fantozzi, pressing ahead in spite of the refusal by some pilots and flight attendants' unions to sign up for the rescue plan. Another obstacle threatening to block the way was the 12 November decision by the European Union that the EUR 300 million loan of 22 April was illegal and had

to be paid back to the Italian Government by Alitalia, not the CAI. Nevertheless, the take-over offer was agreed on 19 November and Alitalia's profitable assets were transferred on 12 December, when CAI paid over the EUR 1.055 billion, EUR 427 million in cash, and taking on EUR 625 million in Alitalia's debts.

At the same time, the administrator put 46 of the airline's aircraft up for sale, which were offered in eight lots. Five lots comprised aircraft from the main fleet, one of which consisted of two Boeing 767-300ER, and three lots each of seven McDonnell Douglas MD-82, and another lot of a single MD-82. Regional aircraft were offered in the three remaining lots, one of four ATR 72-200 turboprops, one of four ATR 72-500, and a third of 14 Embraer ERJ145 twinjets. On 12 January 2009, Air France-KLM bought a 25 per cent stake for EUR 323 million, with an option to purchase additional shares after 2013, and the new Alitalia (Alitalia-branded CAI), which included the merged Air One operations, started life on the following day.

Air One, which had started at Pescara in 1983 as Aliadriatica and adopted the Air One name on 23 November 1995, grew into Italy's second-largest carrier and main competitor to the national airline. It operated many Boeing 737s, series 200, 300 and 400, and later on a handful of Airbus A.320 and A.330. Starting from 29 October 2000, it also had enjoyed a partnership alliance with Lufthansa. On 28 March 2010 it started low-cost flights out of Milan/Malpensa under the title of Air One *Smart Carrier*. By the time of the operational merger into CAI-Alitalia, it was almost bankrupt, but proceeded to retain its identity.

Embraer E190STD EI-RNC *Parco Nazionale Archipelago Toscano* of Alitalia CityLiner

Expansion and the opening of new bases at Venice, Pisa, Catania and Palermo followed, but on 26 August 2014, Alitalia announced that it would shut down Air One, a process that was completed on 30 October that year.

Air One had also set up a regional affiliate on 7 June 2006 under the name of Air One CityLiner, which commenced operations the following month with a fleet of ten Bombardier CRJ900 twin jets between Trieste and Rome, and between Genoa and Naples. It added its first international route between Turin and Paris/Charles de Gaulle in February 2007. Following the operational merger of Air One into Alitalia on 13 January 2009, Air One CityLiner's aircraft began operating on behalf of the national carrier until rebranded as Alitalia CityLiner on 20 April 2011. A brand-new fleet of 11 Embraer E175 and five larger E190 twinjets, respectively with seating for 88 and 100 passengers, was delivered between 23 September 2011 and 22 March 2013. All received Irish registrations

Airbus A330-200 EI-EJM *Giovanni Battista Tiepolo* departing Milan/Malpensa

and were named after national parks. Alitalia CityLiner took up the role previously performed by Alitalia Express. The brand was gradually phased out in favour of Alitalia CityLiner, with the last of its 10 Embraer E170 jets disposed of by March 2013. Alitalia Express was legally merged into Alitalia-CAI on 1 October 2014, and was dissolved on 6 February 2015.

Starting anew

The new, slimmed-down Alitalia-Compagnia Aerea Italiana started operations with only a few of the old fleet, most of which had been disposed of. Taken over were only 11 Airbus A319-100, four Airbus A321-100, two Airbus A330-200, and 12 Boeing 777-200(ER), most of whose ownership was transferred to Irish leasing company Aircraft Purchase Fleet (APF), owned by Carlo Toto, one-time owner of Air One. All were registered in the Irish Republic. The two A330-200, EI-DIP *Gian Lorenzo Bernini* and EI-DIR *Filippo Bruneleschi,* had previously been operated by Air One and joined the Alitalia fleet on 13 January 2009. However, Alitalia now acquired 12 new aircraft, starting on 6 July 2010 with EI-AJG *Raffaello Sanzio,* which entered service on 15 July at Milan/Malpensa. On board the first flight were Alitalia's president, Roberto Colaninno, CEO Rocco Sabelli, and other management and shareholders. With the new A330-200, which had originally been ordered by Air One, Alitalia also introduced the new *Magnifica* business class (28 seats), the new premium economy class *Classica Plus* (21 Seats)' and the renovated economy class (175 seats), named

Airbus A330-200

Classica, for a total seating capacity for 224 passengers. The new business-class seats were arranged in a 1-2-1 layout in two cabins, one with five rows and a mini-cabin with two rows. All featured leather seats that converted into fully-flat beds 533 mm (21 inches) wide, and incorporated a large 390 mm (15.4 inches) TV screen with privacy control, and PC and USB power. Alitalia's wide-body, long-range A330-200 was powered by two 292 kN (65,800 lbf) General

Magnifica business-class introduced on the newly-acquired Airbus A330-200

Boeing 777-200ER I-DIGU departing Rome/Fiumicino

Alitalia's Boeing 777-200ER EI-DDH *Tropea* in SkyTeam colours

Electric CF6-80E-1A4 engines and had a range of 13,450 km (8,355 miles). They were used on services to North and South America and Asia.

Larger than the A330, the first Boeing 777-200ER, I-DISA *Taormina*, had entered the fleet on 23 August 2002. The first Boeing aircraft with fly-by-wire controls, the 'Triple Seven' became the biggest-selling wide-body twin, just ahead of the A330. The Alitalia ER (extended range) variant was powered by two 416 kN (93,700 lbf) General Electric GE90-94B turbofan engines, and achieved a typical range of 13,085 km (8.127 miles) with additional fuel capacity. A total of 293 passengers were accommodated in three classes (30/24/239). The 777 was part of a major re-equipment programme initiated for the new Millennium. Alitalia later also operated a single 777-300ER, which entered service on the Paris Charles de Gaulle-Rome service on 13 April 2017. It was previously operated by Air Austral and was operated with the French registration until reregistered EI-WLA on 23 June 2017 and christened *Roma* on 1 September. It also went on to service the routes to Athens, São Paulo and Buenos Aires. On 28 September it was converted to cargo and made its final flight with Alitalia from New York JFK to Milan/Malpensa on 30 June 2021.

The reshaped airline started operations on 13 January 2009, but in spite of a much-reduced fleet and network, it still carried 21 million passengers in its first year of operations, although at a low load factor of 65.4 per cent. With a few changes during 2009, Alitalia's route network included 73 destinations, of which 51 were in Europe. During the following year, the airline added new long-haul routes to Los Angeles, Seoul, Shanghai and Rio de Janeiro, while gradually adding new or re-establishing previous services to major European destinations. This provided a commensurate increase in passenger numbers for the year to 25 million. One major change was the halving of flights out of Milan/Malpensa, but an increase of flights out of Milan/Linate, Bologna and Catania. But it faced considerable challenges from the word go. Ryanair announced that it would increase its Italian bases to penetrate deeper into the tourist market in the south, easyJet had already begun flying on the lucrative Milan-Rome route, and on 9 February 2009, Lufthansa Italia started serving eight European cities out of Milan, putting pressure on Alitalia's business market in the north. Surprisingly the German intrusion was not a successful one and all operations were halted on 29 October 2011.

But Alitalia soon found itself back on familiar territory, with strikes by flight crew and ground workers leading to cancelled flights, and unfulfilled promises of a return to profitability by 2010. A possible integration of Meridiana Fly operations was mooted on 12 February 2011 but was denied, neither did a plan of 25 January 2012 that was aimed at achieving integration with two other Italian carriers, Blue Panorama and Wind Jet. Although the Italian anti-trust authority gave the green light in July 2012 for Alitalia to acquire Wind Jet, in return for giving up a number of domestic slots, this proved a step too far. Alitalia struggled on amid mounting losses, and when its main fuel supplier threatened to cut off supplies, if a rescue deal was not forthcoming, and ENAC considered grounding the airline, bankruptcy was once more a distinct possibility. Scrambling to save an imminent collapse, Alitalia shareholders agreed on 11 October 2013 to issue new shares worth EUR 300 million, as part of a EUR 500 million rescue package brokered by the government. The difference was to be made up by Poste Italiane SpA, the Italian postal service, which was contributing EUR 75 million, and by various banks. Air France-KLM, which owned 25 per cent of Alitalia, refused to take up its share of the cash call, thus reducing its stake to just 7 per cent, and also dismissed an alternative

Dusk at Milan/Linate

Boeing 747 promoting Bulgari watches

arrangement for a full take-over.

The rescue package was intended as a stop-gap measure to give Alitalia more time to find a strategic investor that would initiate a root-and-branch restructuring programme and keep it flying. In June 2014, cash-rich Abu Dhabi flag-carrier, Etihad Airways, announced that it would be taking a major stake in Alitalia. All formalities for the transfer of operations from Alitalia-CAI to the new corporate holding company, Alitalia-Società Aerea Italiana SpA (Alitalia-SAI), were completed in 23 December 2014 and came into effect on 31 December. Under the deal, Etihad Airways subscribed and paid for the capital increase of EUR 387.5 million for the acquisition of a 49 per cent stake in the airline. The remaining 51 per cent majority stake was held by Alitalia-CAI through Midco, which contributed the agreed assets and liabilities for the continuation of the airline. The most prominent shareholders in CAI were Intesa Sanpaolo and UniCredit banks, Poste Italiane, Roberto Colaninno via IMMSI, and the Benetton family through Atlantia, the company that then controlled both Rome airports, and another running some 60 per cent of Italy's toll highways. Alitalia began operating under its new corporate holding company on 1 January 2015, marking the beginning of yet another chapter in the troubled airline's history. The first flight was operated from New York/J F Kennedy to Milan/Malpensa.

Etihad Airways Airbus A330 in Expo 2015 markings landing at Perth in Western Australia (Darren Koch)

Unfulfilled expectations

It was a new start full of promise. Chairman Luca di Montezemolo insisted that Alitalia will become once again a premium Italian airline recognised worldwide, adding: "The revitalised Alitalia we envision and have started building, will be an asset to this country, and a driver to support the growth of our tourism and our business." But James Hogan, Etihad's chief executive officer, warned that "anything other than rapid, decisive change is simply not an option." The key elements of the new business, with the objective to return to profitability by 2017, were a new three-hub strategy (again), co-operation with existing partners and the creation of new partnerships, the exploration of joint fleet efficiencies, and implementation of a new brand signature, although the name would remain unchanged. The route network was to be reconfigured, with additional long-haul services from Milan/Malpensa, including 13 weekly flights to Abu Dhabi, four flights a week to Shanghai, and additional flights to Tokyo, with new services from Rome to San Francisco, Mexico City, Santiago de Chile, Beijing and Seoul, with increased flights to New York, Chicago, and Rio de Janeiro. Also implemented was an increased connectivity with Etihad Airways' hub in Abu Dhabi, with daily services from Venice, Milan, Bologna and Catania, as well as additional flights from Rome, all allowing onward connections to the Middle East, Africa, the Indian subcontinent, South-East Asia, China and Australia.

The relationships with SkyTeam members, and in particular Air France-KLM and Delta Air Lines, were to be intensified, but already in May 2015, Alitalia announced it would terminate its partnership with Air France-KLM,

stating that there were no longer sufficient advantages for it to continue. New partnerships were created with Air Berlin, branded airberlin, Germany's second-largest airline, and its then subsidiary flyNiki, and Alitalia also planned to work more closely with Air Serbia, owned 49 per cent by Etihad, and Etihad Regional, formerly Darwin Airline. In May 2016, Air Berlin and Alitalia announced the strengthening of their commercial agreement, by offering 25 per cent more flights to Italy, starting on 2 May with a new route from Düsseldorf to Bologna, and also adding capacity from Düsseldorf to Venice and Florence. The two airlines were then operating 1,400 code-share flights on 90 routes, including 750 flights between Germany, Austria, Switzerland and Italy to such destinations as Rome, Milan/Linate, Venice, Bologna and Florence, but this all collapsed when Etihad, a major shareholder in Air Berlin, withdrew its support of the loss-making German airline, which, in spite of a restructuring effort from 28 September 2016, entered insolvency on 15 August 2017 and made its last flight on 27 October. It also meant the end for flyNiki, which was declared bankrupt and ceased all operations on 14 December that same year.

The expected profits for Alitalia never materialised and any hopes of continuing were dashed on 25 April 2017, when Alitalia employees rejected an 8 per cent pay-cut, 1,600 job-cuts and longer working-hours as part of an EUR 2 billion recapitalisation plan, to which the Italian shareholders and Etihad Airways had committed themselves. At that time, Alitalia was reportedly losing some EUR 500,000 a day! On 12 May, Alitalia and Alitalia CityLiner were back in bankruptcy, having filed for *amministrazione straordinaria*

Alitalia jointly promoted Milan's Expo 2015 with Etihad and had one of its own A330, EI-EJM, painted in the special livery

A striking view of Alitalia's Airbus A330-200

(extraordinary administration), in compliance with a decree issued by the *Ministero dello Sviluppo Economico* (Ministry of Economic Development), dated 2 May. The special administrators were charged with devising a survival plan, but, after the government had ruled out renationalising Alitalia, it was officially put up for sale on 17 May. It was the end of the road for Abu Dhabi's Etihad Airways, whose involvement with Alitalia started with high expectations. But, following Alitalia's entry into extraordinary administration, Etihad was no longer prepared to continue to invest without the support of all shareholders.

Expressions of interest were due to be submitted by 5 June, on which date some 32 non-binding offers had been received. This process lasted some three years, during which there was much fencing, skirmishes and manoeuvrings, but no white knight came riding in to save the airline, which continued operating throughout, albeit on a reduced scale.

Several airlines looked, but then turned away. Already in June, easyJet expressed an interest in purchasing Alitalia, as did Ryanair, but neither proceeded. Lufthansa was reported in October 2017 to have offered EUR 500 million to acquire the aircraft, runway slots and aircrew, but this was apparently rejected. Lufthansa, Ryanair and easyJet were only interested in parts of the airline, primarily its fleet and airport slots, which clearly was not acceptable to the administrators. The New York-based private equity group Cerberus Capital Management was said to be prepared to make an offer of between USD 100-400 million if the airline could be comprehensively restructured. It also apparently wanted the Italian Government to retain a stake and ensure that employees would benefit from some form of profit sharing.

In 2018, Delta Air Lines, easyJet (again) and the Italian State railway company, *Ferrovie dello Stato Italiane*,

Airbus A320-200 I-BIMI *Isola La Maddalena* in the newest livery

lodged formal expressions of interest. Talks were initiated in February 2019, but did not go well. While the railway company was apparently prepared to take a stake of up to 49 per cent, both easyJet and Delta put a 15 per cent (EUR 100 million) limit on their involvement, with easyJet wanting only Alitalia's short-haul business and positions at primary airports. Fearing a break-up of the airline, the administrators rejected these proposals. Following a state visit to Rome by Chinese president Xi Jinping in March, China Eastern Airlines said it was prepared to spend up to EUR 100 million for a 10 per cent stake, but neither offer was deemed sufficient to rescue the airline. The deadline of 31 March 2020 came and went without resolution. Italy, as most of Europe, was already facing the Covid-19 pandemic and Alitalia operations were badly hit.

A new dawn?

After months of negotiations, political machinations and the worldwide upheaval of the Covid-19 pandemic, a new state-owned airline was officially established on 9 October 2020. Retaining its well-known brand, Italia Trasporto Aereo (Alitalia-ITA) had assets of EUR 20 million and

a budget of EUR 3 billion, coming entirely from the *Ministero dell'Economia e delle Finanze* (MEF), the Ministry of Economy and Finance. Economy Minister, Roberto Gualtieri, explained that the new company's goal was to lay "the foundations for the launch of Italian air transport, through the choice of top-level managers and great skills able to develop and implement a solid and sustainable business plan." A 2021-2025 Business Plan was approved, which focuses on Rome/Fiumicino as the main hub, and Milan/Linate for business and leisure traffic. In the first year of operations, it was envisaged to operate 61 routes with 52 aircraft, and have some 5,500 employees. Already under

ITA Airways Airbus A320-200 EI-DTE, one of several of the type taken over from Alitalia

pressure from the European Commission, the ambitions for ITA Airways had to be scaled down to no more than 45 aircraft and 4,500 employees, the EC also insisting on a complete separation of the old Alitalia from ITA.

On 26 March 2021, the European Commission approved (yet another) EUR 24.7 million Italian support to compensate Alitalia for further loss of profitability suffered on certain routes due to the coronavirus outbreak between 1 November and 31 December 2020. This followed on from earlier EC decisions for EUR 272.47 million for damage suffered between 1 March and 31 October 2020. Further approvals were made up to and including 30 April 2021 for EUR 52.535 million, which brought the overall total to EUR 350 million. The Commission concluded that these compensations were in line with EU State aid rules.

Plans for the new ITA to start operations in July 2021 foundered on a lack of agreement on the conditions acceptable to the European Union. Although Prime Minister Mario Draghi appeared reluctant for the government to intervene again in the airline's rescue, the fact that ITA would be controlled by the Italian Government, as it was considered a strategic investment, engendered a suspicion of a hidden agenda for renewed state aid. Nevertheless, in September, the EC gave the green light to the new venture and authorised the injection of EUR 1.35 billion of public funds and, significantly, exempted ITA Airways from having to pay back the state aid received by its predecessor.

In the end, Alitalia's long history ended on 14 October 2021, when the last flight from Cagliari touched down at Rome's Fiumicino Airport, flown by the Airbus A320 EI-DSV *Primo Levi*. This event was viewed by many as a sad end to an Italian icon, with others experiencing relief that the bottomless pit that had swallowed nearly EUR 13 billion of government money, was now filled in. But was it? Its replacement, ITA Airways has been very much slimmed down. Only 52 out of 150 aircraft, and 2.800 of 11,000 employees have been retained, and many Alitalia take-off and landing slots have had to be relinquished, with the new airline focusing its operations on the Rome/Fiumicino and Milan/Linate hubs. To prevent its rivals getting their hands on the Alitalia brand, ITA has bought the brand and the website for EUR 90 million! ITA Airways made its first flight on 15 October 2021 when the A320-200 EI-IKU *Fryderyk Chopin* flew from Milan/Linate to Bari. The new state-owned airline serves 44 destinations on 59 routes, which it intends to increase to 74 destinations and 89 routes by 2025, when it expects to record its first profit. On 24 January 2022, ITA Airways announced that it had received an expression of Interest from a partnership of the MSC Group and Lufthansa to acquire the majority of the airline, which also wishes for the Italian Government to retain a minority stake. But already there has been disagreement on how to proceed with several board members resigning from the airline. A new dawn indeed, but will the sun continue to shine?

Alitalia Fleet 1947-2021

Fiat G.12 CA 1947-1949 (4)

18-passenger low-wing cantilever monoplane, powered by three 575 kW (770 hp) Alfa Romeo 128 radial engines, generating a cruising speed of 310 km/h

I-DALF	*Antares*	83	12.05.47-05.10.48	ex MM 60903; leased from Aeronautica Militare
I-DALG	*Altair*	84	28.04.47-26.07.48	ex MM 60904; leased from Aeronautica Militare
I-DALH	*Alcione*	86	16.04.47-08.11.49	ex MM 60906; leased from Aeronautica Militare
I-DALI	*Aldebaran*	81	21.04.47-24.08.48	ex MM 60901; leased from Aeronautica Militare

Savoia Marchetti SM.95C 1947-1953 (8)

20-passenger cantilever monoplane of mixed construction, powered by three 552 kW (740 hp) Bristol Pegasus 48 radial engines, generating a speed of 295 km/h

I-DALJ	*Cristoforo Colombo*	8	30.08.47-31.10.52	to Aeronautica Militare as MM 61812
I-DALK	*Amerigo Vespucci*	9	05.09.47-31.10.52	to Aeronautica Militare as MM 61813
I-DALL	*Marco Polo*	11	30.01.48-31.10.52	to Aeronautica Militare as MM 61814
I-DALM	*Marco Polo*	4	13.05.47-15.09.47	to Aeronautica Militare as MM 61635
I-DALN	*Sebastiano Caboto*	7	26.09.47-31.10.52	to Aeronautica Militare as MM 61811
I-DALO	*Ugolino Vivaldi*	10	14.11.47-27.01.51	crashed in flames on approach to Rome, Italy
I-LAIT	*Sant'Antonio*	19	00.04.50-00.02.51	ex LATI; wfu and to Lebanese International Airlines as OD-ABR 02.06.53
I-LITA	*San Cristoforo*	18	00.04.50-00.02.51	ex LATI; wfu and to Lebanese International Airlines as OD-ABS 02.06.53

Avro 691 Lancastrian Mk.III 1947-1952 (5)

13-passenger cantilever monoplane, powered by four 1,210 kw (1,620 HP) Rolls-Royce Merlin 24/2 piston engines, generating a cruising speed of 450 km/h

I-DALR	*Borea*	1299	07.08.47-05.11.52	ex G-AHCE; wfu
I-AHBX	*Maestrale*	1292	13.02.48 -23.12.49	ex G-AHBX; crashed on landing after engine failure at Dakar/Yoff, Senegal
I-AHBY	*Libeccio*	1293	12.11.47-05.11.45	ex G-AHBY; wfu
I-AHCB	*Grecale*	1296	21.07.47-05.11.52	ex G-AHCB; wfu
I-AHCD	*Scirocco*	1298	17.12.47-05.11.52	ex G-AHCD; wfu

Fiat G.12 LB 1948-1950 (5)

22-passenger low-wing metal monoplane, powered by three 552 kW (740 hp) Bristol Pegasus 48 radial engines, generating a cruising speed of 295 km/h

I-DALA	*Castore*	95	25.01.48-23.06.50	to Aeronautica Militare as MM 61779
I-DALB	*Vega*	96	11.02.48-23.06.50	to Aeronautica Militare as MM 61780
I-DALC	*Polluce*	97	15.03.48-23.06.50	to Aeronautica Militare as MM 61781
I-DALD	*Sirio*	98	25.03.48-23.06.50	to Aeronautica Militare as MM 61782
I-DALE	*Regolo*	99	26.06.48-23.06.50	to Aeronautica Militare as MM 61783

Avro 652A Anson I 1948-1949 (1)

Four-passenger low-wing cantilever monoplane, powered by two 250 kW (335 hp Armstrong Siddeley Cheetah IX piston engines, generating a cruising speed of 255 km/h

I-AHBN			26.07.48-01.01.49	ex G-AHBN;

Douglas DC-4 1950-1955 (4)

40-passenger low-wing, all-metal monoplane, powered by four 1,081 kW (1,450 hp) Pratt & Whitney R-2000-2SD13-G Twin Wasp engines, generating a maximum speed of 450 km/h

I-DALT	*Città di Milano*	10400	25.04.50-13.05.54	ex N88913; to Compagnie Générale de Transports Aétiens (CGTA) as F-BGZK
I-DALU	*Città di Palermo*	10381	18.08.50-11.12.53	ex N88926; to REAL Transportes Aéreos as PP-XFD
I-DALV	*Città di Napoli*	10351	28.04.50-09.12.55	ex N88919; to California Eastern Airways as N1438V
I-DALZ	*Città di Roma*	10403	26.04.50-20.11.53	ex N88914; to REAL Transportes Aéreos as PP-XEF

Douglas DC-6 1957-1962 (3)

64-passenger low-wing, all-metal monoplane, powered by four 1,790 kW (2,400 hp) Pratt & Whitney R-2800-CA15 Double Wasp engines, generating a speed of 500km/h

I-DIMC	43152/161	08.11.58-06.09.62	ex I-LIKE; to Aeronautica Militare as MM 61900
I-DIMS	43216/165	22.07.58-30.12.61	ex I-LADY; to Società Aerea Mediterranea (SAM) as I-DIMS
I-DIMT	43217/166	12.06.58-21.01.66	ex I-LOVE; leased to Central African Airways (CAA) as I-DIMT 19.10.62-28.12.65; to Aeronautica Militare as MM 61923
I-LADY	43216/165	31.10.57-22.07.58	ex LAI; reregistered I-DIMS
I-LIKE	43152/161	31.10.57-08.11.58	ex LAI; reregistered I-DIMC
I-LOVE	43217/166	31.10.57-12.06.58	ex LAI; reregistered I-DIMT

Convair 340 1953-1962 (4)

44-passenger low-wing monoplane, powered by two 1,865 kW (2,500 hp) Pratt & Whitney R-2800-CB16 Double Wasp engines, generating a speed of 465 km/h

I-DOGI*	63	05.05.53-15.04.61	to Aero OY as OH-LTG
I-DOGO*	87	29.06.53-13.09.62	to Yugoslovenski Aerotransport (JAT) as YU-ADM
I-DOGU*	102	24.08.53-13.09.62	to Yugoslovenski Aerotransport (JAT) as YU-AND
I-DUGA*	112	21.12.54-13.09.62	to Yugoslovenski Aerotransport (JAT) as YU-ADL

* all upgraded to 440 standard in 1956

Douglas DC-6B 1953-1966 (11)

68-passenger, low-wing monoplane, powered by four 1,865 kW (2,500 hp) Pratt & Whitney R-2800-CB17 Double Wasp engines, generating a speed of 510km/h

I-DIMA	44251/420	16.11.53-01.05.70	leased to Società Aerea Mediterranea (SAM) as I-DIMA 17.04.61-31.02.64; to Aeronautica Militare as MM61965
I-DIMB	44913/663	07.03.56-01.10.63	to Società Aerea Mediterranea (SAM) as I-DIMB
I-DIMD	44419/491	12.06.58-26.05.61	ex I-LAND; to Società Aerea Mediterranea (SAM) as I-DIMD
I-DIME	44252/442	30.11.54-01.04.61	to Società Aerea Mediterranea (SAM) as I-DIME
I-DIMI	44253/448	22.02.54-14.05.62	to Società Aerea Mediterranea (SAM) as I-DIMI
I-DIMO	44254/456	26.03.54-21.11.61	to Società Aerea Mediterranea (SAM) as I-DIMO
I-DIMP	44418/473	24.06.58-30.12.61	ex I-LYNX; to Società Aerea Mediterranea (SAM) as I-DIMP
I-DIMU	44888/645	05.01.56-13.11.61	to Società Aerea Mediterranea (SAM) as I-DIMU
I-LAND	44419/491	31.10.57-12.06.58	ex LAI; reregistered I-DIMD
I-LYNX	44418/473	31.10.57-24.06.58	ex LAI; reregistered I-DIMP
F-BGSN	44871/611	07.05.60-31.05.60	originally ordered by Alitalia in 1955 but cancelled; leased from UAT-Union Aéromaritime de Transports
F-BIAM	45478/962	01.05.58-30.09.58	leased from UAT-Union Aéromaritime de Transports
PH-DFK	43552/240	23.03.60-10.07.60	leased from KLM Royal Dutch Airlines

Convair 440-75 Metropolitan 1957-1961 (2)

52-passenger low-wing monoplane, powered by two 1,865 kW (2,500 hp) Pratt & Whitney R-2800-CB16 Double Wasp engines, generating a speed of 465 km/h

| I-DOVA | 392 | 07.02.57-23.02.61 | to Aeronautica Militare as MM63898 |
| I-DOVE | 407 | 11.03.57-23.02.61 | to Aeronautica Militare as MM61899 |

Vickers V.700D Viscount 1957-1971 (18)

48-passenger short/medium-range aircraft, powered by four 1,175 kW (1.575 hp) Rolls-Royce Dart RDa3 Mk.510 turboprop engines, generating a speed of 550 km/h

I-LAKE	328	01.10.57-28.03.64	ex LAI; crashed on Monte Somma on approach to Naples
I-LARK	329	01.10.57-24.05.71	ex LAI; to SAETA as HC-AVP
I-LIFE	325	01.10.57-12.05.68	ex LAI; to Somali Airlines as 60S-AAK
I-LIFS	130	30.11.60-05.12.67	ex N7432; to PLUNA as CX-BHAF
I-LIFT	326	01.10.57-06.09.69	ex LAI; wfu
I-LILI	327	01.10.57-01.06.69	ex LAI; to Aerolineas TAO as I-LILI, later HK-1061-X
I-LINS	131	16.12.60-01.10.67	ex N7433; to PLUNA as CX-BHB
I-LIRC	114	16.12.60-12.12.70	ex N7416; to Somali Airlines as 60S-AAN
I-LIRE	116	30.11.60-11.04.68	ex N7418; to BMA-British Midland Airways as G-AWGV
I-LIRG	284	05.10.63-14.01.70	ex N6594C; wfu
I-LIRM	288	30.04.64-13.01.70	ex N6596C; to SAETA as HC-ART
I-LIRP	379	29.04.58-12.08.68	to Somali Airlines as 60S-AAJ
I-LIRS	377	24.03.58-17.12.69	to SAETA as HC-ARS
I-LIRT	118	04.03.65-13.08.68	ex N7420; to Philippine Air Lines (PAL) as PI-C773
I-LITS	119	08.12.60-02.09.69	ex N7421; wfu
I-LIZO	380	15.05.58-13.11.68	to Aerolineas TAO as HK-1058-X

Douglas C-47 (DC-3) 1957-1970 (13)

21-passengers low-wing, all-metal monoplane, powered by two 895 kW (1,200 hp) Pratt & Whitney R-1830-S1C3G Twin Wasp engines, generating a speed of 370 km/h

I-LALO	19484	31.10.57-12.01.65	ex USAAF 42-101021; taken over from LAI; leased to SAM 00.12.61-12.01.65; to Africair as VP-XYP
I-LENE	4325	31.10.57-01.03.65	ex USAAF 41-7826; taken over from LAI; to Ethiopian Airlines as ET-ABQ
I-LEON	4316	31.10.57-06.08.60	ex USAAF 41-7817; taken over from LAI; to Aeronautica Militare as MM61896
I-LICE	6011	31.10.57-30.06.60	ex USAAF 41-18650; taken over from LAI; to Aeronautica Militare as MM61895
I-LIDA	4261	31.10.57-20.06.60	ex USAAF 41-7774; taken over from LAI; to Aeronautica Militare as MM61894
I-LINA	4236	31.10.57-03.08.60	ex USAAF 41-7749; taken over from LAI; to Aeronautica Militare as MM61893
I-LONA	4500	31.10.57-08.02.60	ex USAAF 41-18438; taken over from LAI; to Martin's Air Charter as PH-MAB
I-LORD	4406	31.10.57-29.09.64	ex USAAF 41-18434; taken over from LAI; leased to SAM 00.00.62-29.09.64; to Rhodesia Air Force
I-LORO	4297	31.10.57-20.02.65	ex USAAF 41-7805; taken over from LAI; leased to SAM 00.04.62-20.02.65; to Ethiopian Airlines as ET-ABR
I-LUCE	4387	31.10.57-29.12.59	ex USAAF 41-18349; taken over from LAI; to TAI-Transports Aériens Intercontinentaux as F-BJUT
I-LULA	4291	31.10.57-29.10.60	ex USAAF 41-7799; taken over from LAI; to Aeronautica Militare as MM61897
I-LUNA	4346	31.10.57-09.03.60	ex USAAF 41-7847; taken over from LAI; to Kat Air as OH-VKD
I-NEBB	18964	05.01.70-02.09.70	ex MM61778; leased from Aeronautica Militare

Douglas DC-7C 1957-1966 (6)

105-passenger low-wing monoplane, powered by four 2,536 kW (3,400 hp) Pratt & Whitney R-3350EA1 engines, generating a maximum speed of 650 km/h

I-DUVA	45228/879	08.10.57-25.03.66	to Airlift International as N356AL
I-DUVB	45542/1008	18.07.58-28.04.66	leased to SAM 00.00.61-28.04.66; to International Aerodyne as N6000V
I-DUVE	45229/904	29.11.57-25.03.66	to Airlift International as N357AL
I-DUVI	45230/942	21.02.58-04.05.66	to Spantax as EC-BDL
I-DUVO	45231/945	21.02.58-26.02.60	crashed on climb out of Shannon, Ireland
I-DUVU	45541/999	25.06.58-15.03.66	to Martin's Air Charter as PH-MAK

Douglas DC-8-40 1960-1977 (15)

189-passenger medium-range airliner, powered by four 78.4 kN (17,500 lb) Rolls-Royce Conway 509 turbofan engines, generating a crusing speed of 895 km/h

I-DIWA	*Amerigo Vespucci*	45598/57	28.04.60-10.10.77	to International Air Leases (IAL)
I-DIWB	*Antonio Pigafetta*	45625/144	31.05.61-05.05.72	crashed into Mount Longa on approach to Palermo, Sicily
I-DIWD	*Lanzerotto Malocello*	45631/160	25.03.62-07.07.62	crashed into Davandyachi Hill on approach to Bombay, India

I-DIWE	*Cristoforo Colombo*	45599/73	05.07.60-28.02.70	to Zambia airways as 9J-ABR
I-DIWF	*Antoniotto Usodimare*	45639/159	28.02.62-02.08.68	crashed on approach to Milan/Malpensa, Italy
I-DIWG	*Luca Tarigo*	45660/184	21.05.63-22.12.76	to F B Ayer & Associates as N253FA
I-DIWI	*Giovanni da Verrazzano*	45600/79	27.07.60-27.08.77	to International Air Leases (IAL)
I-DIWL	*Niccolò Zeno*	45682/220	12.03.65-23.10.74	to F B Ayer & Associates as N153AF
I-DIWM	*Ugolino Vivaldi*	45755/222	15.04.65-08.12.76	leased to VIASA on three occasions; to F B Ayer & Associates as N153FA
I-DIWO	*Marco Polo*	45601/107	02.11.60-28.02.77	to F B Ayer & Associates as N453FA
I-DIWP	*Alvise Ca' Da Mosta*	45636/153	03.11.61-15.01.75	to F B Ayer & Associates as I-DIWP
I-DIWR	*Nicoloso da Recco*	45637/157	01.02.62-15.01.75	leased to Zambia Airways as I-DIWR 06.69-06.71; to F B Ayer & Associates as N53AF
I-DIWS	*Leone Pancaldo*	45665/194	12.12.63-07.01.75	wfu; to ARCA Colombia as HK-1855 29.11.76
I-DIWT	*Emanuele Pessagno*	45666/202	14.04.64-08.11.76	to F B Ayer & Associates as N53FA
I-DIWU	*Giovanni Caboto*	45624/139	28.04.61-28.01.77	to F B Ayer & Associates as N353FA

Sud-Aviation SE-210 Caravelle III 1960-1975 *(4)*

80-passenger short-range aircraft, powered by two rear-mounted 50.7kN (11,400 lb) Rolls-Royce Avon Mk.527 turbojet engines, generating a speed of 805km/h

I-DAXA	*Altair*	35	29.05.60-17.02.75	leased to SAM 10.06.68-10.69; wfu
I-DAXE	*Aldebaran*	36	19.05.60-19.04.73	wfu; to Transavia Holland as PH-TVV 26.04.73
I-DAXI	*Antares*	40	10.06.60-31.03.75	wfu; to SAETA as HC-BAE 16.06.75
I-DAXO	*Deneb*	44	18.07.60-19.04.73	wfu and to Transavia Holland as PH-TVW

Sud-Aviation SE-210 Caravelle VI-N 1961-1977 (17)

80-passenger short-range aircraft, powered by two 54.3 kN (12,200 lb) Rolls-Royce Avon Mk 531 turbojet engines, generating a cruising speed of 845 km/h

I-DABA	*Regolo*	71	21.03.61-21.12.76	to Afro Cargo as 9Q-CRU
I-DABE	*Rigel*	72	31.03.61-01.10.75	to SAETA as I-DABE
I-DABF	*Mizar*	179	19.02.65-02.08.69	crashed on approach to marseille/Marignane, France
I-DABG	*Arturo*	205	27.05.66-28.02.77	leased to SAM 05.71-08.71 and 00.73-00.76; wfu and to Aérotour as F-BYAT 17.03.77
I-DABI	*Sirio*	74	22.04.61-28.02.77	leased to SAM 00.69-00.70; wfu
I-DABL	*Formalhaut*	132	15.04.64-21.12.75	leased to SAM 01.04.69-00.12.70 and 00.72-10.74; wfu
I-DABM	*Procione*	143	27.05.64-18.01.77	leased to SAM on three separate occasions; wfu
I-DABP	*Castore*	192	13.04.65-14.01.77	leased to SAM 06.70-10.72; wfu and to Aérotour as F-BAYU 18.03.77
I-DABR	*Bellatrix*	81	19.01.62-19.10.75	wfu
I-DABS	*Dubhe*	106	06.04.62-01.10.76	wfu
I-DABT	*Denebola*	85	02.04.62-01.02.75	transferred to SAM 01.05.68-01.72; subleased to ATI until 00.74;
I-DABU	*Vega*	77	22.05.61-26.09.76	wfu
I-DABV	*Acrux*	146	14.03.63-01.11.68	transferred to SAM
I-DABW	*Betelgeuse*	150	01.04.63-28.09.76	leased to SAM on three occasions; wfu

I-DABZ	*Spica*	82	09.02.62-01.01.75	leased to SAM 00.72-00.74; wfu
I-DAXT	*Polluce*	80	17.10.61-19.02.77	leased to Aerolineas Argeninas as I-DAXT 12.67-29.01.68; wfu
I-DAXU	*Canopo*	79	09.06.61-01.07.75	wfu

Curtiss C-46A Commando (2)

Pressurised cargo /passenger aircraft, powered by two 1,419 kW (2,000 hp) Pratt & Whitney R-2800-51 piston engines, generating a maximum speed of 430 km/h

I-SILA		30271	31.10.62-17.07.68	ex SAM; to AAXICO as N10624
I-SILV		392	04.05.62-17.07.68	ex SAM; to AAXICO as N10623

Douglas DC-9-32 1967-1997 (46)

115-passenger short/medium-range aircraft, powered by two rear-mounted 64kN Pratt & Whitney JT9D-9 turbofan engines, generating a speed of 895 km/h

I-ATJA	*Sicilia*	47641/746	01.10.88-14.11.90	ex ATI-Aero Trasporti Italiani; crashed on approach to Zürich/Kloten
I-ATIU	*Veneto*	47438/545	01.12.89-28.02.95	ex ATI-Aero Trasporti Italiani; reregistered I-RIZP 25.06.90 and I-RIFP 30.11.92; leased to Eurofly and ATI; wfu and to Northwest Airlines as N613NW
I-DIBA	*Isola di Capri*	47038/136	08.08.67-20.03.95	registered N901DC 04.01.83-20.11.87 and I-DIBR 20.11.87-01.12.92; to Northwest Airlines as N601NW via ATS Leasing
I-DIBC	*Isola di Lampedusa*	47233/429	19.11.68-21.05.94	reregistered I-RIBC 15.07.88 and I-RIFC 02.12.92; wfu and to Northwest Airlines as N608NW via ATS Leasing
I-DIBD	*Isola di Montecristo*	47234/435	04.01.69-26.01.95	reregistered I-RIBD 15.07.88 and I-TIFD 02.12.92; wfu and to Northwest Airlines as N609NW via ATS Leasing
I-DIBE	*Isola di Murano*	47046/168	25.09.67-30.06.95	registered N903DC 01.02.83-20.11.87 and I-DIBT 20.11.87-01.12.92; to Northwest Airlines as N602NW via ATS Leasing
I-DIBI	*Isola del Giglio*	47129/225	25.12.67-04.05.96	registered N906DC 01.02.83-20.11.87 and I-DIBW 20.11.87-30.11.92; to Northwest Airlines as N615NW via ATS Leasing
I-DIBJ	*Isola di Capraia*	47235/436	09.01.69-31.12.96	reregistered I-RIBJ 15.07.88 and I-TIFJ 03.12.92; wfu and to Northwest Airlines as N617NW via ATS Leasing
I-DIBK*	*Ercole*	47355/452	12.02.69-12.12.80	to Evergreen International as N932F
I-DIBN	*Isola di Palmaria*	47339/437	11.01.69-17.12.91	reregistered I-RIBN 13.07.88; crashed
I-DIBO	*Isola di Procida*	47237/451	06.02.69-25.06.90	leased to Aermediterranea and ATI; reregistered I-RIZX 25.06.90; wfu and later to Zuliana de Aviaçion as YV-497C
I-DIBQ	*Isola di Pianosa*	47236/450	04.02.69-30.06.93	reregistered I-RIBQ 13.07.88; wfu
I-DIKB	*Isola di Caprera*	47117/196	22.11.87-07.01.80	destroyed by fire during maintenance at Rome/Fiumicino
I-DIKC	*Isola di Ponza*	47128/210	11.12.67-01.03.96	leased to Aermediterranea as N516MD, reregistered I-RIZH 30.05.89 and I-RIFH 02.12.92; wfu and to Northwest Airlines as N614NW via ATS Leasing
I-DIKE	*Isola d'Elba*	47039/154	01.09.67-31.10.92	registered N902DC 18.01.83-20.11.87, then I-DIBS; to McDonnell Douglas
I-DIKF*	*Atlante*	47220/296	03.05.68-28.10.81	to Evergreen International as N935F
I-DIKG*	*Anteo*	47221/305	09.05.68-10.02.72	to Overseas National Airways (ONA) as N938F Gina
I-DIKJ	*Isola di Lipari*	47222/299	03.05.68-15.10.94	registered N43265 04.01.83-01.12.87 and I-DIBZ 01.12.87-27.11.92, then I-DIBP; to Northwest Airlines as N604NW via ATS Leasing

I-DIKL	*Isola di Panarea*	47223/300	30.04.68-30.06.95	registered N2787T 01.02.83-02.12.87 and I-DIBY 02.12.87-27.11.92, then I-DIBM; to Northwest Airlines as N606NW via ATS Leasing
I-DIKM	*Isola di Tavolara/ Positano*	47244/316	25.05.68-13.02.96	leased to ATI 00.10.81-01.06.86; wfu
I-DIKN	*Isola di Nisida*	47225/317	27.05.68-13.07.95	leased to ATI 28.03.82; reregistered N515MD 17.12.83, I-RIZG 14.05.89, then I-RIFG; wfu and to Northwest Airlines as N606NW via ATS Leasing
I-DIKO	*Isloa di Pantelleria*	47047/183	31.10.67-28.02.94	registered N904DC 00.01.83-24.11.87, then I-DIBU; to McDonnell Douglas
I-DIKP	*Isola di Marettimo*	47226/333	28.06.68-29.10.95	leased to ATI 01.04.80-01.05.85; wfu and to McDonnell Douglas as N946VV
I-DIKQ	*Isola di Stromboli*	47227/334	29.05.68-23.12.78	crashed into the sea on approach to Palermo
I-DIKR	*Isola di Torcello/ Piemonte*	47228/355	09.08.68-28.10.96	leased to ATI 16.12.81-07.10.86; wfu
I-DIKS	*Isola di Filicudi/ Basilicata*	47227/356	08.08.68-01.01.97	leased to ATI and Aermediterranea; reregistered I-RIKS 25.06.90 and I-RIFS 27.11.92; wfu and to Northwest Airlines as N616NW via ATS Leasing
I-DIKT	*Isola di Ustica*	47230/395	18.10.68-07.04.82	leased to Aermediterranea, later to ATI
I-DIKU	*Isola d'Ischia*	47101/195	24.11.67-31.03.95	registered N905DC 01.02.83-24.11.87 and I-DIBV 24.11.87-01.12.92, then I-DIBL from 01.12-92; to Northwest Airlines as N603NW via ATS Leasing
I-DIKV	*Isola di Vulcano*	47231/396	19.10.68-16.02.93	reregistered I-RIKV 20.07.88; wfu
I-DIKW	*Isola di Ginnutri*	47283/397	24.10.68-23.10.92	registered N2786S 31.12.82-03.12.87, then I-DIBX; wfu
I-DIKY	*Isola di Alicudi/ Puglia*	47232/428	18.12.68-29.05.94	leased to JAT-Jugoslovenski Aerotransport 11.04.69-25.05.70 and to ATI 01.04.79-114.04.89; reregistered I-RIZY 25.06.90 and I-RIFY 01.12.92; wfu and to Northwest Airlines as N607NW via ATS Leasing
I-DIKZ	*Isola di Linosa*	47311/398	21.10.68-15.01.93	reregistered I-RIKZ 26.07.88; wfu
I-DIZA	*Isola di Palmarola*	47238/465	14.03.69-16.03.95	reregistered I-RIZA 20.07.88; to ValuJet Airlines as N945VV
I-DIZB	*Isola di Maddalena*	47434/537	26.09.69-31.10.93	leased to ATI; reregistered I-RIZJ 19.08.89; wfu
I-DIZC	*Isola di Meloria/ Molise*	47435/540	15.10.69-06.08.95	leased to ATI 28.0570-01.02.91; reregistered I-RIZC 20.06.90 and I-RIFL 01.12.92; wfu and to Northwest Airlines as N611NW via ATS Leasing
I-DIZE	*Isola della Meloria*	47502/574	20.02.70-26.08.96	leased to ATI-Aero Trasporti Italiani 31.05.79-01.09.86; wfu
I-DIZF	*Isola di Spargi/ Cassino*	47519/615	18.02.71-17.08.92	leased to ATI and Aermediterranea; reregistered I-RIZF 23.02.89; wfu
I-DIZI	*Isola di Basiluzzo/ Abruzzo*	47432/525	28.08.69-26.5.95	leased to ATI-Aero Trasporti Italiani 20.05.80-31.07.90; reregistered I-RIZB; wfu
I-DIZO	*Isola del Tino/ Erice*	47518/614	16.02.71-02.08.96	leased at various times to ATI, Alisarda and Aermediterranea; reregistered I-RIZQ 23.02.89 and I-RIFE 03.12.92; wfu and to Northwest Airlines as N619NW via ATS Leasing
I-DIZU	*Isola di Bergeggi/ Valle d'Aosta*	47433/526	15.08.69-09.08.80	leased at vatious times to ATI and Aermediterranea; reregistered I-RIZU 25.06.90 and I-RIFU 27.11.92; wfu and to Northwest airlines as N618NW
I-RIFV	*Lazio*	47533/641	30.10.94-31.12.96	ex I-ATIW; wfu and later to Northwest Airlines as N620NW
I-RIFW	*Lombardia*	47575/680	30.10.94-26.10.96	ex I-ATTY; wfu and to Northwest Airlines as N622NW via ATS Leasing
I-RIZK	*Toscana*	47436/541	01.07.89-29.08.94	ex N873UM; reregistered I-RIFZ; wfu and to Northwest Airlines as N612NW via ATS Leasing

I-RIZL	Emiglia Romana	47437/544	01.06.89-22.08.94	ex N872UM; wfu and later to Aero Republica as HK-3963
I-RIZR	Marche	47544/676	27.03.91-01.05.96	ex I-ATIJ; leased to ATI 00.11.92-30.10.94; reregistered I-RIFM 04.12.92; wfu and to Northwest Airlines as N621NW
I-RIZT	Friuli Venezia Giulia	47591/706	01.11.91-17.04.96	ex I-ATIQ; wfu and later to Northwest Airlines as N623NW via ATS Leasing

* Douglas DC-9-32F

Note: many aircraft were frequently reregistered and some were operated for a short time in US markings

McDonnell Douglas DC-8-62 1967-1981 (11)

189-passenger long-range aircraft, powered by four 80 kN (18,000 lb) Pratt & Whitney JT3D-3b turbofan engines, generating a cruising speed of 895 km/h

I-DIWC*	Titano	45960/347	10.04.68-22.03.81	leased to Zambia Airways as I-DIWC 00.71; wfu; to Minerve as F-GDJM 24.11.82
I-DIWH	Pierluigi da Palestrina	46132/535	24.07.70-04.04.81	wfu; to Aero Perú as OB-R-1249 25.05.82
I-DIWJ	Antonio Vivaldi	45986/379	26.07.68-22.04.81	wfu; to Guy American Airways as N3931G
I-DIWK	Giacomo Puccini	46082/458	14.05.69-07.01.79	to Braniff International as N801BN
I-DIWN	Guiseppe Verdi	45909/307	28.10.67-15.11.78	to Braniff International as N802BN
I-DIWQ*	Ciclope	45961/361	30.06.68-26.03.81	wfu; to Sea & Sun Aviation as N3931A 01.08.83
I-DIWV	Gioacchino Rossini	45910/311	16.11.67-07.05.80	leased to DETA as I-DIWV 25.11.77-30.01.79; to Guy American Airways as N39307
I-DIWW	Arcangelo Corelli	46098/516	12.02.70-28.03.81	wfu; to Guy American Airways as N39305 01.02.83
I-DIWX	Luigi Cherubini	46142/546	12.03.71-07.01.81	wfu; to Aero Perú as OB-R-1210 Armando Revoredo 19.02.81
I-DIWY	Vincenzo Bellini	46027/437	25.02.69-03.04.81	wfu; to Aero Perú as OB-R-1248 25.02.82
I-DIWZ	Gaetano Donizetti	46026/452	30.04.69-15.09.70	crashed on landing at New York/J F Kennedy International, USA

* McDonnell Douglas DC-8-62CF

Boeing 747-100 1970-1981 (2)

366-passenger wide-body long-range aircraft with short upper deck, powered by four 230 kN (51,600 lb) Pratt & Whitney JT9D-7A turbofan engines, generating a speed of 940 km/h

| I-DEMA | Neil Armstrong | 19729/36 | 13.05.70-04.11.81 | to Boullioun Aviation Services as N355AS |
| I-DEME | Arturo Ferrarin | 19730/56 | 01.07.70-17)9.81 | leased to Aer lingus as I-DEME 26.09.76-24.10.76; to Boullioun Aiation Services as N356AS |

Boeing 747-200B 1971-2004 (19)

440-passenger wide-body intercontinental aircraft, powered by four 253 kN (56,900 lb) General Electric CF6-50E2 turbofan engines, generating a speed of 895 km/h

I-DEMB	Carlo Del Prete	20520/190	26.05.72-12.12.80	to Boeing Aircraft Holding Company (BAHC) as N45224
I-DEMC*	Taormina	22506/492	26.11.80-20.09.04	to AirBridgeCargo as VP-BIB
I-DEMD*	Cortina d'Ampezzo	22507/497	12.12.80-05.06.95	to Atlas Air as N516MC
I-DEMF*	Portofino	22508/499	22.12.80-28.12.00	to Atlas Air as N540MC

I-DEMG	Cervinia	22510/533	05.08.81-31.10.01	wfu
I-DEML	Sorrento	22511/536	16.09.81-31.03.02	wfu
I-DEMN	Porto Cervo	22512/542	05.11.81-31.03.02	wfu
I-DEMO	Francesco De Pinedo	19731/120	30.03.71-10.12.81	to Boeing Aircraft Holding Company (BAHC) as N357AS
I-DEMP	Capri	22513/546	03.12.81-31.03.02	wfu
I-DEMR**	Stresa/Titano	22545/545	18.12.81-15.02.04	wfu
I-DEMS	Argentario	22969/575	28.02.83-31.10.01	wfu
I-DEMT	Montecatini	23300/613	29.05.85-14.12.95	wfu
I-DEMU	Geo Chavez	19732/134	07.05.71-19.11.81	to Boeing Aircraft Holding Company (BAHC) as N358AS
I-DEMV	Sestriere	23301/618	24.07.85-15.12.01	wfu
I-DEMW*	Spoleto	23476/647	13.06.86-19.10.95	to Atlas Air as N518MC
I-DEMX**	Ciclope	23286/614	21.05.92-29.02.94	ex D-ABYZ, leased from Lufthansa
I-DEMY	Asolo	21589/345	25.07.90-21.10.01	wfu
N535MC**		21833/423	03.05.98-01.02.99	leased from Atlas Air
N536MC**		21576/334	15.03.03-10.04.06	leased from Atlas Air

* Boeing 747-200B Combi, ** Boeing 747-200F Freighter

McDonnell Douglas DC-10-30 1973-1986 (8)

270-passenger long-range wide-body aircraft, powered by three 227 kN (51,000 lb) General Electric CF6-50C turbofan engines, generating a speed of 895 km/h

I-DYNA	Galileo Galilei	47861/75	06.02.73-27.12.82	to McDonnell Douglas as N3878P
I-DYNB	Giotto di Bondone	47866/149	19.04.74-27.06.85	to Eastern Airlines as N391EA
I-DYNC	Luigi Pirandello	47867/178	18.02.75-11.06.82	leased to Sabena as I-DYNC 12.04 to 11.06.82; to Eastern Airlines as N392EA
I-DYND	Enrico Fermi	47868/200	05.05.75-25.05.83	to Pakistan international Airlines (PIA) as AP-BBL
I-DYNE	Dante Alighieri	47862/88	21.03.73-15.01.86	to Eastern Airlines as N390EA
I-DYNI	Michelangelo Buonarotti	47863/94	20.04.73-28.12.82	to McDonnell Douglas as N3878M
I-DYNO	Benvenuto Cellini	47864/121	13.11.73-29.12.82	leased to Sabena as I-DYNO 16.09-10.82; to McDonnell Douglas as N3878F
I-DYNU	Guglielmo Marconi	47865/135	22.01.74-28.10.83	to Finnair as OH-LHD

Boeing 727-200 Advanced 1976-1985 (18)

155-passenger short/medium-range aircraft, powered by three 66.7 kN (15,000 lb) Pratt & Whitney JT8D-9A turbofan engines, generating a cruising speed of 865 km/h

I-DIRA	Città di Gubbio	21264/1225	07.10.76-06.01.84	to PEOPLExpress as N571PE
I-DIRB	Città di Siracusa	21268/1229	20.12.76-25.08.84	to PEOPLExpress as N575PE
I-DIRC	Città di Aosta	21269/1230	19.11.76-18.08.84	to PEOPLExpress as N576PE
I-DIRD	Città di Bergamo	21661/1394	05.10.78-28.07.84	to PEOPLExpress as N578PE
I-DIRF	Città di Lecce	21662/1421	12.12.78-12.01.84	to PEOPLExpress as N579PE

I-DIRG	*Città di Urbino*	21663/1438	01.02.79-17.07.84	to PEOPLExpress as N580PE
I-DIRI	*Città di Siena*	21265/1226	18.10.76-28.07.84	to PEOPLExpress as N572PE
I-DIRJ	*Città di Verona*	21270/1231	21.12.76-03.04.84	to PEOPLExpress as N577PE
I-DIRL	*Città di Viterbo*	21664/1448	27.02.79-05.01.84	to THY-Türk Hava Yollari as TC-JCK *Erciyes*
I-DIRM	*Città di Genova*	22052/1568	17.01.80-18.12.84	to PEOPLExpress as N581PE
I-DIRN	*Città di Aquileia*	22053/1620	23.05.80-25.02.85	to PEOPLExpress as N582PE
I-DIRO	*Città di Amalfi*	21266/1227	18.10.76-21.06.84	to PEOPLExpress as N573PE
I-DIRP	*Città di Ivrea*	22165/1635	02.07.80-20.02.85	to PEOPLExpress as N583PE
I-DIRQ	*Città di Sassari*	22166/1725	17.03.81-19.11.84	to PEOPLExpress as N584PE
I-DIRR	*Città di Trento*	22167/1752	01.06.81-16.04.85	to PEOPLExpress as N585PE
I-DIRS	*Città di Sulmona*	22168/1770	03.09.81-02.05.85	to PEOPLExpress as N586PE
I-DIRT	*Città di Matera*	22702/1814	20.12.82-24.04.85	to Aviogenex as YU-AKM Pula
I-DIRU	*Città di Ravenna*	21267/1228	20.12.76-26.07.84	to PEOPLExpress as N574PE

Airbus A300B4-200 1980-1998 (12)

238-passenger medium-range wide-body aircraft, powered by two 230 kN (52,000 lb) General Electric CF6-50C2 turbofan engines, generating a speed of 895km/h

I-BUSB*	*Tiziano*	101	28.04.80-14.05.98	to FSBU First Security Bank of Utah as N59101
I-BUSC	*Botticello*	106	29.05.80-14.04.98	to C-S Aviation as N59106
I-BUSD	*Caravaggio*	107	20.06.80-15.01.98	to C-S Aviation as N59107
I-BUSF	*Tintoretto*	123	01.12.80-12.06.97	to C-S Aviation as N59123
I-BUSG*	*Canaletto*	139	28.04.81-20.03.98	to C-S Aviation as N59139
I-BUSH	*Mantegna*	140	00.05.81-00.07.97	to S-C Aviation as N59140
I-BUSJ	*Tiepolo*	142	27.05.81-29.07.97	to S-C Aviation as N68142
I-BUSL	*Pinturicchio*	173	23.02.82-20.03.98	to FSBU First Security Bank of Utah as N68173
I-BUSP**	*Masaccio*	067	30.10.88-00.00.97	ex N207EA; wfu and broken up
I-BUSQ**	*Michelangelo*	118	01.03.89-00.00.97	ex N401UA; wfu and broken up
I-BUSR**	*Cimabue*	120	01.04.89-00.00.97	ex N402UA; wfu and broken up
I-BUST**	*Piero della Francesca*	68	12.07.89-00.00.97	ex N403UA; broken up

* Airbus A300N4-200F; ** A300B4-100

McDonnell Douglas MD-82 1983-2012 (90)

172-passenger short/medium-range aircraft, powered by two rear-mounted 89 kN (20,000 lb) Pratt & Whitney JT8D-217A turbofan engines, generating a speed of 875km/h

I-DACM	*La Spezia*	49971/1755	30.10.94-06.02.09	ex ATI; to WFBN-Wells Fargo Bank Northwest as N971AG
I-DACN	*Rieti*	49972/1757	30.10.94-06.02.09	ex ATI; to WFBN-Wells Fargo Bank Northwest as N972AG
I-DACP	*Padova*	49973/1762	30.10.94-14.05.10	ex ATI; to Bulgarian Air Charter as LZ-LDP
I-DACQ	*Taranto*	49974/1774	31.10.90-19.03.08	wfu and stored
I-DACR	*Carrara*	49975/1775	31.10.90-06.10.12	wfu and stored

I-DACS	*Maratea*	53053/1806	21.12.90-25.10.12	wfu and stored
I-DACT	*Valtellina*	53054/1856	10.05.91-11.12.10	wfu and stored
I-DACU	*Brindisi*	53055/1857	30.10.94-28.12.09	ex ATI; to Bank of Utaha as N530SV
I-DACV	*Riccione*	53056/1880	30.10.94-30.11.11	ex ATI; wfu and stored
I-DACW	*Vieste*	53057/1894	05.08.91-13.01.09	wfu and stored
I-DACX	*Piacenza*	53060/1944	20.12.91-01.12.08	wfu and stored
I-DACY	*Novara*	53059/1942	16.12.91-28.12.09	wfu and to Servisair as D2-FGI 04.10
I-DACZ	*Castelfidardo*	53058/1927	29.10.91-26.10.12	to Bulgarian Air Charter as LZ-LDT
I-DAND	*Trani*	53061/1957	30.10.94-26.07.12	ex ATI; wfu and stored
I-DANF	*Sassari*	53062/1960	30.10.94-01.03.12	ex ATI; wfu and stored
I-DANG	*Benevento*	53176/1972	30.10.94-18.06.12	ex ATI; leased to Eurofly 01.04-29.10.95; wfu and stored
I-DANH	*Messina*	53177/1973	30.10.94-13.01.09	ex ATI; leased to Eurofly 01.04-29.10.95; wfu and stored
I-DANL	*Cosenza*	53178/1994	30.10.94-16.08.10	ex ATI; cancelled from register
I-DANM	*Vicenza*	53179/1997	30.10.94-20.10.10	ex ATI; to Pennant Aviation as N247PA
I-DANP	*Fabriano*	53180/2002	16.06.92-20.10.10	to Pennant Aviation as N251PA
I-DANQ	*Lecce*	53181/2005	30.10.94-01.09.12	ex ATI; wfu and stored
I-DANR	*Matera*	53203/2007	30.10.94-13.01.09	ex ATI; wfu and stored
I-DANU	*Trapani*	53204/2009	30.09.92-01.10.12	ex ATI; wfu and to Bulgarian Air Charter as LZ-LDU 17.04.13
I-DANV	*Forte dei Marmi*	53205/2028	30.09.92-13.01.09	wfu and stored
I-DANW	*Siena*	53206/2034	30.11.92-09.06.12	wfu and stored
I-DATA	*Gubbio*	53216/2048	21.03.93-11.06.10	to Bulgarian Air Charter as LZ-LDN
I-DATB	*Bergamo*	53221/2079	14.04.94-22.06.10	to Bulgarian Air Charter as LZ-LDE
I-DATC	*Foggia*	53222/2080	02.05.94-05.07.12	wfu
I-DATD	*Savona*	53223/2081	16.05.94-31.12.08	wfu and stored
I-DATE	*Grosseto*	53217/2053	30.10.94-20.10.12	ex ATI; wfu and stored
I-DATF	*Vittorio Veneto*	53224/2084	03.06.94-21.05.10	to Bulgarian Air Charter as LZ-LDB
I-DATG	*Arezzo*	53225/2086	26.07.94-14.01.12	to Caspian Airlines as EP-CPU
I-DATH	*Pescara*	53226/2087	26.07.94-31.12.08	wfu and stored
I-DATI	*Siracusa*	53218/2060	30.10.94-27.10.12	ex ATI; wfu and stored
I-DATJ	*Lunigiana*	53227/2103	26.01.95-28.10.10	to Pennant Aviation as N259PA
I-DATK	*Ravenna*	53228/2104	31.01.95-13.01.09	to Bulgarian Air Charter as LZ-LDM
I-DATL	*Alghero*	53229/2105	21.02.95-13.01.09	to Bulgarian Air Charter as LZ-LDL
I-DATM	*Cividade del Friuli*	53230/2106	28.02.95-23.10.12	wfu and stored
I-DATN	*Sondrio*	53231/2107	23.03.95-07.06.05	to McDonnell Douglas Finance Corporation as N772BC
I-DATO	*Reggio Emilia*	53219/2062	02.06.93-21.06.11	to Bank of Utah as N219AP
I-DATP	*Latina*	53232/2108	31.03.95-06.07.05	to Copa Airlines as HK-4399X
I-DATQ	*Modena*	53233/2110	28.04.95-13.01.09	to Engage Aviation LLC as N261PH
I-DATR	*Livorno*	53234/2111	24.05.95-13.01.09	wfu and stored
I-DATS	*Foligno*	53235/2113	30.06.95-28.12.09	wfu and stored
I-DATU	*Verona*	53220/2073	31.03.94-28.12.09	wfu and stored; to Servisair asD2-ATU 13.05.10
I-DAVA	*Cuneo*	49215/1253	30.10.94-23.04.04	ex ATI; leased to Eurofly 01.04-29.10.95 and later sold to Eurofly
I-DAVB	*Ferrara*	49216/1262	30.10.94-16.04.06	ex ATI; to Itali Airlines

I-DAVC	*Lucca*	49217/1268	30.10.94-07.06.04	ex ATI; to Eurofly
I-DAVD	*Mantova*	49218/1274	30.10.94-07.05.04	ex ATI; to Eurofly
I-DAVF	*Oristano*	49219/1310	30.10.94-28.07.04	ex ATI; to Eurofly
I-DAVG	*Pesaro*	49220/1319	30.10.94-14.02.05	ex ATI; to Eurofly
I-DAVH	*Salerno*	49221/1330	30.10.94-22.01.05	ex ATI; to Eurofly
I-DAVI	*Assisi*	49430/1334	15.01.87-18.11.04	to Eurofly
I-DAVJ	*Parma*	49431/1377	23.06.87-31.10.06	to Itali Airlines
I-DAVK	*Pompei*	49432/1378	23.06.87-04.10.04	to Eurofly
I-DAVL	*Reggio Calabria*	49433/1428	30.10.94-06.02.09	ex ATI; leased to Bulgarian Air Charter as LZ-LDL; to WFBN-Wells Fargo Bank Northwest as N943AG
I-DAVM	*Caserta*	49434/1446	01.03.88-31.12.08	to WFBN-Wells Fargo Bank Northwest as N434AG
I-DAVN	*Volterra*	49435/1504	30.10.94-28.01.99	ex ATI; destroyed beyond repair in hard landing at Catania
I-DAVP	*Gorizia*	49549/1544	30.10.94-02.06.09	ex ATI; to WFBN-Wells Fargo Bank Northwest as N59AG
I-DAVR	*Pisa*	49550/1584	30.10.94-13.01.09	ex ATI; leased at various times to Eurofly, Bulgarian Air Chater as LZ-LDR, and Kish Air as I-DAVR; wfu and stored
I-DAVS	*Catania*	49551/1586	30.10.94-06.02.09	ex ATI; to WFBN-Wells Fargo Bank Northwest as N551AG
I-DAVT	*Como*	49552/1597	30.10.94-26.10.12	ex ATI; wfu and stored
I-DAVU	*Udine*	49794/1600	30.10.94-06.02.09	ex ATI; to WFBN-Wells Fargo Bank Northwest as N794AG
I-DAVV	*Pavia*	49795/1639	30.10.94-03.05.10	ex ATI; to Bulgarian Air Charter as LZ-LDW
I-DAVW	*Camerino*	49796/1713	30.10.94-02.06.09	ex ATI; to Wintech Industries as N796AG
I-DAVX	*Asti*	49969/1719	30.10.94-31.12.08	ex ATI; to WFBN-Wells Fargo Bank Northwest as N969AG
I-DAVZ	*Brescia*	49970/1737	30.10.94-06.02.09	ex ATI; to WFBN-Wells Fargo Bank Northwest as N970AG
I-DAWA	*Roma*	49192/1126	16.12.83-28.12.08	to Safair as ZS-
I-DAWB	*Cagliari*	49197/1138	27.05.84-01.05.08	wfu and stored
I-DAWC	*Campobasso*	49198/1142	26.06.84-28.11.08	wfu and stored
I-DAWD	*Catanzaro*	49199/1143	29.06.84-29.12.08	wfu and stored
I-DAWE	*Milano*	49193/1127	16.12.83-19.12.08	to Aergo Leasing as I-DAWE
I-DAWF	*Firenze*	49200/1147	24.07.84-12.01.09	to Aergo Leasing as I-DAWF
I-DAWG	*L'Aquila*	49201/1148	30.07.84-22.01.09	to Aergo Leasing as I-DAWG
I-DAWH	*Palermo*	49202/1170	30.11.84-31.12.08	wfu and later to Aergo Leasing as I-DAWH
I-DAWI	*Ancona*	49194/1130	24.02.84-20.01.09	to Aergo Leasing as I-DAWI
I-DAWJ	*Genova*	49203/1174	03.07.85-31.12.08	ex ATI; wfu and later to Aergo Leasing as I-DAWJ
I-DAWL	*Perugia*	49204/1179	19.02.85-31.12.08	wfu and later to Aergo Leasing as I-DAWL
I-DAWM	*Potenza*	49205/1184	27.02.85-31.12.08	to Aergo Leasing as I-DAWM
I-DAWO	*Bari*	49195/1136	11.05.84-10.01.09	to Aergo Leasing as I-DAWO
I-DAWP	*Torino*	49206/1188	15.03.85-31.12.08	to Aergo Leasing as I-DAWP
I-DAWQ	*Trieste*	49207/1189	20.03.85-07.01.09	to ILFC-International Lease Finance Corporation as N461LF
I-DAWR	*Venezia*	49208/1190	25.03.85-21.04.04	wfu and stored
I-DAWS	*Aosta*	49209/1191	02.04.85-22.10.08	wfu and to Air Albatros as 9A-CDM 11.02.09
I-DAWT	*Napoli*	49210/1192	30.10.94-31.12.08	ex ATI; wfu and later to Aergo Leasing
I-DAWU	*Bologna*	49196/1137	20.05.84-02.12.08	to TARA Aerospace as I-DAWU
I-DAWV	*Trento*	49211/1202	30.10.94-31.12.08	ex ATI; wfu and stored, later to Aergo Leasing

I-DAWW	*Riace*	49212/1233	30.10.94-23.04.04	ex ATI; to Eurofly
I-DAWY	*Agrigento*	49213/1243	30.10.94-30.06.04	ex ATI; to Eurofly
I-DAWZ	*Avellino*	49214/1245	30.10.94-23.04.04	ex ATI; to Eurofly

Airbus A300B2-200 1988-1997 (2)

238-passenger medium-range wide-body aircraft, powered by two 230 kN (52,000 lb) General Electric CF^-50C2 turbofan engines, generating a speed of 895km/h

I-BUSM	*Raffaello*	049	01.09.88-09.02.96	ex N291EA; wfu and broken up 22.08.07
I-BUSN	*Giotto*	051	21.12.88-28.12.96	ex N292EA; wfu and broken up 23.08.07

Boeing 737-200C 1991-1993 (2)

Cargo short-range narrow-body aircraft, powered by two 66.7 kN (15,000 lb) Pratt & Whitney JT8D-9A turbofan engines, generating a cruising speed of 800 km/h

EI-ASD	20219/208	06.06.92-31.03.93	leased from Aer Lingus
EI-ASE	20220/215	14.04.91-28.05.93	leased from Aer Lingus; sub-leased to Hunting Air Cargo 15.12.92-28.05.93

McDonnell Douglas MD-11 1991-2009 (8)

325-passenger long-range wide-body aircraft, powered by three 273.5 kN (61,500 lb) General Electric CF6-80C2D1F turbofan engines, generating a maximum speed of 940 km/h

I-DUPA**	*Tetro all Scala/*			
	Gioacchino Rossini	48426/468	27.03.92-10.07.05	reregistered EI-UPA
I-DUPB*	*Valle dei Templi/*			
	Pietro Mascagni	48431/534	30.04.93-10.06.04	to WFBN-Wells Fargo Bank Northwest as N431LT
I-DUPC	*Vincenzo Bellini*	48581/565	05.05.94-28.05.04	to WFBN-Wells Fargo Bank Northwest as N581LT
I-DUPD	*Gaetano Donizetti*	48630/567	10.06.94-09.06.04	to WFBN-Wells Fargo Bank Northwest as N630LT
I-DUPE**	*Arena di Verona/*			
	Guiseppe Verdi	48427/471	27.11.91-27.10.05	reregistered EI-UPE
I-DUPI**	*Fontana di Trevi/*			
	Giacomo Puccini	48428/474	12.12.91-31.08.05	reregistered EI-UPI
I-DUPO**	*Canal Grande/*			
	Niccolò Paganini	48429/500	17.07.92-31.08.05	reregistered EI-UPO
I-DUPU**	*Ponte Veccio/*	48430/508	17.08.92-25.07.06	reregistered EI-UPU
	Antonio Vivaldi			
EI-UPA***		48426/468	10.07.05-10.01.09	ex I-DUPA; to Pegasus Aviation Financial Co (PAFCO) as EI-UPA
EI-UPE***		48427/471	27.10.05-08.01.09	ex I-DUPE; to Pegasus Aviation Financial Co (PAFCO) as EI-UPE
EI-UPI***		48428/474	31.08.05-10.01.09	ex I-DUPI; to Pegasus Aviation Financial Co (PAFCO) as EI-UPI
EI-UPO***		48429/500	31.08.05-10.01.09	ex I-DUPO; to Pegasus Aviation Financial Co (PAFCO) as EI-UPO
EI-UPU***		48430/508	25.07.06-10.01.09	ex I-DUPU; to Pegasus Aviation Financial Co (PAFCO) as EI-UPU

* MD-11C (Combi), ** MD-11C (Combi) later converted to full freighter; *** MD-11F freighter

Airbus A321-100 1994-2021 (23)

230-passenger short/medium-range aircraft, powered by two 147 kN (33,000 lb) CFM International CFM56-5B1 turbofan engines, generating a speed of 850 km/h

I-BIXA	Piazza del Duomo MILANO	477	18.03.94-18.09.14	wfu
I-BIXB	Piazza Castello TORINO	524	23.05.95-18.11.10	reregistered EI-IXB
I-BIXC	Piazza del Campo SIENA	526	23.05.95-17.11.10	reregistered EI-IXC
I-BIXD	Piazza Pretoria PALERMO	532	27.06.95-23.11.10	reregistered EI-IXD
I-BIXE	Piazza di Spagna ROMA	488	27.05.94-03.09.14	wfu
I-BIXF	Piazza Maggiore BOLOGNA	515	07.09.95-05.11.10	reregistered EI-IXF
I-BIXG	Piazza dei Miracoli PISA	516	21.09.95-24.11.10	reregistered EI-IXG
I-BIXH	Piazza dell Signoria GUBBIO	940	26.01.99-09.02.10	reregistered EI-IXH
I-BIXI	Piazza San Marco VENEZIA	494	07.06.94-16.11.10	reregistered EI-IXI
I-BIXJ	Piazza del Municipio NOTO	959	26.02.99-08.02.10	reregistered EI-IXJ
I-BIXK	Piazza Ducale VIGEVANO	1220	31.05.00-09.02.10	reregistered EI-IXK
I-BIXL	Piazza del Duomo LECCE	513	31.01.96-15.07.19	wfu
I-BIXM	Piazza di San Francesco ASSISSI	514	28.02.96-21.11.18	wfu; to DAE Captial as LZ-AWS
I-BIXN	Piazza del Duomo CATANIA	576	01.03.96-08.10.19	wfu and broken up
I-BIXO	Piazza Plebiscito NAPOLI	495	20.07.94-11.11.10	reregistered EI-IXO
I-BIXP	Carlo Morelli	583	02.04.96-26.12.19	wfu and broken up
I-BIXQ	Domenico Colapietro	586	12.02.97-15.11.19	wfu; to Castlelake as EI-ROE
I-BIXR	Piazza del Campidoglio ROMA	593	25.02.97-28.04.20	wfu; to Castlelake as 9H-AHW
I-BIXS	Piazza San Martino LUCCA	595	02.04.97-07.05.20	wfu
I-BIXT	Piazza del Signori VICENZA	765	23.01.98-30.06.12	to Asian Wings Airways as XY-AGN
I-BIXU	Piazza della Signoria FIRENZE	434	04.11.94-10.11.10	reregistered EI-IXU
I-BIXV	Piazza del Rinascimento URBINO	819	06.05.98-11.02.10	reregistered EI-IXV

I-BIXZ	*Piazza del Duomo ORVIETO*	848	27.07.98-10.02.10	reregistered EI-IXZ
EI-IXB	*Piazza Castello TORINO*	524	18.11.10-31.10.13	ex I-BIXB; wfu
EI-IXC	*Piazzo del Campo SIENA*	526	17.11.10-09.11.13	ex I-BIXC; wfu
EI-IXD	*Piazza Pretoria PALERMO*	532	23.11.10-19.02.13	ex I-BIXD; wfu
EI-IXF	*Piazza Maggiore BOLOGNA*	515	07.09.95-05.11.10	ex I-BIXF; wfu
EI-IXG	*Piazza dei Miracoli PISA*	516	24.11.10-25.05.13	ex I-BIXG; wfu
EI-IXH	*Piazza della Signoria GUBBIO*	940	09.02.10-04.03.21	ex I-BIXH; wfu
EI-IXI	*Piazza San Marco VENEZIA*	494	16.11.10-02.11.13	ex I-BIXI; wfu
EI-IXJ	*Piazza del Municipio NOTO*	959	08.02.10-31.07.20	ex I-BIXJ; wfu
EI-IXK	*Piazza Ducale VIGEVANO*	1220	09.02.10-04.03.21	ex I-BIXK; wfu
EI-IXO	*Piazza Plebiscito NAPOLI*	495	11.11.20-30.09.13	ex I-BIXO; wfu
EI-IXU	*Piazza della Signoria FIRENZE*	434	10.11.10-30.09.14	ex I-BIXU; wfu
EI-IXV	*Piazza del Rinascimento URBINO*	819	11.02.10-12.03.21	ex I-BIXV; wfu
EI-IXZ	*Piazza del Duomo ORVIETO*	848	10.02.10-11.09.20	ex I-BIXZ; wfu

Boeing 767-300ER 1995-2012 (14)

290-passenger wide-body medium- to long-range airliner, powered by two 764 kN (61,500 lb) General Electric CF6-80C2B6F turbofan engines, generating a speed of 900 km/h

I-DEIB	*Pier Paolo Racchetti*	27376/560	21.01.95-08.04.08	ex VH-ITA; leased to G-OITA 24.07.95-21.02.97; to VARIG-Viaçao Aérea Rio-Grandense as PR-VAG
I-DEIC	*Alberto Nassetti*	27377/561	21.01.95-03.09.08	ex VH-ITB; leased to G-OITB 21.07.95-24.03.97; to TAM Linhas Aéreas as PT-MSR
I-DEID	*Marco Polo*	27468/584	06.07.95-10.06.08	ex G-OITC; to TAM Linhas Aéreas as PT-MSQ
I-DEIF	*Cristoforo Colombo*	27908/578	07.08.95-11.08.09	ex G-OITF; to Omni Air International as N351AX
I-DEIG	*Francesco Agello*	27918/603	26.02.96-28.09.12	ex G-OITG; wfu
I-DEIL	*Arturo Ferrarin*	28147/611	13.05.96-28.01.10	ex G-OITL; to Omni Air International as N378AX
EI-CRD	*Giovanni da Verrazzano*	26259/534	18.09.01-09.12.11	wfu
EI-CRF	*Umberto Nobile*	25170/542	09.12.01-01.05.12	wfu
EI-CRL	*Leonardo da Vinci*	30008/743	22.03.99-18.03.09	wfu
EI-CRM	*Amerigo Vespucci*	30009/746	08.04.99-20.02.11	wfu
EI-CRO	*Francesco de Pinedo*	29383/747	16.04.99-17.12.08	to International Lease Finance Corp (ILFC) as N171LF

EI-CTW	Roberto Pau	30342/774	23.05.02-09.09.04	to Aeroflot as VP-BWQ Mikhail Lermontov
EI-DBP	Duca degli Abruzzi	26389/459	17.06.03-21.10.12	ex C-GGBJ; wfu
EI-DDW	Sebastiano Caboto	26608/559	08.01.04-25.10.12	ex N979PG; wfu

Airbus A320-200 1999-2021 (54)

150-passenger narrowbody airliner, powered by two 120 kN (27,000 lb) CFM International CFM56-5B4 turbofan engines, generating a speed of 830 km/h

I-BIKA	Johann Sebastian Bach	951	11.03.99-15.10.21	to ITA Airways
I-BIKB	Wolfgang Amadeus Mozart	1226	30.05.00-04.11.10	reregistered EI-IKB
I-BIKC	Zefiro/Torre di Pisa	1448	11.10.03-16.03.21	wfu; to ITA Airways 01.08.21
I-BIKD	Maestrale/Maschio Angioino-Napoli	1457	27.09.03-20.06.21	wfu and stored
I-BIKE	Franz Liszt	999	27.05.99-13.05.13	to Jetcom as OE-IJC
I-BIKF	Mole Antonelliana	1473	25.05.01-27.07.11	leased to Eurofly 01.06.01-04.12.03; reregistered EI-IKF
I-BIKG	Scirocco	1480	06.11.02-27.07.11	reregistered EI-IKG
I-BIKI	Girolamo Frescobaldi	1138	18.01.00-30.03.21	wfu and stored
I-BIKL	Libeccio	1489	06.11.02-17.11.10	reregistered EI-IKL
I-BIKO	George Bizet	1168	01.03.00-15.10.21	to ITA Airways
I-BIKU	Fryderyk Chopin	1217	30.05.00-02.11.10	reregistered EI-IKU
I-WEBA		3138	01.10.14-11.01.18	to Indigo as VT-IHH
I-WEBB	Ippolito Nievo	3161	04.10.14-19.01.18	leased to Air One 07.03.10-01.10.14; to Brussels Airlines as OO-SNJ
EI-DSA	Palazzo dei Normanni PALERMO	2869	13.01.09-14.03.21	to ITA Airways
EI-DSB	Tomasi de Lampedusa	2932	13.01.09-07.07.17	to Allegiant Air as N271NV
EI-DSC	Lorenzo de Medici	2995	13.01.09-08.12.17	leased to Air Berlin as EI-DSC 26.03-01.07.17; to Allegiant Air as N272NV
EI-DSD	Edmondo de Amicis	3076	13.01.09-11.10.17	to Allegiant Air as N273NV
EI-DSE	Antonio Fogazzaro	3079	13.01.09-12.10.17	to Allegiant Air as N274NV
EI-DSF	Emilio Salgari	3080	13.01.09-18.03.15	to Air Berlin as D-ABZN
EI-DSG	Elio Vittorini	3115	13.01.09-12.10.21	to ITA Airways 15.10.21
EI-DSH	Cecco Angiolieri	3178	07.03.10-07.05.15	to Air Berlin as D-ABZL
EI-DSI	Carlo Emilio Gadda	3213	13.01.09-17.12.14	to Air Berlin as D-ABZK
EI-DSJ	Ignazio Silone	3295	13.01.09-03.04.15	to Air Berlin as D-ABZJ
EI-DSL	Ignazio Silone	3343	01.11.14-15.10.21	to ITA Airways
EI-DSM	Cesare Beccaria	3362	13.01.09-10.06.15	to Congo Airways as 9Q-CLU Patrice-emery Lumumba
EI-DSN	Vicenzo Monti	3412	13.01.09-25.06.15	to Congo Airways as 9Q-CKD M zee Laurent Désiré Kabila
EI-DSO	Luigi Capuana	3464	13.01.09-12.11.14	to Air Berlin as D-ABZE
EI-DSP	Ippolito Nievo	3482	28.03.10-12.01.15	to Air Berlin as D-ABZF

EI-DSU	Beppe Fenoglio	3563	13.01.09-15.10.21	to ITA Airways
EI-DSV	Primo Levi	3598	13.01.09-15.10.21	leased to Air Berlin as EI-DSV 25.03-22.08.17; to ITA Airways
EI-DSW	Vasco Pratellini	3609	13.01.09-15.10.21	to ITA Airways
EI-DSX	Trilussa	3643	01.11.14-15. 10.21	leased to Air Berlin as EI-DSX 26.03-28.09.17; to ITA Airways
EI-DSY	Aldo Palazzeschi	3666	01.11.14-15.10.21	to ITA Airways
EI-DSZ		3695	01.10.14-15.10.21	leased to Air Berlin as EIO-DSZ 25.03-28.09.17; to ITA Airways
EI-DTA	Ada Negri	3732	13.01.09-15.10.21	to ITA Airways
EI-DTB	Giacomo Leopardi	3815	17.03.09-15.10.21	to ITA Airways
EI-DTC	Dante Alighieri	3831	06.04.09-20.12.14	to Pegasus Airlines as TC-DCF
EI-DTD	Alessandro Manzoni	3846	02.04.09-19.09.21	to DAE Capital 05.11.21
EI-DTE	Francesco Pertrarca	3885	07.05.09-15.10.21	to ITA Airways
EI-DTF	Giovanni Boccaccio	3906	19.05.09-11.10.21	to DAE Capital 09.11.21
EI-DTG	Ludovico Ariosto	3921	02.07.09-15.10.21	to ITA Airways
EI-DTH	Torquato Tasso	3956	25.09.09-02.04.21	wfu and stored
EI-DTI	Niccolò Machiavelli	3976	25.09.09-15.09.21	wfu and stored
EI-DTJ	Giovanni Pascoli	3978	25.09.09-03.07.21	wfu and stored
EI-DTK	Giovanni Verga	4075	24.03.10-15.10.21	to ITA Airways
EI-DTL	Gabriele D'Annunzio	4108	23.04.10-15.10.21	to ITA Airways
EI-DTM	Giuaeppe Ungaretti	4119	29.04.10-15.10.21	to ITA Airways
EI-DTN	Ugo Foscolo	4143	25.03.10-15.10.21	to ITA Airways
EI-DTO	Città di L'Aquila	4152	25.03.10-15.10.21	to ITA Airways
EI-EIA	Elsa Morante	4195	09.07.10-15.10.21	to ITA Airways
EI-EIB	Città di Fiumicino	4249	08.07.10-15.10.21	to ITA Airways
EI-EIC	Leonardo Sciascia	4520	10.12.10-08.01.21	wfu and stored
EI-EID	Umberto Saba	4523	08.12.10-12.12.20	wfu and stored
EI-EIE	Carlo Goldoni	4536	20.12.10-15.01.21	wfu and stored
EI-IKB	Wolfgang Amadeus Mozart	1226	03.11.10-15.10.21	ex I-BIKB; to ITA Airways
EI-IKF	Grecale	1473	26.07.11-15.10.21	ex I-BIKF; to ITA Airways
EI-IKG	Scirocco	1480	28.07.11-26.07.21	ex I-BIKG; wfu and stored
EI-IKL	Libeccio	1489	16.11.10-15.10.21	wx I-BIKL; to ITA Airways
EI-IKU	Fryderyk Chopin	1217	02.11.10-15.10.21	ex I-BIKU; to ITA Airways

Boeing 747-400F 2000-2002 (1)

Cargo long-range wide-body aircraft, powered by four 262.5 kN (59,000 lb) General Electric CF6-80C2BSF turbofan engines, generating a cruising speed of 935 km/h

N409MC		30558/1242	01.07.00-01.01.02	leased from Atlas Air

Airbus A319-100 2002-2021 (22)

150-passenger short/medium-range aircraft, powered by two 120 kN (27,000 lb) CFM International CFM56-5B5 turbofan engines, generating a speed of 850 km/h

I-BIMA	Isola d'Elba	1722	19.06.02-15.10.21	to ITA Airways
I-BIMB	Isola del Giglio	2033	23.09.03-22.11.10	reregistered EI-IMB
I-BIMC	Isola di Lipari	2057	29.10.03-15.11.10	reregistered EI-IMC
I-BIMD	Isola di Capri	2074	28.11.03-12.11.10	reregistered EI-IMD
I-BIME	Isola di Panarea	1740	27.06.02-10.11.10	reregistered EI-IME
I-BIMF	Isole Tremiti	2083	28.11.03-07.11.10	reregistered EI-IMF
I-BIMG	Isola di Pantelleria	2086	04.12.03-19.11.10	reregistered EI-IMG
I-BIMH	Isola di Ventotene	2101	06.02.04-30.11.10	reregistered EI-IMH
I-BIMI	Isola di Ponza	1745	19.07.02-25.11.10	reregistered EI-IMI
I-BIMJ	Isola di Caprera	1779	08.08.02-30.11.10	reregistered EI-IMJ
I-BIML	Isola La Maddalena	2127	01.03.04-01.12.10	reregistered EI-IML
I-BIMO	Isola d'Ischia	1770	19.0702-28.11.10	reregistered EI-IMO
EI-IMB	Isola del Giglio	2033	22.11.10-15.10.21	to ITA Airways
EI-IMC	Isola di Lipari	2057	15.11.10-15.10.21	to ITA Airways
EI-IMD	Isola di Capri	2074	12.11.10-15.10.21	to ITA Airways
EI-IME	Isola di Panarea	1740	10.11.10-15.10.21	to ITA Airways
EI-IMF	Isole Tremiti	2083	07.11.10-15.10.21	to ITA Airways
EI-IMG	Isola di Pantelleria	2086	19.11.10-15.10.21	to ITA Airways
EI-IMH	Isola di Ventotene	2101	30.11.10-15.10.21	to ITA Airways
EI-IMI	Isola di Ponza	1745	25.11.10-15.10.21	to ITA Airways
EI-IMJ	Isola di Caprera	1779	30.11.10-15.10.21	to ITA Airways
EI-IML	Isola La Maddalena	2127	01.12.10-15.10.21	to ITA Airways
EI-IMM	Vittorio Alfieri	4759	29.06.11-15.10.21	to ITA Airways
EI-IMN	Carlo Collodi	4764	05.08.11-15.10.21	to ITA Airways
EI-IMO	Isola d'Ischia	1770	28.11.10-15.10.21	to ITA Airways
EI-IMP	Italo Svevo	4859	04.11.11-21.04.21	wfu; to Bulair as LZ-MAA 03.09.21
EI-IMR	Italo Calvino	4875	04.11.11-21.04.21	wfu and stored
EI-IMS	Giuseppe Parini	4910	17.11.11-15.10.21	to ITA Airways
EI-IMT	Silvio Pellico	5018	14.06.12-01.10.21	to Orix Aircraft Management LTd 28.10.21
EI-IMU	Pietro Verri	5130	23.05.12-21.04.21	wfu and stored
EI-IMV	Filippo Tommaso Marinetti	5294	16.01.13-15.10.21	to ITA Airways

EI-IMW		5383	04.12.12-15.10.21	to ITA Airways
EI-IMX		5424	17.01.13-15.10.21	to ITA Airways

Boeing 777-200ER 2002-2021 (11)

305-passenger wide-body airliner, powered by two 417 kN (93,700 lb) General Electric GE90-90B2 turbofan

I-DISA	Taormina	32855/413	23.08.02-10.01.13	reregistered EI-ISA
I-DISB	Porto Rotondo	32859/426	28.01.03-22.03.12	reregistered EI-ISB
I-DISD	Cortina s'Ampezzo	32860/439	08.05.03-15.07.11	reregistered EI-ISD
I-DISE	Portofino	32856/421	25.10.02-19.12.12	reregistered EI-ISE
I-DISO	Positano	32857/424	26.11.02-28.12.12	reregistered EI-ISO
I-DISU	Madonna di Campiglio/ Alberto Nasetti	32858/425	12.12.02-08.04.20	wfu and stored
EI-DBK	Ostuni	32783/455	10.10.03-24.11.21	wfu and stored
EI-DBL	Sestriere	32781/459	14.11.03-13.12.21	wfu and stored
EI-DBM	Argentario	32782/463	12.12.03-20.12.21	wfu and stored
EI-DDH	Tropea	32784/477	15.05.04-03.12.21	wfu and stored
EI-FNI	Lampedusa	28688/436	27.02.17-31.08.21	ex VN-A141; wfu and stored
EI-ISA	Taormina	32855/413	10.01.13-11.10.21	ex I-DISA; wfu and stored
EI-ISB	Porto Rotondo	32859/426	22.03.12-12.10.21	ex I-DISB; wfu and stored
EI-ISD	Cortina d'Ampezzo	32860/439	15.07.11-13.11.21	ex I-DISD; wfu and stored
EI-ISE	Portofino/Pier Paolo Rachetti	32856/421	19.12.12-18.03.20	ex I-DISE; wfu and stored
EI-ISO	Positano	32857/424	28.12.12-20.04.20	ex I-DISO; wfu and stored

Airbus A330-200 2009-2021 (14)

250-passenger wide-body long-Range airliner, powered by two 316 kN (71,100 lb) General Electric CF6-80E1A3 turbofan engines, generating a speed of 875 km/h

I-EJGA	Artemisia Gentileschi	825	01.06.15-21.03.20	ex A6-AGA; wfu and stored
I-EJGB	Francesco Borromini	831	05.06.15-23.03.20	ex A6-AGB; wfu and stored
EI-DIR	Filippo Brunelleschi	272	13.01.09-04.04.21	ex A6-EYV; wfu and stored
EI-DIP	Gian Lorenzo Bernini	339	13.01.09-06.08.20	ex A6-EYW; wfu and stored
EI-EJG	Raffaello Sanzio	1123	06.07.10-15.10.21	to ITA Airways
EI-EJH	Sandro Botticelli	1135	23.07.10-15.10.21	to ITA Airways
EI-EJI	Canaletto	1218	15.04.11-26.03.21	wfu and stored
EI-EJJ	Michelangelo Merisi da Caravaggio	1225	19.05.11-05.05.21	wfu and stored
EI-EJK	Giotto	1252	15.09.11-15.10.21	to ITA Airways
EI-EJL	Piero della Francesca	1283	30.01.12-15.10.21	to ITA Airways

EI-EJM	*Giovanni Battista Tiepolo*	1308	14.05.12-15.10.21	to ITA Airways
EI-EJN	*Il Tintoretto*	1313	29.05.12-15.10.21	to ITA Airways
EI-EJO	*Tiziano*	1327	11.07.12-15.10.21	to ITA Airways
EI-EJP	*Michelangelo Buonarotti*	1354	22.10.12-15.10.21	to ITA Airways

Boeing 777-300ER 2017-2021 (1)

365-passenger wide-body airliner, powered by two 513 kN (115,300 lb) General Electric GE90-115B turbofan engines, generating a maximum speed of 945 km/h

EI-WLA	*Roma*	35783/786	01.09.17-15.09.21	ex F-ONOU; wfu and stored

Alitalia Express Fleet 1996-2013

ATR 42-300 1996-2007 (9)

48-passenger high-wing regional aircraft, powered by two 1,343 kW (1,800 hp) Pratt & Whitney Canada PW120 turboprop engines, generating a cruising speed of 500 km/h

I-ATRD	*Lago Trasimeno*	032	01.11.96-28.11.99	ex Avianova; to SiFly as I-ATRD
I-ATRF	*Flumendosa*	034	01.11.96-19.08.02	ex Avianova; to Air Industria as I-ATRF
I-ATRG	*Lago Maggiore*	042	01.11.96-11.12.06	ex Avianova; to UTair Aviation as VP-BCD 08.09.07
I-ATRJ	*Lago di Bolsena*	057	01.11.96-04.05.07	ex Avianova; to UTair Aviation as VP-BCG
I-ATRL	*Fiume Adige*	068	25.10.96-27.07.06	ex Avianova; to UTair Aviation as VP-BCF 08.09.07
I-ATRN	*Arno*	020	01.11.96-10.05.00	ex Avianova; to Air Mandalay as F-OHOT 17.11.00
I-ATRP	*Lago di Garda*	021	01.11.96-17.01.00	ex Avianova; to Air Mandalay as F-OHOS 08.08.00
I-NOWA	*Fiume Po*	051	25.10.96-11.12.06	ex Avianova; to Utair Aviation as VP-BCA 27.03.07
I-NOWT	*Fiume Tevere*	054	25.10.96-27.09.06	ex Avianova; to Utair Aviation as VP-BCB 04.07

ATR 72-500 1999-2013 (12)

70-passenger high-wing regional aircraft, powered by two 1,954 kW (2,620 hp) Pratt & Whitney Canada PW127F turboprop engines, generating a cruising speed of 510 km/h

I-ATLR	*Fiume Tevere*	701	12.12.02-12.11.09	to NAC-Nordic Aviation Capital as OY-EDC
I-ATMC	*Fiume Arno*	588	27.07.99-14.10.09	to NAC-Nordic Aviation Capital as G-CGFT
I-ATPA	*Lago Trasimeno*	626	21.12.99-14.10.10	to Asian Wings Airways as XY-AIS
I-ATPM	*Fiume Po*	705	26.03.03-14.10.09	to NAC-Nordic Aviation Capital as G-CGFX
I-ATRO	*Lago di Bracciano*	423	22.12.05-31.03.08	ex EI-CLB; to MAS-Magellan Aviation Services as EI-CLB 01.07.10
I-ATRQ	*Fiume Simeto*	428	22.12.05-31.03.08	ex EI-CLC; to MAS-Magellan Aviation Services as I-ATRQ 03.09.09
I-ATRR	*Fiume Piave*	432	22.12.05-15.04.08	ex EI-CLD; to MAS-Magellan Aviation Services as I-ATRR 03.03.10
I-ATRS	*Fiume Volturno*	467	22.12.05-25.11.08	ex EI-CMJ; to Air Contractors as EI-CMJ 28.05.10
I-ATSL	*Lago di Garda*	592	30.07.99-11.11.08	to Air Bagan as XY-AIK 12.09.09

I-ATSM	*Lago di Nemi*	702	12.12.02-09.09.09	to Borajet as TC-YAD 02.12.09
EI-CLB	*Lago di Bracciano*	423	01.11.96-22.12.05	reregistered I-ATRO
EI-CLC	*Fiume Simeto*	428	01.11.96-22.12.05	reregistered I-ATRQ
EI-CLD	*Fiume Piave*	432	01.11.96-22.12.05	reregistered I-ATRR
EI-CMJ	*Fiume Volturno*	467	01.11.96-22.12.05	reregistered I-ATRS
YR-ATR		555	17.12.12-02.02.13	ex OY-CJT; wet-leased from Carpatair
YR-ATS		533	21.12.12-02.02.13	ex N533AT; wet-leased from Carpatair; damaged beyond repair on landing at Rome

Embraer ERJ145LR 2000-2008 (14)

50-passenger regional aircraft, powered by two 33.1 kN (7,587 lb) Rolls-Royce AE 3007A1 turbofan engines, generating a cruising speed of 850 kn/hspeed

I-EXMA	*Giosuè Carducci*	145250	18.04.00-11.04.08	to Dniproavia as UR-DPB 19.11.10
I-EXMB	*Salvatore Quasimodo*	145330	20.10.00-01.12.08	to Dniproavia as UR-DPA 02.05.11
I-EXMC	*Emilio Gino Segrè*	145436	23.05.01-29.10.08	to Dniproavia as UR-DNZ 10.09.10
I-EXMD	*Eugenio Montale*	145445	31.05.01-31.10.08	to Dniproavia as UR-DNV 21.06.10
I-EXME	*Guglielmo Marconi*	145282	30.06.00-31.03.08	to Dniproavia as UR-DNY 02.09.10
I-EXMF	*Giulio Natta*	145641	25.09.02-29.10.08	to Dniproavia as UR-DNR 20.04.10
I-EXMG	*Daniel Bovet*	145652	25.10.02-27.10.08	to Dniproavia as UR-DNS 07.05.10
I-EXMH	*Camillo Golgi*	145665	04.12.02-21.11.08	to Dniproavia as UR-DNN 11.04.10
I-EXMI	*Grazia Deledda*	145286	12.07.00-30.03.08	to Dniproavia as UR-DNX 15.08.10
I-EXML	*Ernesto Teodoro Moneta*	145709	08.05.03-28.10.08	to Dniproavia as UR-DNT 01.06.10
I-EXMM	*Anna Magnani*	145738	11.07.03-28.10.08	to Dniproavia as UR-DNU 01.07.10
I-EXMN	*Vittorio de Sica*	145750	01.10.03-00.09.08	to Enhance Aero Group as F-WKXN
I-EXMO	*Luigi Pirandello*	145299	09.08.00-02.04.08	to Enhance Aero Group as F-WKXO
I-EXMU	*Enrico Fermi*	145316	20.09.00-28.03.08	to Dniproavia as UR-DNW 04.08.10

Embraer E170LR 2004-2012 (6)

72-passenger regional aircraft, powered by two 63 kN (14,200 lb) General Electric CF34-8E turbofan engines, generating a speed of 800 km/h

EI-DFG	*Via Appia*	17000008	24.03.04-07.12.11	to Régional as F-HBXK
EI-DFH	*Via Aurelia*	17000009	23.04.04-07.07.12	to Régional as F-HBXL
EI-DFI	*Via Cassia*	17000010	20.05.04-20.01.12	to Régional as F-HBXM
EI-DFJ	*Via Flaminia*	17000011	30.06.04-16.05.12	to Régional as F-HBXN
EI-DFK	*Via Salaria*	17000032	30.06.04-30.12.11	to Régional as F-HBXO
EI-DFL	*Via Tiburtina Valeria*	17000036	16.07.04-18.11.11	to Régional as F-HBXP

Alitalia CityLiner Fleet 2011-2021

Bombardier CRJ900ER 2011-2012 (10)

90-seat short/medium-range regional aircraft, powered by two 64.5kN General Electric CF34-8C5 turbofan engines, generating a speed of 830km/h

EI-DOT	15066	20.04.11-00.11.12	wfu; to Mesa Airlines as N241LR 17.04.14
EI-DOU	15068	20.04.11-13.10.12	wfu; to Mesa Airlines as N943LR 16.05.14
EI-DRI	15076	20.04.11-00.11.12	wfu; to Mesa Airlines as N242LR 28.04.14
EI-DRJ	15077	20.04.11-18.06.12	wfu; to Mesa Airlines as N945LR 07.05.14
EI-DRK	15075	20.04.11-00.11.12	wfu; to Mesa Airlines as N944LR 05.06.14
EI-DUK	15104	20.04.11-11.10.12	wfu; to Mesa Airlines as N946LR 27.05.14
EI-DVP	15116	20.04.11-00.11.12	wfu; to Mesa Airlines as N947LR 18.06.14
EI-DVR	15118	20.04.11-00.11.12	wfu; to Mesa Airlines as N948LR 03.07.14
EI-DVS	15119	20.04.11-00.11.12	wfu; to Mesa Airlines as N950LR 26.06.14
EI-DVT	15123	20.04.11-00.11.12	wfu; to Mesa Airlines as N951LR 16.07.14

Embraer E175STD 2011-2021 (15)

78-passenger regional aircraft, powered by two 63 kN (14,200 lb) General Electric CF34-8E turbofan engines, generating a crusing speed of 800 km/h

EI-RDA	Parco Nazionale del Gran Paradiso	17000330	31.10.11-24.04.20	wfu and stored
EI-RDB	Parco Nazionale dello Stelvio	17000331	13.11.11-14.10.21	wfu and stored
EI-RDC	Parco Nazionale delle Cinque Terre	17000333	01.03.12-14.10.21	wfu and stored
EI-RDD	Parco Nazionale d'Abruzzo	17000334	26.03.12-30.09.21	wfu and stored
EI-RDE	Parco Nazionale dell'Etna	17000335	16.04.12-07.10.21	wfu and stored
EI-RDF	Parco Naturale Dolomiti Friulano	17000337	22.06.12-09.10.21	wfu and stored
EI-RDG	Parco Nazionale dell'Asinara	17000338	26.06.12-11.10.21	wfu and stored
EI-RDH	Parco Delta del Po	17000339	26.06.12-03.11.21	wfu and stored
EI-RDI	Parco Storico Monte Sole	17000340	26.06.12-11.10.21	wfu and stored
EI-RDJ	Parco Nazionale del Circeo	17000342	04.07.12-08.04.20	wfu; to Falko Regional Aircraft as G-CLVH 24.12.20
EI-RDK	Parco Nazionale del Gargano	17000343	05.07.12-20.04.20	wfu; to Falko Regional Aircraft as G-CLVK 24.12.20
EI-RDL	Parco Nazionale della Val Grande	17000345	24.08.12-29.04.20	wfu; to Falko Regional Aircraft as G-CLVN 30.12.20
EI-RDM	Parco Nazionale della Majella	17000346	30.08.12-26.11.20	wfu; to Falko Regional Aircraft as G-CLVT 24.12.20
EI-RDN	Parco Nazionale dell'Alta Murgia	1700347	22.03.13-11.10.21	wfu and stored

| EI-RDO | *Parco Regionale della Maremma* | 1700348 | 22.03.13-21.11.21 | wfu and stored |

Embraer E190STD 2011-2021 (5)

100-passenger regional aircraft, powered by two 89 kN (20,000 lb) General Electric CF34-10E turbofan engines, generating a cruising speed of 830 km/h

EI-RNA	Parco Nazionale del Vesuvio	19000470	23.09.11-31.01.21	wfu and stored
EI-RNB	Parco Nazionale del Pollino	19000479	09.10.11-14.10.21	wfu and stored
EI-RNC	Parco Nazionale Arcipelago			
	Toscano	19000503	16.12.11-28.11.21	wfu and stored
EI-RND	Parco Nazionale Dolimiti			
	Bellunesi	19000512	12.03.12-30.09.21	wfu and stored
EI-RNE	Parco Nazionale della Sila	19000520	23.04.12-31.10.21	wfu and stored

Aermediterranea-Linee Aeree Mediterranee Fleet 1981-1985

Douglas DC-9-30 1981-1985 (8)

115-passenger short/medium-range aircraft, powered by two rear-mounted 64kN Pratt & Whitney JT9D-9 turbofan engines, generating a speed of 895 km/h

I-ATIH	*Lido degli Estensi*	47553/642	00.05.82-01.04.85	lsd from ATI-Aero Trasporti Italiani
I-ATIQ	*Sila*	47591/706	00.11.81-01.04.85	lsd from ATI-Aero Trasporti Italiani
I-ATJB	*Riviera del Conero*	47653/760	00.12.81-01.04.85	lsd from ATI-Aero Trasporti Italiani
I-DIBO	*Conca d'Oro*	47237/451	01.07.81-01.04.85	lsd from Alitalia; to ATI-Aero Trasporti Italiani as I-DIBO *Conca d'Oro*
I-DIKS	*Isola di Filicudi*	47229/356	00.06.82-01.04.85	lsd from Alitalia; to ATI-Aero Trasporti Italiani as I-DIKS *Basilicata*
I-DIKT	*Isola di Ustica*	47230/395	07.04.82-01.04.85	lsd from Alitalia; to ATI-Aero Trasporti Italiani as I-DIKT *Trentino Alto Adige*
I-DIZF	*Dolomiti*	47519/615	30.06.81-01.04.85	lsd from Alitalia; to ATI-Aero Trasporti Italiani as I-DIZF *Cassino*
I-DIZO	*Isola del Tino*	47518/614	01.11.81-27.03.82	lsd from Alitalia; to ATI-Aero Trasporti Italiani as I-DIZO *Erice*
N516MD	*Isola di Ponza*	47128/210	17.12.83-01.05.84	lsd from Alitalia

ATI-Aero Trasporti Italiani Fleet 1969-1994

Fokker F.27-200 Friendship 1964-1986 (16)

50-passenger high-wing airliner, powered by two 1,678 kW (2,250 hp) Rollos-Royce Dart Mk 532 turboprop engines, generating a cruising speed of 460 km/h (290 mph)

I-ATIB		10289	15.12.65-00.04.75	to Ibis A/S as LN-DAS
I-ATIC**	Polluce	10349	24.01.68-18.12.85	lsd to Servizio Radiomisure 21.01.74-00.12.84; to SAS Scandinanvian Airlines as SE-ITH *Visbur Viking*
I-ATID		10320	30.01.67-16.03.74	to Centre national d'etudes des télécommunications (CNET) as F-SEBF
I-ATIF	Mar Atlantico	10321	22.02.67-12.08.86	lsd to Servizio Radiomisure 30.09.74-00.12.77; to SAS Scandinanvian Airlines as LN-RNX *Visbur Viking*
I-ATIG		10288	03.12.65-14.04.73	to PIA-Pakistan International Airlines as AP-AXB
I-ATIL		10324	28.03.67-o1.01.77	to Compagnie européene de recherches as OO-PSF
I-ATIM		10249	06.05.64-15.05.74	operated for Kingdom of Libya Airlines 06.66-09.69; to NLM CityHopper as PH-KFG *Koos Abspoel*
I-ATIN**	Castore	10350	24.01.68-05.04.86	lsd to Servicio Radiomisure 26.03.74-00.12.85; to SAS Scandinavian Airlines as SE-ITI *Vidar Viking*
I-ATIP		10251	25.05.64-16.04.72	crashed in thundrestorm near Ardinello di Amaseno
I-ATIR		10301	29.04.66-30.10.72	crashed at Poggiorsini on approach to Bari
I-ATIS		10256	22.07.64-00.11.74	to NLM CityHopper as PH-KFH *Koene Dirk Parmentier*
I-ATIT*		10363	08.05.68-25.05.69	crashed on landing at Reggio di Calabria
I-ATIV**	Mar Tirreno	10419	27.10.69-20.08.85	to SAS Scandinavian Airlines as LN-RNY *Vatnar Viking*
I-ATIZ**	Mar Ligure	10420	11.11.69-28.09.85	to SAS Scandinavian Airlines as OY-KAD *Vigleik Viking*
PH-ARO*		10270	25.07.69-26.11.69	lsd from Fokker
PH-FSD		10137	25.04.66-30.04.67	lsd from Fokker

* Fokker F.27-400; ** F.27-600

Douglas DC-9-32 1969-1994 (30)

115-passenger short/medium-range aircraft powered by two rear-mounted 64kN Pratt & Whitney JT9D-9 turbofan engines, generating a speed of 895 km/h

I-ATIA		47431/420	24.07.69-00.09.85	to McDonnell Douglas as N506MD
I-ATIE	Toscana	47436/541	08.10.69-00.12.86	reregistered N873UM
I-ATIH		47553/642	09.12.71-00.06.90	reregistered I-RIZS
I-ATIJ	Marche	47544/676	18.10.72-27.03.91	to Alitalia
I-ATIK	Sardegna	47477/613	00.02.71-00.01.86	to McDonnell Douglas as N508MD
I-ATIO	Emilia Romagna	47437/544	27.10.69-29.10.86	reregistered N872UM
I-ATIQ	Friuli Venezia Giulia	47591/706	28.09.73-27.03.91	reregistered I-RIZT
I-ATIU	Veneto	47438/545	07.11.69-01.12.89	to Alitalia
I-ATIW	Lazio	47533/641	02.12.71-20.06.90	reregistered I-RIZV
I-ATIX	Calabria	47474/600	00.12.70-00.10.85	to McDonnell Douglas as N507MD
I-ATIY	Lombardia	47575/680	13.12.72-26.03.91	reregistered I-RIZW
I-ATJA	Sicilia	47641/746	19.09.74-01.10.88	to Alitalia
I-ATJB	Riviera del Conero	47653/760	09.01.75-26.03.91	reregistered I-RIZN
I-ATJC		47667/l/776	22.02.75-14.09.79	crashed near Sarroch on approach to Cagliari
I-DIBO	Conca d'Oro	47237/451	01.04.85-01.12.88	to Alitalia
I-DIBX	Isola di Giannutri	47283/397	00.12.92-00.03.93	lsd from Alitalia
I-DIKM	Positano	47224/316	00.10.81-01.06.86	leased from Alitalia

I-DIKN	*Isola di Nisida*	47225/317	28.03.82-17.12.83	lsd from Alitalia; reregistered N515MD
I-DIKP	*Isola di Marettimo*	47226/333	01.04.80-01.05.85	lsd from Alitalia
I-DIKR	*Piemonte*	47228/355	16.12.81-07.10.86	lsd from Alitalia
I-DIKS	*Basilicata*	47227/356	01.04.85-25.06.90	ex Aermediterranea; reregistered I-RIKS
I-DIKT	*Trento Alto Adige*	47230/395	01.04.85-26.06.90	ex Aermediterranea; reregistered I-RIKT
I-DIKY	*Puglia*	47232/428	01.04.79-14.04.89	lsd from Alitalia
I-DIZB	*Umbria*	47434/537	30.06.70-20.10.86	lsd from Alitalia; reregistered N871UM
I-DIZC	*Molise*	47435/540	28.05.70-20.06.90	lsd from Alitalia; reregistered I-RIZC
I-DIZE	*Isola di Meloria*	47502/574	31.05.79-01.09.86	lsd from Alitalia
I-DIZF	*Cassino*	47519/615	01.04.85-15.04.87	ex Aermediterranea; to Alitalia
I-DIZI	*Abruzzo*	47432/525	20.05.80-30.07.90	lsd from Alitalia; reregistered I-RIZB
I-DIZO	*Erice*	47518/614	29.09.70-01.03.87	lsd from Alitalia
I-DIZU	*Valle d'Aosta*	47433/526	09.04.80-25.06.90	lsd from Alitalia; reregistered I-RIZU
I-RIFM	*Marche*	47544/676	04.12.92-30.10.94	to Alitalia
I-RIFP	*Veneto*	47438/545	01.10.93-30.10.94	lsd from Alitalia
I-RIFU	*Valle d'Aosta*	47433/526	27.11.92-24.10.94	ex I-RIZU; to Alitalia
I-RIFV	*Lazio*	47533/641	27.11.92-30.10.94	ex I-RIZV; to Alitalia
I-RIFW	*Lombardia*	47575/680	27.11.92-30.10.94	ex I-RIZW; to Alitalia
I-RIKS	*Basilicata*	47227/356	25.06.90-01.10.92	ex I-DIKS; to Alitalia
I-RIKT	*Isola di Ustica*	47230/395	26.06.90-30.01.93	ex I-DIKT; to McDonnell Doulgas
I-RIZB	*Abruzzo*	47432/525	30.07.90-31.07.90	ex I-DIZI; to Alitalia
I-RIZC	*Molise*	47435/540	20.06.90-01.02.91	ex I-DIZC; to Alitalia
I-RIZJ	*Umbria*	47434/537	19.08.89-01.11.90	ex N871UM; to Alitalia
I-RIZN		47653/760	26.03.91-28.09.94	ex I-ATJB; to Zuliana de Aviació as YV-496C
I-RIZR	*Marche*	47544/676	00.11.92-04.12.92	reregistered I-RIFM
I-RIZS		47553/642	00.06.90-00.09.94	ex I-ATIH; to Jet Fleet as N136AA
I-RIZT	*Friuli Venezia Giulia*	47591/706	27.03.91-01.11.91	ex I-ATIQ; to Alitalia
I-RIZU	*Valle d'Aosta*	47433/526	25.06.90-27.11.92	ex I-DIZU; reregistered I-RIFU
I-RIZV	*Lazio*	47533/641	20.06.90-27.11.92	ex I-ATIW; reregistered I-RIFV
I-RIZW	*Lombardia*	47575/680	26.03.91-27.11.92	ex I-ATIY; reregistered I-RIFW
N515MD	*Isola di Nisida*	47225/317	17.12.83-01.04.85	lsd from Alitalia
N871UM	*Umbria*	47434/537	20.10.86-19.08.89	ex I-DIZB; reregistered I-RIZJ
N872UM	*Emilia Romagna*	47437/544	29.10.86-01.06.89	to Alitalia
N873UM	*Toscana*	47436/541	00.12.86-01.07.89	ex I-ATIE; to Alitalia

ATR 42-300 1986-1990 (10)

48-passenger high-wing regional aircraft, powered by two 1,343 kW (1,800 hp) Pratt & Whitney Canada PW120 turboprop engines, generating a cruising speed of 500 km/h

I-ATRB	*Ravello*	020	10.07.86-30.05.89	to Olympic Aviation as SX-BIX
I-ATRC	*Asolo*	021	24.07.86-30.05.89	to Olympic Aviation as SX-BIY
I-ATRD	*Siracusa*	032	06.01.87-01.11.89	to Avianova as I-ATRD *Lago Trasimeno*

I-ATRF	Siena	034	11.12.86-15.12.89	to Avianova as I-ATRF *Flumendosa*
I-ATRG	Bergamo	042	10.04.87-21.04.90	to Avianova as I-ATRG *Lago Maggiore*
I-ATRH	Verona	046	00.05.87-15.10.87	crashed into Monte Crezzo
I-ATRJ	Ravenna	057	15.07.87-24.03.90	to Avianova as I-ATRJ *Lago di Bolsena*
I-ATRK	Gubbio	067	09.02.88-18.09.89	to Avianova as I-ATRK
I-ATRL	Urbino	068	16.02.88-01.07.90	to Avianova as I-ATRL *Fiume Adige*
I-ATRM	Viterbo	114	15.11.88-17.08.89	to Avianova as I-ATRM
I-ATRP	Asolo	021	04.01.90-14.03.90	to Avianova as I-ATRP *Lago di Garda*

McDonnell Douglas MD-82 1984-1994 (40)

172-passenger short/medium-range aircraft, powered by two rear-mounted 89 kN (20,000 lb) Pratt & Whitney JT8D-217A turbofan engines, generating a speed of 875km/h

I-DACM	La Spezia	49971/1755	14.09.90-30.10.94	to Alitalia as I-DACM
I-DACN	Rieti	49972/1757	21.09.90-30.10.94	to Alitalia as I-DACN
I-DACP	Padova	49973/1762	27.09.90-30.10.94	to Alitalia as I-DACP
I-DACU	Brindisi	53055/1857	10.05.91-30.10.94	to Alitalia as I-DACU
I-DACV	Riccione	53056/1880	28.06.91-30.10.94	to Alitalia as I-DACV
I-DAND	Trani	53061/1957	17.01.92-30.10.94	to Alitalia as I-DAND
I-DANF	Vicenza	53062/1960	24.01.92-30.10.94	to Alitalia as I-DANF
I-DANG	Benevento	53176/1972	24.02.92-30.10.94	to Alitalia as I-DANG
I-DANH	Messina	53177/1973	04.03.92-30.10.94	to Alitalia as I-DANH
I-DANL	Cosenza	53178/1994	30.04.92-30.10.94	to Alitalia as I-DANL
I-DANM	Vicenza	53179/1997	26.05.92-30.10.94	to Alitalia as I-DANL
I-DANQ	Lecce	53181/2005	26.06.92-30.10.94	to Alitalia as I-DANQ
I-DANR	Matera	53203/2007	01.07.92-30.10.94	to Alitalia as I-DANR
I-DANU	Trapani	53204/2009	01.07.92-30.10.94	to Alitalia as I-DANU
I-DATE	Grosseto	53217/2053	01.04.93-30.10.94	to Alitalia as I-DATE
I-DATI	Siracusa	53218/2060	03.05.93-30.10.94	to Alitalia as I-DATI
I-DAVA	Cuneo	49215/1253	18.02.86-30.10.94	to Alitalia as I-DAVA
I-DAVB	Ferrara	49216/1262	20.03.86-30.10.94	to Alitalia as I-DAVB
I-DAVC	Lucca	49217/1268	29.04.86-30.10.94	to Alitalia as I-DAVC
I-DAVD	Mantova	49218/1274	21.05.86-30.10.94	to Alitalia as I-DAVD
I-DAVF	Oristano	49219/1310	09.10.86-30.10.94	to Alitalia as I-DAVF
I-DAVG	Pesaro	49220/1319	19.11.86-30.10.94	to Alitalia as I-DAVG
I-DAVH	Salerno	49221/1330	30.12.86-30.10.94	to Alitalia as I-DAVH
I-DAVL	Reggio Calabria	49433/1428	21.01.88-30.10.94	to Alitalia as I-DAVL
I-DAVN	Volterra	49435/1504	05.10.88-30.10.94	to Alitalia as I-DAVN
I-DAVP	Gorizia	49549/1544	19.12.88-30.10.94	to Alitalia as I-DAVP
I-DAVR	Pisa	49550/1584	24.04.89-30.10.94	to Alitalia as I-DAVR
I-DAVS	Catania	49551/1586	03.05.89-30.10.94	to Alitalia as I-DAVS
I-DAVT	Como	49552/1597	08.06.89-30.10.94	to Alitalia as I-DAVT

I-DAVU	*Udine*	49794/1600	20.06.89-30.10.94	to Alitalia as I-DAVU
I-DAVV	*Pavia*	49795/1639	12.10.89-30.10.94	to Alitalia as I-DAVV
I-DAVW	*Camerino*	49796/1713	29.05.90-30.10.94	to Alitalia as I-DAVW
I-DAVX	*Asti*	49969/1719	14.06.90-30.10.94	to Alitalia as I-DAVX
I-DAVZ	*Brescia*	49970/1737	31.07.90-30.10.94	to Alitalia as I-DAVZ
I-DAWJ	*Genova*	49203/1174	18.12.84-03.07.85	to Alitalia as I-DAWJ
I-DAWT	*Napoli*	49210/1192	08.04.85-30.10.94	to Alitalia as I-DAWT
I-DAWV	*Trento*	49211/1202	24.05.85-30.10.94	to Alitalia as I-DAWV
I-DAWW	*Riace*	49212/1233	04.11.85-30.10.94	to Alitalia as I-DAWW
I-DAWY	*Agrigento*	49213/1243	04.11.85-30.10.94	to Alitalia as I-DAWY
I-DAWZ	*Avellino*	49214/1245	18.12.85-30.10.94	to Alitalia as I-DAWZ

Sud-Aviation SE-210 Caravelle VI-N 1971-1976 (2)

80-passenger short-range aircraft, powered by two 54.3 kN (12,200 lb) Rolls-Royce Avon Mk 531 turbojet engines, generating a cruising speed of 845 km/h

I-DABT	*Denebola*	085	00.00.71-18.03.72	sub-lsd from SAM
I-DABV	*Acrux*	146	00.00.72-00.00.76	sub-lsd from SAM

SAM-Società Aerea Mediterranea Fleet 1961-1977

Douglas DC-6B 1961-1972 (9)

68-passenger, low-wing monoplane, powered by four 1,865 kW (2,500 hp) Pratt & Whitney R-2800-CB17 Double Wasp engines, generating a speed of 510km/h

I-DIMA	44252/420	17.04.61-31.02.64	lsd from Alitalia
I-DIMB	44913/663	01.10.63-09.09.72	lsd from Alitalia; to AAXICO as N4913R
I-DIMD	44419/491	26.05.61-00.08.72	lsd from Alitalia; to AAXICO as N4419R
I-DIME	44252/442	01.04.61-30.04.69	lsd from Alitalia; destroyed on landing at Bari/Palese
i-DIMI	44253/448	14.05.62-00.08.69	lsd from Alitalia; to Aeronautica Militare as MM61964
I-DIMO	44254/456	21.11.61-08.03.62	lsd from Alitalia; crashed into Monte Velino while returning to Rome from Khartoum
I-DIMP	44418/473	30.12.61-00.08.69	lsd from Alitalia; to Aeronautica Militare as MM61987
I-DIMS*	43216/165	30.12.61-12.06.65	ex I-LADY; lsd from Alitalia; to Aeronautica Militare as MM61922
I-DIMU**	44888/645	13.11.61-24.07.72	lsd from Alitalia; to Zantop International Airlines as N4888R

* Douglas DC-6; ** converted to DC-6A/B cargo

Douglas C-47 (DC-3) 1961-1965 (3)

21-passengers low-wing, all-metal monoplane, powered by two 895 kW (1,200 hp) Pratt & Whitney R-1830-S1C3G Twin Wasp engines, generating a speed of 370 km/h

I-LALO	19484	00.12.61-12.01.65	lsd from Alitalia
I-LORD	4496	00.00.62-29.09.64	lsd from Alitalia

I-LORO		4297	00.04.62-20.02.65	lsd from Alitalia

Douglas DC-7C 1961-1966 (1)

105-passenger low-wing monoplane, powered by four 2,536 kW (3,400 hp) Pratt & Whitney R-3350EA1 engines, generating a maximum speed of 650 km/h

I-DUVB		45542/1008	00.00.61-28.04.66	lsd from Alitalia

Sud-Aviation SE-210 Caravelle VI-N 1968-1977 (10)

80-passenger short-range aircraft, powered by two 54.3 kN (12,200 lb) Rolls-Royce Avon Mk 531 turbojet engines, generating a cruising speed of 845 km/h

I-DABG	*Arturo*	205	00.05.71-00.00.76	lsd from Alitalia
I-DABI	*Sirio*	074	00.00.69-00.00.70	lsd from Alitalia
I-DABL	*Fomalhaut*	132	01.04.69-00.10.74	lsd from Alitalia
I-DABM	*Procione*	143	00.00.69-00.00.76	lsd from Alitalia
I-DABP	*Castore*	192	00.06.70-00.10.72	lsd from Alitalia
I-DABT	*Denebola*	085	01.05.68-00.00.74	lsd from Alitalia; sub-lsd to ATI 00.00.01-18.03.72
I-DABV	*Acrux*	146	01.11.68-25.01.77	lsd from Alitalia; sub-lsd to ATI 00.00.72-00.00.76
I-DABW	*Betelgeuse*	150	01.04.69-00.00.74	lsd from Alitalia
I-DABZ	*Spica*	082	00.00.72-00.00.74	lsd from Alitalia
I-DAXA	*Altair*	035	10.06.68-00.10.69	lsd from Alitalia

Some Caravelles were leased to SAM on several occasions

Airbus A320-200 EI-DSW in Jeep Renegade livery (Anna Zvereva)

Alitalia Flight School Fleet 1963-1967 and 1980-2006

Aermacchi MB.326D 1963-1967 (4)

Two-seat basic jet trainer, powered by a single 17.8 kN (4,000 lb) thrust Bristol Siddeley Viper 623-42 turbojet, generating a maximim speed of 890 km/h (553 mph)

I-ADIA	6291/61	27.05.63-12.12.66	crashed into the ground near Cellino San Marco
I-ADIE	6392/62	03.06.63-00.00.67	to Aeronautica Militare as MM54266
I-ADIO	6293/63	08.07.63-00.00.67	to Aeronautica Militare as MM54267
I-ADIU	6294/64	16.07.63-00.00.67	to Aeronautica Militare as MM54268

Piaggio P.166DL-3 1981-1990 (2)

Eight-passenger high-wing utility aircraft, powered by two 450 kW)600 hp) Lycoming LTP101-600 turboprop engines, generating a maximum speed of 400 km/h (250 mph)

I-PIAC	*Città di Iglesias*	465/114	09.03.81-00.07.90	to Guardia di Finanza as MM25171
I-PIAE	*Città di Olbia*	466/115	15.01.81-00.07.90	to Guardia di Finanza as MM25172

Piper PA-42-720 Cheyenne IIIA 1986-2006 (5)

Eight passenger light aircraft, powered by two 537 kW (720 hp) Pratt & Whitney Canada PT6A-61 turboprop engines, generating a maximum cruising speed of 565 km/h (350 mph)

I-TREP	*Città di Arbatax*	42-5501045	05.05.87-22.03.06	to Aircraft Guarant Title & Trust as N56MV
I-TREQ	*Città di Macomer*	42-5501046	10.06.87-22.03.06	to Air Alliance Express as D-ITWO
I-TRER	*Città di Fertilia*	42-5501047	17.07.87-22.03.06	Air Alliance Express as D-IAAE
N4118M		42-5501016	00.00.86-11.08.87	lsd from Piper Aircraft Corporation
N420TS		42-8001088	00.00.86-00.07.87	lsd from Piper Aircraft Corporation

SIAI-Marchetti SF.260C 1980-1997 (7)

Three-seat light training aircraft, powered by a single 190 kW (260 hp) Textron Lycoming O-540 piston engine, generating a cruising speed of 300 km/h (190 mph)

I-LELB	*Città di Alghero*	563/41-001	21.10.80-10.10.91	to Servair as I-LELB
I-LELC	*Città di Cagliari*	566/41-002	21.10.80-09.10.91	to Finvellant as I-LELC
I-LELD	*Città di Nuoro*	567/41-003	21.10.80-09.10.91	to Finvellant as I-LELD
I-LELF	*Città di Oristano*	568/41-004	03.11.80-09.10.91	to Finvellant as I-LELF
I-LELG	*Città di Sassari*	735/41-005	12.03.86-30.01.97	to Giuseppe Demarie as I-LELG
I-LELH*		764	01.04.84-09.05.97	to ICARO-Impresa Commerciale Aeronautica Romagnole as I-LELH
I-LELM*		765	18.03.89-04.11.97	to Locafit as I-LELM

* SIAI Marchetti SF-260D

The Alitalia brand through the years

Immediately after its foundation on 16 September 1946 as one of two major airlines in Italy, the other was LAI, Alitalia launched a nationwide competition to find a trademark for the new airline. The winning entry centred on a dark-blue and sky-blue winged arrow, the *freccia alata*, to denote speed, based on a symbol that had been used by the Italian military squadrons in the First World War. An alternative version had the word Alitalia forming the shaft of the arrow. Alas it made little impression when applied to the aircraft and had low visibility. The name Alitalia was applied in italic capital letters, in a triple-line font, which again was subdued and diminished its visibility. The winged arrow was displayed on the tailfin together with a small Italian flag, but was replaced with the advent of jet aircraft by the Italian tricolore covering the entire tail.

While the winged arrow was graphically not the most original design, nor did it create a memorable visual impact on the aircraft, it had, nevertheless, served the airline for more than 20 years. But in 1969, Alitalia employed Walter Landor to create a distinctive icon of Italian culture, one that was to be easily remembered and would immediately be associated with Alitalia across the world. This, Landor clearly achieved with its stylised 'A' in the colours of the green, white and red Italian flag, and a shape that perfectly fitted the aircraft tail units. The prominent new titles, also repeating the stylised 'A' on the forward fuselage above the green cheatline over the windows running from the tail to the nose of the aircraft, also provided a considerable aesthetic enhancement over the previous lettering.

In 1981, the liveries of the airline's ATI and Aermediterranea subsidiaries were harmonised with the parent company, but with different colours, with ATI's tail colours in dark and light blue, and those of Aermediterranea in red and yellow.

In 2005, Alitalia's logotype was slightly restyled by Saatchi & Saatchi to make it more contemporary and imbue a sense of dynamism, while keeping its full and immediate recognisability and, in 2015, Alitalia once again turned to Landor for the next phase of its evolution as a rejuvenated global airline by introducing a brand-new identity, said to be a young and seductive new look to represent the airline's ambitions, utilising the design elements of the airline's previous iconic livery, and to represent the best of Italy on the world stage. To reflect longevity and the airline's history, the stylised tail logo, which has characterised Alitalia since its first major rebrand was updated and refined, retaining the same green, red, and white colours. The new logotype was modernised and a more dominant 'A' was introduced - a bold statement of the heights the airline was striving to reach and its long experience in aviation.

According to the design consultancy, by increasing the number of primary colour tones used on the logo's palette, the modernised livery now portrayed greater depth and richness. Inspired in part by the striking lines on Formula 1 racing cars, striations were added to the red triangular interior of the Alitalia 'A', creating a pinstripe effect, which was said to reflect exclusivity, attention to detail, and a strong focus on design. Aircraft fuselages were then painted in a calm ivory, reflective of understated Italian style, and progressively banded rearward to create an impression of movement, speed and unhindered progress. The new branding was also extended to the cabin décor of the airline's modern fleet.

Alitalia Express

Alitalia
CITYLINER

SKYTEAM

Alitalia
CARGO

SKYTEAM

Alitalia

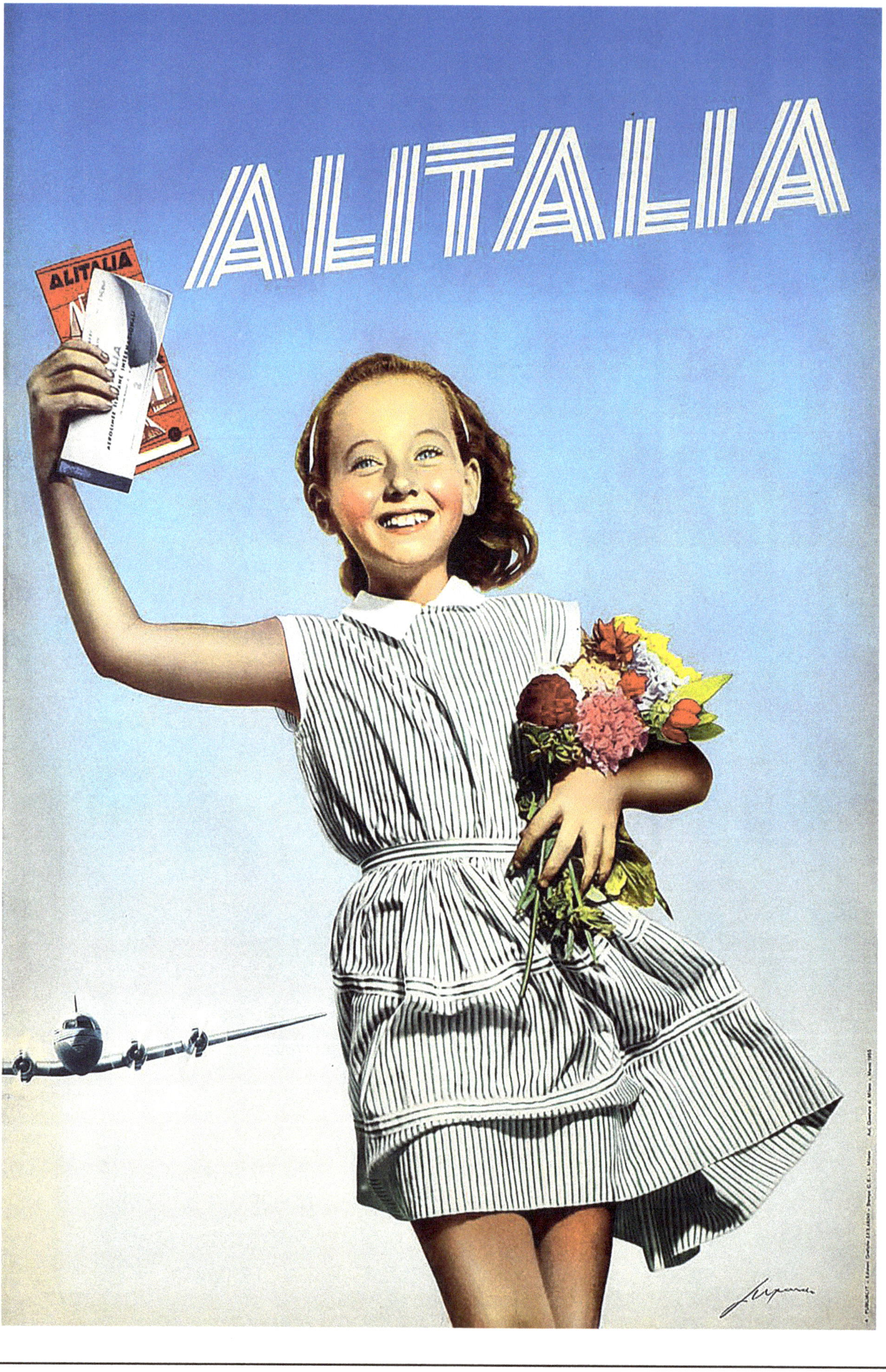
ALITALIA
ALITALIA

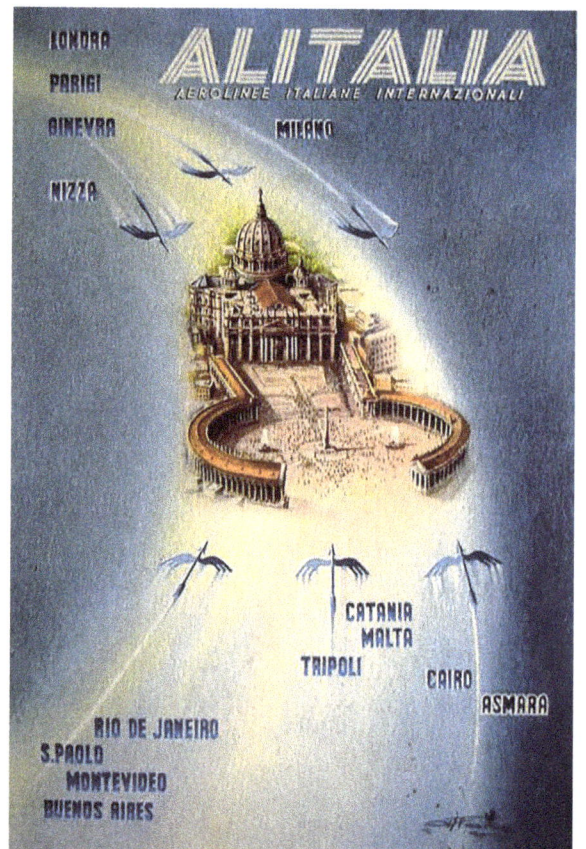

The Italian Post office issued a special set of stamps commemorating Alitalia's 25th Anniversary 1946-1971

McDonnell Douglas MD-82 I-DAVZ in special McDonald's paintscheme (Roberto Falciola)

Airbus A319-100 EI-IMI in a special livery promoting the Friuli Venezia Giulia region in northeastern Italy (Anna Zvereva)

Index

Symbols

12o Stormo Bombardemento Terrestre 77

A

B

C

D

E

F

www.ingramcontent.com/pod-product-compliance
Lightning Source LLC
Chambersburg PA
CBHW040318100426
42811CB00012B/1479